travelsph
holidays

CW00361991

SOUTH AFRICA
with Travelsphere

I am delighted to present this beautifully
illustrated and exhaustive guide with my
compliments and best wishes.

I hope it will prove a source of valuable
information before your visit; add greatly to
your enjoyment and understanding of this
fascinating country while you are there with
us; and prove to be a delightful souvenir of what
is sure to be a most memorable tour.

Director

TRAVELSPHERE LTD
COMPASS HOUSE, ROCKINGHAM ROAD
MARKET HARBOROUGH, LEICESTERSHIRE LE16 7QD
PHONE 01858 410 818

THE TRAVEL

All Travelsphere tours are planned and operated by ourselves. We do not just book our customers onto tours operated by another company. In this way we have full control of standards.

A feature of many Travelsphere holidays is a local departure by our exclusively chartered coaches from major towns across the country.

All our Far Away Places tours are fully escorted. Our Tour Managers are specially selected not just for their knowledge of the area visited but also their ability to create a happy and relaxed atmosphere for each and everyone of our clients.

On our resort based holidays o Tour Managers are waiting to me our customers at their destinati and we have representatives on ha at departure air and sea ports.

HERE TOUCH

We know from long experience that our customers love to see as much as they can when they visit a new country - particularly a distant one.

Our itineraries are planned to give the opportunity to see the very best each region has to offer yet provide the right balance between touring and rest days.

THE BENEFITS OF

Today it's fashionable to buy everything direct - whether banking services, insurance, fine wines or fine art. The benefits are seen as improved service and better value.

However, 20 years ago, Travelsphere were among the pioneers of direct sell holidays. We have always been keen to deal direct with our customers and have never chosen to sell through travel agents.

We believe this benefits our clients in a number of ways. Most obviously in the price they pay for their holiday. If we sold through travel agents we would have to increase the price of the holidays by between 10 and 15% - just to cover the commission all tour operators have to pay travel agents for selling their holidays!

We also believe we give a better service. When you deal with us you talk directly with the people who plan and operate the tour so our staff have specialist knowledge about our holidays. And in the unlikely event

BOOKING DIRECT

ything going wrong you will never
d yourself as piggy in the middle
tween travel agent and operator. You
ow exactly who you are dealing with
en you book direct withTravelsphere.

lso it is more convenient. We
e as near to you as your
ephone. There is no need to
ake a special journey or stand
a queue at a travel agent's.
st give us a ring. We even
fer extended opening hours
that we are here when you
nt us.

FULLY BONDED FO

The political changes in South Africa in recent years have resulted in a huge upsurge of interest in this incredibly beautiful and varied country. Our tour includes so many of the best sights you'll read about in this book: the stunning beauty of the Garden Route, the historic culture of the tribal kingdoms of Zululand and Swaziland and the thrilling sights and sounds of big game in the Kruger National Park.

Travelsphere is a privately own company, founded in 1977. T company employed just six peo and carried 3,000 passengers in first season. Today over 150 peo are employed in our purpose bu offices in Market Harborough a we are among the top twenty U tour operators.

YOUR PROTECTION

he company has always been a
ly bonded member of ABTA and
lds an Air Travel Organisers
:ence issued by the Civil Aviation
thority. This means that come
at may our customers' money and
eir holidays are totally protected.
e are also members of the
ssenger Shipping Retail Agent
heme and the Group Travel
rganisers Association.

TRAVELSPHERE'S DIRECT SELL PROGRAMME INCLUDES:

FAR AWAY PLACES

Including Australia, New Zealand, the Far East, India, China, Jordan and the Holy Land, the Middle East and South America.

USA & CANADA

A choice of a dozen or more tours including *the* classic West Coast Tour and specialist tours of the National Parks, the Deep South, New England and Canada in the Fall and the Canadian Rockies.

EUROPE

Our programme covers every major holiday area. There is a choice of travel arrangements: overnight Continental travel for economy and more time at the destination, overnight hotel stops to break the journey, and flights to your coach so you can tour distant destinations without an over long coach journey.

CHANNEL ISLANDS

We have specialised in Channel Island holidays on Jersey and Guernsey for many years. You can choose from local coach departures with a crossing by sea or air, flights from regional airports, or take your own car.

CHRISTMAS BREAKS

More and more people each year decide to 'get away' for Christmas. Whether you are looking for happy company to share the festive season, or bringing all the family with you, we have a wide choice of destinations at home and abroad.

CRUISES

Our close links with the major cruise companies and the sheer number of cruises which we book allow us to offer exceptional value. When you book a cruise with Travelsphere you can book early to be sure of your date and cabin - and still enjoy big savings.

PHONE OUR BROCHURE HOTLINE FREE ON 0800 19 14 18

for current copies of any of our brochures

Look out for our promotional vehicle as it tours the country. It is seen here at the Dover terminal.

SOUTH AFRICA

EX AFRICA SEMPER ALIQUID NOVI

Out of Africa always something new

PLINY The Elder
(23–79 AD)

SOUTH AFRICA

by
Gary Mead

Photography by
Gideon Mendel

British Library Cataloguing-in-Publication Data
A catalogue record for this book is available from the British Library

Distribution in the United Kingdom, Ireland and Europe by
Hi Marketing Ltd, 38 Carver Road, London SE24 9LT, United Kingdom

Grateful acknowledgement is made to authors and publishers for permissions granted:
Little Brown and Company for *A Long Walk to Freedom* by Nelson Mandela © 1994 Nelson Rolihlahla Mandela; Penguin Books for *Penguin Dictionary of South African Quotations* © 1994 Jennifer Crwys-Williams; Ravan Press (Pty) Ltd for *Sketches in the Social and Economic History of the Witwatersrand. Vol. I, 1886–1914* by Charles Van Onselen © 1982 Charles Van Onselen and for *The Return of the Anasi Bird* edited by Tim Couzens and Essop Patel © 1982 Tim Couzens and Essop Patel; Martin Secker & Warburg Limited for *Riotous Assembly* by Tom Sharpe © 1971 Tom Sharpe; Michael Joseph Ltd for *Move Your Shadow* by Joseph Lelyveld © 1985 Joseph Lelyveld; Heinemann Educational Books for *The Will to Die* by Can Themba © 1972 Mrs Anna Themba.

Editor: Stefan Cucos
Designer: Harvey Symons
Maps: Tom Le Bas
Contributing Editor: Robin Hallett
Index: Don Brech

Front cover photography: Jon Resnick
Photography by Gideon Mendel, except for: Africana Museum, Johannesburg 94, 96; Boschendal Estate Wines, Drakenstein 247, 250; Bernard Clark, Pretoria 174; Local History Museum, Durban 82; Mayibuye Centre, University of the Western Cape 98, 122, 141, 175; Museum Afrika, Johannesburg 1, 65, 66, 76–7, 88, 144; Sarah Murray 102 (bottom), 127; Tom Nebbia 106, 110, 111, 158, 210–11, 214, 215, 218, 219 (bottom left), 219 (bottom right), South African Tourist Board 254 (top); Lorne Sulcas 114, 219 (top), 254 (left), 255; Wines of South Africa 246

Printed in Hong Kong

Preface & Acknowledgements

This book is not so much a guide to everything that can be seen and done in South Africa—to do that would require several volumes—but is conceived rather as a tool to help the reader/traveller to make priorities. To that end, it has included several appendices, listing where to turn to for focused information once your plans have taken shape, which ideally should happen even before setting foot in the country. South Africa is vast; unless you have limitless time available, you cannot experience all it has to offer on one short trip.

A number of people and organizations gave considerable support in the research and writing of this book. Inadvertent errors of fact and deliberate assertions of judgement are, of course, solely my responsibility.

Bill Nasson, Charles van Onselen and Ian Phimister, three of South Africa's finest historians and most acerbic wits, were—as always—admirably dedicated to the cause of scepticism. They unstintingly gave time, insight and experience, as only true friends can. Bill and Anne Nasson provided the best possible billet in Cape Town, one which I regret not being able to pass on to fellow travellers.

Roger Matthews, the enormously wise *Financial Times* correspondent in Johannesburg, together with his wife Jane, were the most generous and kindest of hosts, as well as sharp observers of South Africa's rapidly-changing complexities. JDF Jones, former foreign, arts and managing editor of the *Financial Times*—friend and colleague—was tremendously encouraging and gave freely of his invaluable insights into a country he knows so well and loves so much. Grzegorz and Gera Drymer were, as always, wonderfully enthusiastic and full of good ideas. Thanks also to Mick Dowd for all his support.

I am immensely grateful to Leslie Boyd and Mike Nayler at Anglo American Corporation, to South African Airways and the Budget car rental company; without their crucial contributions it would not have been possible to complete this book. At The Guidebook Company Magnus Bartlett and Stefan Cucos were always honest, supportive and loyal.

But my greatest appreciation is of my wife Jane, and our daughter Freya, not just for their unquestioning support and confidence, but for creating the framework in which it was possible to tackle such a task. The book is lovingly dedicated to them.

Gary Mead

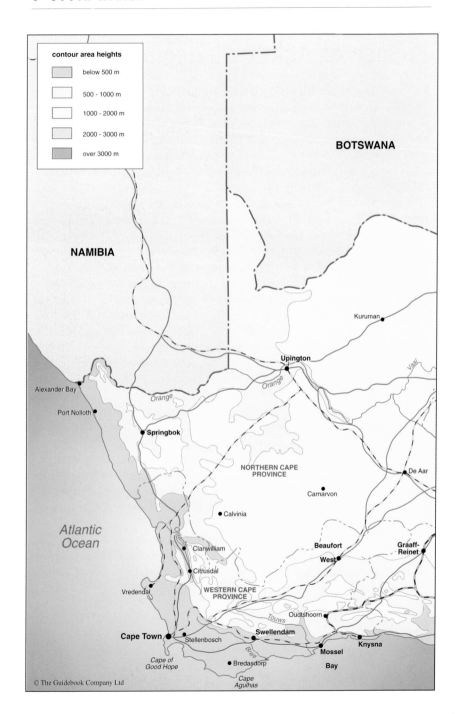

contour area heights

below 500 m

500 - 1000 m

1000 - 2000 m

2000 - 3000 m

over 3000 m

BOTSWANA

NAMIBIA

Kuruman

Vaal

Upington

Alexander Bay

Orange

Orange

Port Nolloth

Springbok

NORTHERN CAPE
PROVINCE

De Aar

Carnarvon

Calvinia

Atlantic
Ocean

Beaufort
West

Graaff-
Reinet

Clanwilliam

Orange

Citrusdal

Vredendal

WESTERN CAPE
PROVINCE

Touws

Oudtshoorn

Cape Town

Stellenbosch

Swellendam

Knysna

Bree

Mossel

Cape of
Good Hope

Bredasdorp

Bay

© The Guidebook Company Ltd

Cape
Agulhas

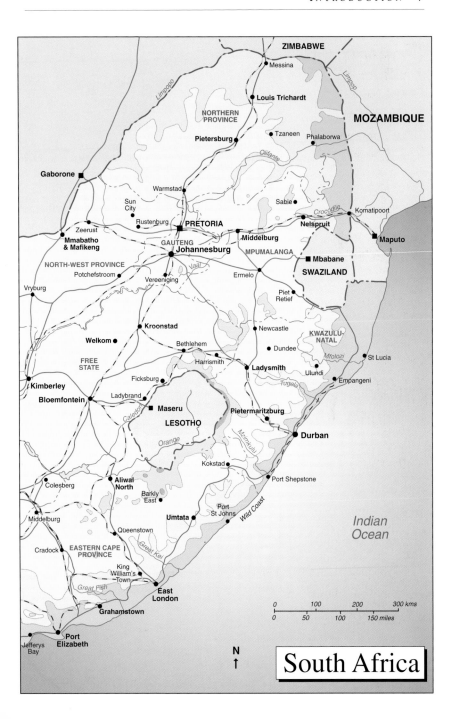

South Africa

Contents

Durban: a Zulu rickshaw driver

Introduction

'I have fought against white domination, and I have fought against black domination. I have cherished the ideal of a democratic and free society in which all persons live together in harmony and with equal opportunities. It is an ideal which I hope to live for and to achieve. But if needs be, it is an ideal for which I am prepared to die.'

Nelson Mandela, speaking at his trial in April 1964.

South Africa is one of the most physically beautiful countries on earth. From Table Mountain in Cape Town, to the lush verdant interior of KwaZulu-Natal, up through the sumptuous Drakensberg mountains, to Mpumalanga and the enormous stretches of bushveld, the country is blessed with a cornucopia of natural riches. Thousands of miles of unpolluted beaches; cities and towns with amenities and entertainments sufficient to satisfy even the most exigent tastes; a wealth of flora and fauna to rival anywhere—South Africa has it all.

As if in mockery of their creation of this semi-paradise, the gods also decided to endow the country with a host of peoples who have been perpetually at odds with one another. Even the release in 1990 of Nelson Mandela from his 27-year incarceration has not stemmed political violence, though its focus has now moved from black-versus-white, to conflicts between activists of Mandela's African National Congress and the largely Zulu Inkatha Freedom Party led by Mangosuthu Buthelezi. For the moment, the optimism that greeted the April 1994 elections, the country's first democratic poll, from which the ANC emerged with an overall majority, still remains, despite the as-yet unsatisfied pent-up expectations of most black South Africans.

The next major test for the country is likely to be the succession to Mandela as president; he is due to step down for the next elections, in 1999. His popularity has done as much as anything to help the various competing groups within the country to put aside their differences. Once he is no longer there, those temporarily supressed but unresolved conflicts may well surface again.

Mandela's release was not only a crowning triumph for the aspirations of all black South Africans, and a signal to the international community that South Africa was on the brink of becoming a truly democratic nation. It also came as an enormous relief to tourists and travellers the world over—it became morally acceptable once more to travel to one of the world's geographically most delightful regions. For many years the ANC had called for those who opposed apartheid to boycott all

South African products and services—including tourism. The country was never sealed off, but travellers who liked to pack their conscience in their luggage and not leave it behind at home declined to visit.

The ANC today naturally wants to encourage as many visitors from overseas as possible, as tourism provides a much-needed source of foreign revenue. But under the country's skin, in one fundamental sense change has yet to happen. In the past, visitors marvelled at the relatively low cost of living in South Africa. That, ironically, holds true today, as the bulk of the service industry still depends on poorly-paid black South Africans. One's conscience can be easier today: those who carry your luggage, clean your room and launder your clothes may be as badly-paid and housed as ever, but at least they have the right to vote.

A vast country—bigger than Belgium, France, Germany, Italy and the Netherlands put together, or than Texas and California combined—South Africa has a total area of 1.228 million square kilometres. It occupies the southernmost part of the African continent, stretching latitudinally from 22 degrees south to 35 degrees south, and longitudinally from 17 degrees east to 33 degrees east. To the north, it borders Namibia, Botswana, Zimbabwe, with Mozambique and Swaziland to the north-east. Completely enclosed within it is the independent kingdom of Lesotho. Its coastline stretches for 2,945 kilometres. On its west coast is the Atlantic Ocean; on its southern and eastern coast is the Indian Ocean.

In 1995 it was estimated by the South African government that 41.24 million people lived in the country, more than five million of them white, but the vast majority black, from a variety of different indigenous peoples. Despite the huge land area, most people live in and around the country's 22 officially proclaimed cities, with 80 per cent of the urban population in four main industrial areas—the south-western Cape, Gauteng (comprising the area around Johannesburg and Pretoria), the stretch between Durban and Pietermaritzburg, and the Port Elizabeth/Uitenhage area in the eastern Cape.

The country is not only very diverse geographically; it also is the home of many different ethnic groups and 11 officially-recognized languages. Over the centuries immigrants have come from Britain, China, the Netherlands, Portuguese territories, eastern Europe, India and many other countries. Certain immigrant communities have situated themselves in particular places. Durban, for example, feels like an Indian city, whereas Johannesburg, where migrant mine workers have for decades come to seek work, is home to a multitude of different black African communities. In Cape Town there is a relatively close-knit Islamic community—Cape Malays—of as many as 250,000 people, whose ancestors were slaves brought from Indonesian islands in the late 17th century.

In other words, South Africa has long been a multi-racial society, if not a society in which all races were permitted freedom. That has begun to change. In his first address to the nation after being elected president in 1994, Nelson Mandela said in Cape Town: 'You have mandated us to change South Africa from a country in which the majority lived with little hope, to one in which they can live and work with dignity, with a sense of self-esteem and confidence in the future.' Much has still to be done, but with continuing goodwill on all sides, Mandela's vision may come to fruition.

A street scene in Hillbrow, one of Joburg's toughest suburbs

Streetlife in Johannesburg

Table Mountain

(Main picture) *Moslem prayers at Durban's Grey Street mosque;*
(inset) *Venda: the traditional 'python god dance'*

A Frank A–Z of Facts and Fancies

AFFIRMATIVE ACTION

Also sometimes referred to as positive or reverse discrimination, Affirmative Action became a buzz-phrase of post-apartheid South Africa. Affirmative Action—henceforth AA—was a concerted effort by the state, and to varying degrees private business, to redress the wrongs of apartheid by appointing non-whites to senior government and commercial positions.

Easier said than done. Most adult black South Africans in the 1990s had been taught under apartheid's 'Bantu education' system—aimed at rendering them fit only for the most menial tasks. Ironically, this means that in contemporary South Africa if you are a well-educated non-white person, private and public employers will, in their anxiety to demonstrate their new-found political correctness, stumble over themselves in the rush to offer you a job.

Apartheid is dead but old habits die hard. The many persistent white racists loathe AA. More thoughtful critics, many of whom were vigorous and open opponents of apartheid, are also worried about it. They claim that academic, commercial, governmental and other standards are in danger of being eroded, because poorly-qualified non-white South Africans are nevertheless being appointed to important posts, purely because of skin colour. This minefield of conflicting views is an inevitable by-product of the apartheid era and the effort to demolish it with alacrity.

It is profoundly ironic that this process is almost a perfect mirror-image of what happened under apartheid—when whites, especially Afrikaners, frequently got jobs, particularly in the state sector, on the basis of their skin colour. Almost a perfect mirror-image, but not quite. For the gravy train ushered in by the electoral victories of the ANC—and there has been plenty of gravy, with well-paid government posts proliferating like plankton—is at least travelling in the direction of national unity, rather than ethnic segregation.

Nevertheless, in some quarters in South Africa even to dispute the wisdom of AA is widely—and perhaps inevitably—regarded by black South Africans as racist. It is not unusual to hear in contemporary South Africa the argument that non-whites cannot be racist, by definition, because to be racist implies having power. As black South Africans don't have power, the worst they can be is prejudiced.

At that stage the debate begins to resemble a medieval scholastic exercise in considering how many angels are able to cavort on the head of a pin.

Maybe the last word on AA should go to South Africa's leading satirist, Pieter-Dirk Uys (*see* UYS *on page 52*). Uys, one of nature's anarchists, describes it as a 'necessary process of bending over blackwards.'

AIDS

No-one knows how many AIDS sufferers there are in South Africa. This is partly because no-one knows exactly how many people there are. A figure of 40 million was bandied about in 1996, but that was informed guesswork. The borders with neighbouring African countries are vast and sparsely patrolled; since apartheid's collapse South Africa has exerted an even stronger pull on Africans seeking to earn money or escape their own country. It's very easy for people to hop over the border fences. In June 1995 the Health Ministry said there were 1.2 million HIV positive people, projecting an increase to as much as 6.4 million by 2005. It's going to be a major problem.

AIRLINES

One airline dominates flights to and within South Africa—the national airline, South African Airways. SAA operates the latest generation of Boeing 747s on its flights to Europe, meaning that nearly all of them are non-stop. On international routes its quality of service is world-class; the airline has won Executive Travel magazine's 'Best Airline to Africa' annual award on six occasions. It's not the cheapest way to travel within the country, but prices are not outrageous—eg about R500 for a one-way economy ticket between Cape Town and Johannesburg. If speed is a priority then flying is a necessity. SAA has many international offices. Addresses, telephone and fax numbers of the most important are in an appendix on page 310.

In October 1996 Virgin Airlines also started a new, direct service between London and Johannesburg, providing much needed extra capacity and competition.

Most major airports are quite some distance from city centres. If not hiring a car or being collected on arrival, think twice about taking a taxi; it's expensive. A taxi-fare from Johannesburg International Airport to the city centre can be as high as R140; for a quarter of that you can pick up a regular, secure bus service. The same is true of other cities.

Flying times between Johannesburg and some major international destinations:—

Bombay: . . . . .8 hours 40 minutes	Nairobi: . . . . .4 hours
Buenos Aires: . . . . .11 hours	New York: . . . . .17 hours 30 minutes
Frankfurt: . . . . .11 hours	Perth: . . . . .9 hours 15 minutes
Hong Kong: . .13 hours 15 minutes	Rio de Janeiro: . . . . .9 hours
London: . . . .10 hours 30 minutes	Singapore: . . . . .10 hours 15 minutes
Miami: . . . . .18 hours	

A selection of international airline telephone numbers in Johannesburg (the telephone code for which is 011)

Aeroflot:	726 8070
Air Canada:	880 8931
Air France:	880 8055
Air India:	442 4421
Air New Zealand:	886 7270
Air Portugal:	337 1660
Alitalia:	880 9259
American Airlines:	880 6370
Austrian Airways:	482 3670
British Airways:	441 8600
Canadian Airlines:	339 4865
Cathay Pacific:	883 9226
China Airlines:	880 7125
Delta Airlines:	403 5702
El Al:	880 3232
Finnair:	339 4865
Gulf Air:	447 8690
Iberia:	907 1632
Japan Airways:	442 8015
KLM:	881 9696
Korean Air:	339 4865
Lufthansa:	484 4711
Malaysia Airlines:	880 9614
Quantas:	884 5300
Sabena:	331 8166
Singapore:	880 8560
SAA:	356 1111
Swissair:	484 1980
Thai Airways:	883 9068
Varig:	331 2471
Virgin:	886 6121

Domestic airlines (besides SAA) in South Africa fly various destinations around the country. For further information call the companies concerned on the following Johannesburg telephone numbers:

Comair 921 0222
Sun Air: 394 5555
SA Airlink: 394 2430

A is also for Airports, the names of some of which appear to be undergoing a partial transformation in South Africa—with the emphasis on partial. Thus Johannesburg's airport was long called Jan Smuts (after the South African statesman), but has now officially been rather dully re-christened 'Johannesburg International Airport'. This is somewhat confusing, as—at time of writing—all motorway signs to the airport still indicate 'Jan Smuts'. Moreover, all locals still refer to it as Jan Smuts. The same is true at Durban and Cape Town, whose airports are now officially known as Durban and Cape Town International Airport, having previously been Louis Botha and D F Malan.

It isn't entirely clear why Botha, Smuts and Malan have lost their airports, when equally politically incorrect figures such as P W Botha, H F Verwoerd and B J Vorster still have theirs—at George, Port Elizabeth, and Kimberley, respectively. These are the names and telephone numbers of the country's main domestic airports:

Ben Schoeman (East London): ....(0431) 44 5299
B J Vorster (Kimberley): ....(0531) 851 1241
Cape Town International: ....(021) 934 0407
Grand Central (Johannesburg domestic): ....(011) 805 3166
H F Verwoerd (Port Elizabeth): ....(041) 34 4333
Johannesburg International: ....(011) 975 9963
J B Hertzog (Bloemfontein): ....(051) 47 3811
Lanseria (Johannesburg domestic): ....(011) 659 2750
Durban International: ....(031) 361 1111
Margate: ....(03931) 20560
Nelspruit: ....(01311) 43192
Pierre van Ryneveld (Upington): ....(054) 31 1364
Pietermaritzburg: ....(0331) 958 2546
Pietersburg: ....(0152) 29 52011
P W Botha (George): ....(0441) 76 9310
Rand (Johannesburg domestic): ....(011) 827 8884
Richards Bay: ....(0351) 98 8413
Skukuza (in Kruger Park): ....(01311) 65611
Wonderboom (Pretoria): ....(012) 57 1188

ALCOHOL

Most drinking is done by South Africans either at home or in restaurants. Pubs and bars exist, but most of those outside of hotels can be shabby, seedy places, though a pub culture is developing slowly, aided perhaps by the fact that with the ending of economic and other sanctions, a wide range of international beers is now available. Pubs open at 10.00 am and generally close in the early hours.

Township shebeens—unlicensed drinking dens, some of them quite classy—are still the most popular social outlet for many black South Africans. But unless accompanied by a local black companion who really knows the score, don't go looking for shebeens; they can be very dangerous places.

South African beers tend to be light, lager-style brews, generally rather gassy and uninteresting except as thirst-quenchers. A couple of interesting exceptions are the (somewhat yeasty) beers from the small local brewery Mitchells, and Castle Milk Stout, a dark beer, less gassy and with greater flavour than the indistinguishable lagers. South Africa is awash in beer, sadly most of it second rate.

That is not true of wine, which (mostly due to its cultural image is a relative expense for black South Africans) is still predominantly a white middle-class drink. Most restaurants are licensed to sell alcohol; the best have excellent cellars.

Most shopping centres have at least one Bottle Store, selling alcohol and also fruit juices and other items. Bottle stores open from 08.00–18.00, though some in large cities close later. Saturday opening hours are from 08.30–14.00; some stay open until 16.00. They do not open on Sundays, when alcohol is on sale only in pubs, bars, hotels and restaurants. Some larger supermarkets also sell wine during licensing hours.

ANTIQUES

Prices for antiques are high, well up to international standards; it's hard to find a real bargain. The South African Antique Dealers Association, PO Box 729, Fontainebleau, 2032, telephone (011) 792 5627, fax (011) 793 3020, gives a list of reputable dealers.

BABIES, CHILDREN

South Africa is generally a child-friendly society, with one exception; most private game reserves and many of the expensive hotels and country lodges stipulate no children. Children can also be frowned upon in some restaurants where the emphasis is more on style than food. There are plenty of those.

BANKING

Banks hours are 09.00–15.30 Monday-Friday, and 08.30–11.00 on Saturdays. Major local banks are Allied, First National, Nedbank, Standard Bank, Trustbank, United

Bank and Volkskas. Travellers' cheques may be cashed at any bank and at certain major travel agencies, and are accepted at many hotels and shops. Opening a bank account is not a simple matter, involving lots of paperwork and time wasting. Best use travellers' cheques and credit cards, both widely acceptable. Foreign currency may only be exchanged at a bank. Automatic Teller Machines are located at most large branches.

Johannesburg central numbers for the major banks:

Allied, Trustbank, United and Volkskas
are all part of the ABSA group, phone: ....(011) 225 9111
First National: ....(011) 632 9111
Nedbank: ....(011) 630 7111
Standard:..(011) 636 9111

Ballooning, Hang Gliding, Microlighting and Parachuting

It's possible to do all of these. For details, contact the Aero Club of South Africa (telephone 011 805 0366) and the South African Hang Gliding and Paragliding Association (telephone and fax 011 609 1678).

Biltong

Should this come under I for Indigestible? Biltong is dried meat, sometimes spiced with pepper, sometimes sliced or cut into chunks, but often left in large lumps for the purchaser to cut, chew, hacksaw or blowtorch. The meat might be beef, or game, or ostrich, or any combination. Sometimes fatty, usually requiring considerable mastication, it's used as a snack or picnic item, or just when the craving for dead animal comes upon one. On sale everywhere, enjoyed by all sectors of society, biltong is quintessentially South African. Some believe it was invented to divert attention from the dullness of the local beer, its natural accompaniment.

BMW

One of the strongest indications that South Africa is genuinely returning to the international fold is that you find South Africans cracking hoary old jokes you have already heard in your own country. Hence the BMW quip. BMW of course is a famous brand of German motorcar. But in contemporary South Africa it also stands for 'Break My Window'—an ironic reference by local cynics to the clear preference shown by car thieves for BMWs.

BUREAUCRACY

Under apartheid, South Africa was not only an undemocratic but also a heavily bureaucratic country, with a bloated civil service with cast-iron job security for low-skilled, inefficient whites. That is being rapidly dismantled—and another being constructed. Known by local sceptics as the 'gravy train' this new state-administered edifice has one simple difference; it's all about reversing the sins of apartheid by creating consultative bodies, think-tanks, directorates of this and institutes of that. One egregious example of the new gravy train kicked off in early 1996, a R82.5m (£13.75m) 'transformation' of parliament; it wasn't very clear what that money would be spent on, apart from hefty salaries for politically correct paper-pushers.

Fortunately, unlike many other African or developing countries, South Africa is not a bureaucratic nightmare for visitors, and the common or garden aspects of tourism—sending mail, buying travel tickets, hiring equipment and so on—are very painless. But for a countervailing tendency, see later entries in this section on VAT and VISAS.

CAR HIRE

Hiring a vehicle in South Africa is expensive. The established internationally-known firms charge as much as £200 ($330) for one week's hire of a small manual vehicle, (including unlimited mileage and insurance).

But hiring a car is pretty much a necessity if you want to get off the beaten track or be freed from relatively slow means of transport such as buses or trains. It's a big country; there are more than 200,000 kilometres of national and provincial high-ways, 85,000 of which are tarred.

If you are driving during the summer months, over long distances, then try to hire a car with air conditioning—particularly if your journeys involve going through areas of potential security risk, such as remote rural districts, impoverished townships, or downtown Johannesburg, where it is sensible to have the windows closed.

Of the large firms, Budget Rent-A-Car is thoroughly recommended for its com-bination of competitive rates, quality of service, range of vehicles and countrywide network. Budget's toll-free number in Johannesburg is 0800-016622; reservations for all parts of the country can be made on that number.

Numbers for the dozens of other hire companies can be found in the Yellow Pages, or from tourist information bureaus.

CHILDREN

See under BABIES, CHILDREN

CINEMAS
South African cinemas are generally wonderful—spacious leg room, capacious and comfortable seats, excellent sound systems, wide screens, marvellous air conditioning. So marvellous that you should take with you a sweater or jacket; it can get very chilly. See later entry under COMPUTICKET.

CLIMATE
A southern hemisphere country, South Africa's midwinter is June–July, midsummer is December–January. But the country has a sunny, healthy climate all year round. Winters around Cape Town can be chilly and wet, while around Johannesburg they will often be cool but much drier. Summers are hot everywhere, and very humid along the Natal coast and eastern Cape.

AVERAGE MAXIMUM TEMPERATURES (CELSIUS)

Month	Cape Town	Johannesburg	Durban	Kruger National Park
January	26.5	26.3	27.2	31.4
February	27.1	25.6	27.5	30.6
March	25.8	24.3	26.9	30.1
April	23	22.1	25.6	28.6
May	19.9	19.1	24.1	27.0
June	18.5	16.5	22.5	25.0
July	17.2	16.4	22.0	25.0
August	18.1	19.8	22.4	26.0
September	19.1	22.8	22.9	28.5
October	21.5	25.0	23.6	29.0
November	24.0	25.3	24.9	30.0
December	25.5	26.1	26.2	30.0

CLOTHING
By and large South Africans dress casually, though for business purposes a suit and tie for men and smart dress for women signify seriousness of intent. 'Upmarket' restaurants often exercise a 'smart casual' dress code—a jacket for men, including, possibly, a tie.

In summer—approximately October to April—cool cotton clothes are best, with a jacket or jumper for evenings when the temperature drops. In winter, temperatures can still reach 20°C in most of the country, but nights can be cold, particular in the Cape. In summer and winter there can also be severe storms and very heavy rainfall in many parts of the country.

In game reserves, camouflage colours are best, to avoid being spotted by animals and to deter insects, which seem to be attracted to bright colours (including white).

At hotel pools topless bathing is not acceptable, though on many beaches going topless is now very common and unlikely to be frowned upon. As always, it's best to get a feel for what others are doing.

Sunburn and sunstroke can be serious problems. Always take adequate protection, both in winter and summer; lotions are essential, sunhats useful.

All but the smallest hotels offer a rapid laundry service, and coin-operated laundries, where clothes can be washed and ironed at very reasonable rates (thanks to cheap labour) can be found dotted around towns and cities.

COACHES

A relatively economical and safe method of travelling round the country is by bus or coach. Various inter-city bus companies offer comfortable, frequent services between the major cities. One drawback is the need to book your ticket at least 24 hours in advance; buying a ticket on the day of departure is not possible except for very short distance, local routes. On the other hand, this generally ensures no unseemly struggling for seats.

Translux, part of the state-run Transnet transport company, operates a service of luxury coaches on cross-country routes, (most of them no smoking) and stopping at various places. The most important routes include the following—this is just a selection and you should contact the company for information concerning minor routes.

- **Cape Town–Pretoria, via Bloemfontein**
  Departs Cape Town daily at 17.45, arrives Pretoria at 12.50;
  Departs Pretoria 17.00, arrives Cape Town 12.00.
  One-way fare R280.

- **Cape Town–Pretoria, via Kimberley**
  Departs Cape Town daily at 14.00 (except Monday and Wednesday),
  arrives Pretoria 08.00;
  Departs Pretoria daily at 14.00 (except Tuesday and Thursday),
  arrives Cape Town 08.45.
  One-way fare R280.

- **Cape Town–Durban,** daily, (via Bloemfontein and Pietermaritzburg):
  Departs Cape Town 12.00, arrives Durban 08.00;
  Departs Durban 12.00, arrives Cape Town 08.15.
  One-way fare R290.

- **Cape Town–Port Elizabeth** (coastal route):
  Departs Cape Town daily at 08.00, arrives Port Elizabeth 18.00;
  Departs Port Elizabeth daily at 08.00, arrives Cape Town 18.00;
  Additional service:
  Departs Cape Town every Tuesday, Thursday, Saturday and Sunday
  at 18.00, arrives Port Elizabeth 06.00,
  Departs Port Elizabeth every Monday, Wednesday, Friday and Saturday
  at 20.30, arrives Cape Town 08.00.
  One-way fare R115.

- **East London–Pretoria,** daily:
  Departs East London at 18.00, arrives Pretoria 07.00;
  Departs Pretoria at 18.00, arrives East London 07.00.
  One-way fare R200.

Translux accepts reservations by telephone; children under three (but not occupying a seat) go free, children between three and 12 are half adult fares. Reservations can be made up to three months in advance. Translux coaches on all routes have reclining seats, air conditioning, music and toilets; some routes also have videos, and a hostess service dealing with on-board refreshments.

For reservations or more information concerning Translux routes, the following are its main office telephone numbers:

Bloemfontein:	(051) 408 3242;	fax 408 3431
Cape Town:	(021) 405 3333;	fax 405 2545
Durban:	(031) 361 8333;	fax 361 7963
East London:	(0431) 44 2333;	fax 43 0471
Johannesburg:	(011) 774 3333;	fax 774 3318
Knysna:	(0445) 21361;	fax 21971
Port Elizabeth:	(041) 507 3333;	fax 507 2299
Pretoria:	(012) 315 2333;	fax 315 2299
Uitenhage:	(041) 994 2223;	fax 994 2223
Welkom:	(057) 916 3252;	fax 916 3251
24 hours:	(011) 774 3333	

Translux now also operates a travel pass system. Called the Lux Pass, it offers unlimited travel on the entire Translux network, getting off and on wherever and whenever wished. The pass covers periods of 7, 10, 15 days (which must be used in the course of one month, and costing R895, R1,270, and R1,540 respectively), and 21 or 30 days (which must be used in the course of two months and cost R2,170 and R2,720 respectively).

Another company worth trying for economical bus travel is the Cape Town-based The Baz Bus, a round South Africa budget bus catering particularly for backpackers, youth hostellers and those on a tight budget. For R520, it offers a round circuit from Cape Town to Swellendam, George, Knysna, Plettenberg Bay, Jeffrey's Bay, Port Elizabeth, Kenton-on-Sea, Hamburg, East London, Umtata, Port Shepstone, Durban, the Drakensberg mountains, Johannesburg, Kimberley, Beaufort West and back to Cape Town, calling in at a host of youth hostels en route. The service runs all year, using what the company calls 'semi-luxury' buses, the ticket is valid for four months, and passengers can get on and off where they choose. For reservations and further details, telephone (021) 439 2323 or fax (021) 439 2343.

Other long-distance coach companies are Greyhound; telephone (011) 403 6400, fax (011) 339 8372: and Impala; telephone (011) 974 6561, fax (011) 974 1346.

Comma

One quirk of South African speech and the printed word is that where many nations use a point to indicate a decimal place (eg, 6.7 per cent, 1.3 million), South Africans use a comma instead (eg 6,7 per cent, 1,3 million), and will actually say 'six comma seven per cent' instead of 'six point seven per cent'.

Communications

See under Post and Communications on page 41

Computicket

One of the joys of South Africa is a service called Computicket. This is a computer-linked network of more than 300 outlets which sells tickets for more than 40,000 nationwide cultural events such as cinema and theatre, as well as bus tours and lotteries. You can, for example, buy a ticket for a movie in Johannesburg when you are in Cape Town—or any combination you can think of. A great time-saver.

Credit Cards

All internationally recognized credit and charge cards are widely accepted, including American Express, Bank of America, Diners, MasterCard, Standard Bank Card and Visa. Johannesburg numbers for the major cards are as follows:

American Express:	(011) 358 4000
Diners Club:	(011) 337 3244
MasterCard and Visa:	(011) 498 4699

Curios

Turn any street corner, round any bend, and you will bump into a curio shop or street trader. At least, that's what it feels like. Masks, stone or wood carved heads, animals and human figures, bent-wire objects, beadwork, ornaments of a hundred different varieties—a magpie's delight. What you should bear in mind is that 99 per cent of the stuff sold in established shops and even roadside or street corner traders is mass-produced, lacking any individuality or originality and not particularly authentic. As decorative clutter goes, it's high calibre.

If you want authentic pieces of township craft-work, you have to delve deep into the countryside to find it. It's still there, particularly objects made from bits and pieces of scrap rubbish, magically transformed into a windmill, or an aeroplane, or motor-car. There is no means of telling how best to find it—except to say that the more you deviate from the regular tourist routes, the more likely you are to encounter it.

If you don't have time to explore in that way, then head for the one shop in the centre of Cape Town which has a wonderful range of authentic, unusual African— not just South African—artifacts and craft work. Patronized by David Bowie (among other stars, according to the staff) it's called African Image and is situated on the corner of Church and Burg streets; telephone (021) 238 385, fax (021) 221575.

Currency

South Africa's currency is the Rand, which is divided into 100 cents. A fully con-vertible currency, the exchange rate in late 1996 was R7.15 to £1.

In 1996 South Africa still had (widely ignored and broken) exchange controls, meaning in theory all currency must be declared on entering as well as leaving the country; in practice, you will be very unlucky to be asked how much you are bring-ing in. The maximum South African currency in cash that can be brought in is R500; an unrestricted amount of travellers cheques is permitted. A maximum of R500 may be exported—though checks seem to be non-existent at most border points.

New notes and coins have been introduced recently. New banknotes are in denominations of R10, R20, R50, R100 and R200; you won't see any old banknotes. Old and new coins are 1c, 2c, 5c, 10c, 20c, 50c, and R1, while there are also new R2 and R5 denominations. Old R2 coins are still sometimes found and are accepted. Some new high denomination coins bear superficial similarities to old lower denominations; watch your change.

There is no currency black market to speak of, though given the absurd restriction on the amount of South African currency that can be exported, people are sometimes interested in private money exchanges, which is illegal.

CUSTOMS ALLOWANCES

You may import 400 cigarettes, 250 grammes of tobacco and 50 cigars; one litre of spirits, two litres of wine; 50ml of perfume and 250ml of toilet water. Personal effects are admitted duty-free, though you may be required to open parcels. Cigarettes and alcohol are very cheap inside the country; perfumes are not.

DOOM

D is for Doom—nothing to do with the Apocalypse. Doom is the brand name of one of the country's leading and most effective anti-mosquito prophylactics. Stock up, not so much to avoid contracting malaria (the risk is quite small) but in order to get a good night's rest.

DRIVING

Driving can be a hair-raising experience. What follows is a comprehensive guide to surviving and enjoying the experience.

Generally it is advisable to possess an international driving licence, though car hire companies and traffic cops will usually accept a driving licence issued in an English-speaking country but check with the car hire company first. Drive on the left side of the road—vehicles are right-hand drive; on a roundabout or traffic circle, traffic approaching from the right has right of way.

Roads are identified by number. National highways are prefixed with the letter N; the N1 route, for example, is the main north-south highway between Cape Town, Johannesburg, Pretoria and beyond. Regional highways are prefixed by the letter R, and metropolitan roads by the letter M. Dirt roads—some of which are very good, others appalling—are prefixed by the letter D.

Speed limits: 120 kilometres per hour on national highways and freeways (though sometimes lower—watch for indicating signposts); 100 kilometres on rural roads; 60 kilometres in built-up areas. Road signs indicating distances and speed limits are in kilometres. Exceeding the speed limit can incur heavy on-the-spot fines. Traffic police have discretionary powers and sometimes let off tourists who have committed minor speeding offences. Seat belts must be worn by the driver and front seat passenger.

Drink-driving laws are more lax than in many countries; the local highway code says 'the liquor limit is not more than three beers or three glasses of wine or two tots of spirits. The alcohol content of your blood may not exceed 0.08g per 100ml of blood.' In practice, it's common for South Africans to exceed those already generous limits, but penalties can be stiff.

One irritation is that for some daft reason route-direction signs are often situated on the far side of a junction, which can mean you miss your exit unless you are watching carefully; allow plenty of time for turn-offs.

Another is the 'four-way stop' junction, found everywhere and in the most unlikely of places. At such junctions, vehicles from all four directions are required to stop at the junction; there then often follows a few seconds of (dangerous) uncertainty as the four drivers try to work out who goes first, second, third and last. The traffic light is a useful device, invented to resolve such quandaries. The highway code states that at a four-way stop 'the vehicle that stops first is the first to drive on when it is safe to do so.' That's the principle; the practice can be chaotic.

One important rule is that if driving on a single-lane road and another driver is going faster than you and wishes to overtake, you should move over to the left, crossing the unbroken yellow line which marks the edge of the road when it is safe to do so, allowing the faster vehicle to pass you. It's also etiquette momentarily to put on your hazard warning indicators once you have passed a vehicle that has moved across to let you pass, as a form of thank-you.

Night driving can be testing; few stretches of the national highways are lit, and in the rural areas there often are no cats' eyes, to mark lanes. In the rural areas you also face the hazard of wandering animals, incautious pedestrians and vehicles with poor or no tail-lights. Unless you really must, avoid driving after dark in rural areas or on anything except N routes. Dirt-road driving can also be gruelling and considerably slows up journey times.

There are many filling stations in towns and cities, but if driving long distances in the rural areas it's a good idea to fill up whenever your fuel gauge drops below half. Filling stations only take cash for fuel; credit cards are not acceptable. In larger places they operate a 24-hour service, otherwise they are normally open from 07.00–19.00. Petrol is sold in litres and pump attendants are normally present to deliver the fuel, clean the windows, check the oil, water and air in the tyres. If you tip the attendant a few Rands it will be much appreciated.

A number of national highways are subject to tolls; at the time of writing the total toll for any of the motorways was not higher than R20.

The Automobile Association (AA) is the country's biggest motor club: its breakdown toll-free number is 0800 010101. The AA's services are free to members of all AA clubs worldwide. Non-members may use the AA in cases of need, but for a fee.

DRUGS

It is a criminal offence both to possess and trade in certain drugs; anyone found guilty of such an offence can expect serious penalties. You will encounter at least the word *dagga*, if not the substance itself. *Dagga* is the local name for marijuana, the most commonly used—across all social and economic classes—illegal drug in South Africa, which has an ideal climate for its production.

It seems the police are these days turning a blind eye to people caught with small quantities of *dagga* which is evidently for their own consumption and not for trading. Another factor to bear in mind is that in the Eastern Cape and KwaZulu-Natal—prime spots for *dagga* production—it is suspected that much of the *dagga* trade is controlled by (very poorly paid) members of the police force.

Other proscribed drugs include heroin, cocaine and their derivatives. Many medicines—such as painkillers—that would be prescription-only elsewhere are available over the counter. Check the contents thoroughly before use.

ELECTRICITY

It is probably a good idea to take an adaptor for electrical appliances. The supply is 220/240 volts AC, 50 cycles. Only sockets with round three-pronged plugs are used.

FIREARMS

One of the more depressing things about South Africa is the amount of personal weaponry around—in 1996 one person in 13 had a licensed firearm, besides all the countless illegally-owned guns. Given the crime level it will probably be impossible to wean many South Africans from their pistols and rifles.

The preferred weapon of black radicals—and now of black criminals—used to be the AK-47 semi-automatic rifle, largely because it was cheap and easy to obtain. It's a bit bulky for muggers, who generally go for pistols or knives; there is a thriving underground weapons trade in the townships. Many whites now possess handguns, carrying them about their person, in their cars and in their bedside tables, on semi-permanent alert for burglars and other criminals, most of whom (it is politically incorrect to point out) derive from the country's underclass amongst the urban black population.

Should any visitor wish to be crazy enough to import a personal weapon, that's perfectly possible by obtaining a permit from the customs official upon entry. The permit is valid for 180 days and the visitor must be able to prove legal ownership of the gun. To buy a gun legally in South Africa you have to prove to the gunshop that you have permanent residence, and then complete paperwork for the police who should check that there are no outstanding criminal charges against you.

FLY-FISHING

FOSAF (The Federation of South African Fly-fishers) has representatives in several provinces. In KwaZulu-Natal, call (0331) 42 1038; in Free State (05816) 2 1106; in Gauteng (011) 887 8787; and in the Western Cape (021) 434 0285.

GUILT

After the end of World War II it was almost impossible to find anyone in Germany who had actually supported the Nazis. A similar miracle occurred in South Africa, where immediately apartheid was officially dead it was very difficult to find anyone who had even thought apartheid might have had its good points.

A related piece of magic also occurred; many whites after the watershed 1994 elections found that it was entirely possible to verbalize a revulsion for apartheid, without necessarily changing their behaviour towards non-white South Africans.

HEALTH

South Africa does not have a national health scheme. Visitors should get adequate medical (and other personal travel) insurance before arriving in the country. Public hospitals are generally overcrowded but medical skills are among the highest in the world. Private hospitals—very expensive—offer a much higher standard of comfort, though not of treatment. Doctors can be found via telephone directories and are listed under 'Medical Practitioners'. Most hospitals have accident and emergency facilities, and are listed under H in telephone directories. There are no requirements for vaccination certificates from visitors, except for those coming from a yellow fever area in Africa or parts of South America, such as Brazil.

While South Africa is fortunately free of many of the awful diseases found elsewhere in Africa, there are two that can cause problems—malaria and bilharzia. It's strongly recommended that visitors to the Mpumalanga lowveld, the Kruger National Park and most game reserves in KwaZulu-Natal take anti-malarial tablets. The endemic areas (where malaria always occurs) are the low altitude areas of the northern and eastern Transvaal, and northern KwaZulu-Natal. The epidemic areas (where malaria only occurs sporadically during the periods following summer rains) are adjacent to the Molopo, Kuruman, and Lower Orange rivers in the northern Cape, (see Malaria Zone map, page 58). Reports of a new and virulent strain of malaria, resistant to some forms of anti-malaria treatment, crossing from neighbouring Mozambique. Consult your physician before travelling to South Africa.

To combat the merely irritating aspect of the mosquito there are various excellent non-prescription insect repellants (*see* Doom earlier in this section), but wearing long-sleeved shirts and trousers and socks after dusk will also help. Mosquitoes also hate air-conditioning.

Bilharzia is a weakening ailment caused by ingesting the eggs of a parasitic worm that inhabits slow-moving fresh water. It's easily avoided. Do not wade through or bath in motionless inland waters—such as ponds—in KwaZulu-Natal, Gauteng, Mpumalanga and the Eastern Cape. If in doubt, don't enter the water. The only exceptions are rapidly flowing water or lakes at high altitudes. Some rivers and dams in the affected regions specify that they are bilharzia-free, but check first. Diagnosing bilharzia can be quite difficult, as the symptoms are often vague and diffused; the good news is that once detected it responds well to drugs.

Other things to watch for are ticks, venomous snakes, and scorpions. Ticks can be avoided by not walking through long grass, or if you do, by wearing long trousers tucked into socks and boots. Tick-bite fever can be quite debilitating though normally not seriously injurious. Snake bites and scorpion stings are rare and can be avoided by exercising care when in rural areas; be careful where you step and look before you sit down, especially near shady rocks or boughs of trees on the ground. If bitten by a snake, try to see what the snake looks like, and seek medical attention. A tourniquet placed above the bite will help prevent the venom spreading. For a scorpion sting, an ice-pack is probably the best emergency remedy.

Occasionally you may hear of a red tide alert along coastal areas. It's a slightly misleading term as the water discolorations may be brown, orange, purple or yellow as well as red. The discoloration is caused by dense concentrations of microscopic organisms called phytoplankton. Along South Africa's coast it's generally a specific group of phytoplankton called dinoflagellates. Red tides usually occur along the Cape west or south coasts in late summer and autumn, when the prevailing southerly winds cause cold, nutrient-rich water to rise up from deeper ocean layers. The increased nutrient levels in turn create a rapid increase in dinoflagellate quantities. Some dinoflagellates produce some of the most potent toxins known to man. Filter-feeders such as mussels, clams and oysters can accumulate toxic phytoplankton in their digestive systems and can cause illness or even death to consumers such as birds, marine mammals and man. Cooking only slightly diminishes the toxicity of affected shellfish because the toxins are generally heat stable. Care should be exercised in the collection of shellfish. If in doubt, contact the Red Tide Hotline on (021) 439 4380 for a 24-hour answering service that provides information concerning outbreaks of red tide detected by the Sea Fisheries Research Institute.

Tap water in most parts of the country is chemically treated and safe to drink. Fresh fruit, salads and vegetables are safe to eat. But to avoid diseases such as hepatitis it is obviously best to exercise care when in areas of obvious serious social deprivation, such as townships or some of the very remote rural areas, where local sanitation may not be perfect.

HIKING

Call the Hiking Federation of South Africa on (telephone and fax) (011) 886 6524, and the National Hiking Way Board, on (012) 343 1991, or fax (012) 320 0949.

Hitchiking

Hitchhiking is a risky business at the best of times, and in contemporary South Africa very few white South Africans will either hitchhike or give lifts to hitchhikers, of any colour. The inexperienced traveller should not hitchhike in South Africa; it's just not worth the risk.

As for giving lifts to hitchhikers, that's a slightly more complicated issue. Many black schoolchildren (normally identifiable by crisp black-and-white uniforms) are forced to travel long distances to schools in the rural areas; up to 50 kilometres each way between home and school is not uncommon. These children hitch out of dire necessity and giving three or four of them a lift is unlikely to be risky—though communication may be a problem. Similarly single women, mothers with small children and elderly people probably pose no risk. It is sad but true that all other categories of hitchhiker may pose an unacceptable level of risk; you just can't be sure.

Holidays

In 1996 there were 12 national public holidays:

January 1 . . . .New Year's Day;	June 16 . . . . .Youth Day;
March 21 . . . .Human Rights Day;	August 9 . . . . . . .National Women's Day;
April 5 . . . . . .Good Friday;	September 24 . .Heritage Day;
April 8 . . . . . .Family Day;	December 16 . . .Day of Reconciliation;
April 27 . . . . .Freedom Day;	December 25 . . .Christmas Day;
May 1 . . . . . . .Workers' Day;	December 26 . . .Goodwill Day.

Apart from the two days around Easter, these holidays normally fall on the same day each year.

A word of warning concerning School Holidays. The most important occur during December and January, give or take a week or two either end; it varies between provinces. This period is when all South African families hit the road. Most of the game parks, beach resorts, country retreats and cheaper hotels will be completely packed with locals getting away from it all—all at the same time. If you intend travelling to the country during these months, book well in advance; and expect to feel like the whole of South Africa is looking for an elephant on precisely the same stretch of road in the Kruger Park as you are on.

Horse Safaris

The Southern African Association for Horse Trails and Safaris can be reached on the telephone number (011) 788 3923.

HUMOUR

It may be the climate, it may be apartheid, it may be any one of a hundred complex things, but for some reason South Africa lacks a sophisticated comic culture. There are notable rare exceptions—*see* UYS, PIETER-DIRK, later in this section.

However there is one post-apartheid joke worth preserving for posterity. In January 1996 much fuss was caused by the removal from parliament in Cape Town of portraits of white South African political figures, many of them implicated in the building and development of apartheid. Their portraits were replaced by contemporary art, much of it critical of the apartheid era. Commenting on the removal of the stuffy paintings of white politicians, an SABC journalist remarked that 'they were obviously taken down because hanging's too good for them'.

HUNTING

Hunting of some wildlife, under strict regulation, is legal. When using a firearm it is illegal to hunt with a spotlight or any artificial light; to hunt from a public road; to hunt during the hours of darkness; in a public place; to use a firearm that uses a rim-fire cartridge with a calibre of less than 5.6mm; to use an automatic firearm (ie one that fires more than two shots without having to be re-loaded by hand); to hunt with a dog (except when hunting season is open or when using a dog to search for or follow wounded animals); or to hunt birds from a boat.

There are many protected species, but surprisingly it is possible to hunt a wide range of creatures, including the 'big five' (elephant, white rhino, lion, leopard and buffalo), for which a number of strictly controlled hunting permits, limiting the numbers killed, is annually available.

To find out more, contact the following organisations:
SA HUNTERS AND GAME CONSERVATION ASSOCIATION:
PO Box 18108 Pretoria North 0116. Tel: (012) 565 4856; fax: (012) 565 4910.
PROFESSIONAL HUNTERS ASSOCIATION:
telephone (011) 706 7724; fax (011) 706 2014; PO Box 770, Cramerview, Johannesburg 2060.

INFLATION

Where prices are given in this book they should be taken as a guide only. They were accurate in mid-1996, but annual inflation in 1995 was officially 6.4 per cent and there is wide consensus that by 1998 it would have returned to double figures. Take annual inflation rates into account when calculating the cost of any prices quoted in this book.

IMBONGI

An *imbongi* (plural form, *iimbongi*) is a traditional oral 'praise' poet, dressed in tribal costume, whose social function is to recite improvised and impromptu poems saluting—and sometimes criticizing—a chief or other bigwig.

In contemporary South Africa, where there is a cottage industry of resurrecting once significant practices that have become completely de-contextualised, *iimbongi* have made a vigorous, if thoroughly anachronistic, comeback. Since the establishment of democratic government no important social, political or cultural function is complete without the performance of an *imbongi*.

At Nelson Mandela's presidential inauguration on 10 May 1994, for example, there were two *iimbongi* to chant/sing, one of whom managed to yoke together the thoughts of Fidel Castro, Yasser Arafat, Boutros Boutros-Ghali and Muammar Gadaffi, in his adoration of Mandela. When the South African cricket team thrashed England in early 1996, Mandela came to the closing ceremony in Port Elizabeth. The whole of South Africa sat glued to the television set and watched an impatient and embarrassed South African cricket official signal to an interminable *imbongi* to wind up, and get off.

JUICE

J is for juice, as in fruit juices. The wine-tasting routes in and around the Cape are well-known; teetotalers are well-served by the Cape fruit routes. There are at least four day-long drives you can do from Cape Town, taking you through beautiful countryside and some of the finest fruit-growing areas of the world.

• THE FOUR PASSES FRUIT ROUTE: 316 KILOMETRES ROUND-TRIP

Take the N2 from Cape Town, stopping off at the village of Grabouw. Then take the R321 over Viljoen's Pass to Vyeboom, an apple and pear growing centre. Then take the R45 to Franschhoek, a fruit-growing as well as wine centre, where you can call in at the Bien Donné estate, which acts as an information centre for this particular route. Then continue along the R45, turning left onto the R310, through Pniel and the Helshoogte Pass to Stellenbosch, where you can visit the national fruit research centre, Infruitec. Then back to Cape Town.

• THE BREEDE RIVER FRUIT ROUTE: 432 KILOMETRES ROUND-TRIP

Take the N1 from Cape Town to Worcester—itself a beautiful old town—and take the R60 to Robertson, where besides grapes, the area is well-known for its apricots, peaches and nectarines. At Robertson you can either turn off to the small, 19th-century village of McGregor, or go onto the R317 to Bonnievale, driving along the banks of the Breede River, or continue on the R60 to Ashton, a major centre of fruit-canning, particularly peaches. Taking the R62 from Ashton you will arrive at Montagu, via Cogmans Kloof Pass. Montagu is another charming small town, where you have a choice of direction: either turn right onto the R62, to Barrydale, then taking the R324 via one of the country's most beautiful mountain passes, the Tradouw Pass, then head towards Swellendam and back to cape Town via the N2; or take the R318 from Montagu through Burger Pass, observing on one side the fertile Breede River valley and on the other the start of arid Great Karoo. The road rejoins the N1 and you return to Cape Town through the stunningly beautiful Hex River valley.

• THE PAARL FRUIT ROUTE: 150 KILOMETRES ROUND-TRIP
Take the N1 to Paarl, on the Berg River, then head towards Wellington on the R44. The area is a centre for production of deciduous, berry and citrus fruits, and Wellington is also the site of the South African Dried Fruit Co-op. There are many roadside stalls selling jams, chutneys, pickles, preserves and fresh fruits in season. Then drive north to Riebeek Kasteel, turning off to Malmesbury and thence back to Cape Town via the N7.

• THE CERES FRUIT ROUTE: 275 KILOMETRES ROUND-TRIP
Take the N1 and then R44 routes from Cape Town to Wellington, and then follow the R303 to Ceres, which is on the banks of the Dwars River. This locality produces pears, plums, apples, apricots, peaches, cherries and much other fruit. From Ceres return down the R303, turning off towards Wolseley. Then take the R46 to Tulbagh, severely damaged by an earthquake in 1969 but since restored to its original prettiness. From Tulbagh you can return on the R44 to Wellington, Paarl and rejoin the N1 back to Cape Town.

MADIBA

One of the fascinating developments of the immediate post-apartheid era is how a whole nation—well, almost whole—has come to believe it has an almost personal relationship with its president, Nelson Mandela. Almost everyone refers to him as 'Madiba,' a term that accords him respect while also suggesting familiarity, as though he were an elderly much-loved uncle. Mandela has encouraged this attitude in various ways, including permitting (in 1996) Pretoria's tourist authorities to use his face, garbed in different styles, including, bizarrely enough, as a Boer commando leader, on promotional advertising, see page 151.

The nadir of this game was reached in January 1996 when Cosmopolitan magazine nominated him South Africa's sexiest and most eligible bachelor—a couple of months before his divorce from Winnie. 'He's everything a woman could want in a man—mega-powerful, kind, modest, considerate and with a great sense of humour. Not to mention the cutest dimples, the world's most winning smile and funky dress sense.'

Media

By local standards, Cosmopolitan is a shining example of intellectual prowess. Local newspapers, magazines, radio and television are, with one or two exceptions, dire.

Of the English-language press, *Business Day* is the leading local business and finance daily newspaper, providing fairly comprehensive if not particularly probing coverage; the *Financial Mail* is a dense, *Economist*-style weekly magazine; in Johannesburg and further afield *The Star* is good for news and local information, though its features and editorials appear to know only two modes, bland or blustering; the *Mail & Guardian* (a weekly) is the best-written and most consistently absorbing newspaper in the country; and a new Sunday newspaper, *Sunday Independent*, tries to strike a more intelligent pose than the bulk of local printed journalism. *Drum*, an English-language colour monthly magazine, is worth reading for an insight into the concerns of black South Africans. Most newspapers carry comprehensive details of local films, theatre, restaurants and other cultural events. An excellent, unusual, irregularly-published colour magazine to look out for is *ADA* (Art, Design, Architecture), published in Cape Town but available nationally; it's the best place to pick up on local trends, issues and personalities.

Television and radio are largely dominated by the state-owned South African Broadcasting Corporation (SABC), an institution deeply tarnished in the past by its unthinking adherence to the apartheid regime. SABC is now frantically trying to reinvent itself. It has changed its spots, but under the skin is still the same animal in terms of production quality. Its TV broadcasting consists largely of US imports or risibly weak locally-produced game shows or talk shows, where third-rate presenters chat to second-rate stars. News and analysis programmes generally are slack. Many South Africans now scarcely watch SABC TV, preferring instead one of the cable or satellite broadcasters. SABC1 broadcasts in English, Xhosa and Zulu; SABC2 in Afrikaans and Sotho; and SABC3 entirely in English.

The dozens of radio stations around the country tend to blur into one, most playing a diet of pop records that failed to make it big 15 or more years ago, interspersed with tedious, ranting phone-in programmes. SABC's SAfm has a reasonably interesting diet of talk shows and news, but travellers doing lots of driving should take plenty of cassette tapes. One exception to the general awfulness of local radio is a strange station called Radio Safari, which can be picked up on the FM band in and around the Kruger Park. If you ignore the stilted delivery, the hammy acting, and script-writing which assumes the listener has a mental age of 10, Radio Safari is excellent for one reason—it broadcasts nothing but items about the flora and fauna of the area, and thus is an extremely easy way of picking up knowledge and information.

MEASUREMENT
The metric system of weights and measurements is used.

MK
MK stands for Umkhonto we Sizwe, or Spear of the Nation, which was the ANC's underground military wing. According to the journalist Arthur Goldstuck, MK was 'rated the second least effective guerilla army in history, but that's only because the Manchester United Supporters' Club was also counted.'

Now disbanded, a number of its former members have been integrated into the South African National Defence Force (SANDF). As the SANDF itself came under budgetary pressures following the 1994 elections, former MK members were offered instead of SANDF membership a cash payment of between R12,734 and R42,058, (equivalent to £2,1222 and £7,000), depending on length of service.

OPENING HOURS
O is for opening hours, the absurdity thereof. There is no consistency of opening hours for public buildings, museums and suchlike, which is particularly irritating when it comes to the (otherwise praiseworthy) publicity associations and tourist information bureaus (see the relevant appendix on pages 315–18). In general, shops are open from 09.00–17.00 during the week and half-day on Saturday; some close for an hour at lunch, as do just about all publicity associations and tourist information bureaus. In general the latter are closed all day Sunday.

OUTDOOR MARKETS
There are many outdoor markets dotted across the country. Here is a list of some of the better ones.

BLOEMFONTEIN
Art market at Loch Logan on Henry Street, the first Saturday of each month.
CAPE TOWN
Antiques and bric-a-brac, on Church Street between Burg and Long Streets, Monday–Saturday.
Flea market, at Green Point Common, on Sundays and Public Holidays.
JOHANNESBURG
Arts and crafts, at the Upper Mall, in Rosebank, every Sunday.
Flea market, at Fisherman's Village, Bruma Lake, Marcia Street, Tuesday-Sunday.
Organic produce, arts and crafts, clothing, at Culross Road, in Bryanston, on Thursday and Saturday from 09.00–13.00, and Tuesday nights nearest the full moon, between 18.00–21.00.

KIMBERLEY
Art market, on Jan Smuts Boulevard, opposite Oppenheimer Gardens, the last Saturday of each month.

PORT ELIZABETH
Art market, at St Georges Park, on the first Sunday of each month between 09.00–17.00.

PRETORIA
Flea market, on Burnett Street, Hatfield, on Sundays between 09.00–16.00.
Flea market, outside State Theatre on Church Street, on Saturdays between 08.00–13.00.

PERSONAL SAFETY

South Africa has the reputation of being a violent country. Like many reputations, this one is full of contradictions. Personal security for travellers need not be a problem providing some basic rules are followed.

One of the country's miracles is that despite centuries of ill-treatment by whites, the average black South African is not automatically anti-white. However, it is true that in some circumstances you will, if you are white, get a much warmer reception from some black South Africans once they learn you are from overseas. Much of the violence the country has experienced and occasionally still suffers is politically-motivated and carried out between rival criminal or political black groups, in black townships and rural areas. You will not encounter this unless very stupid or very unlucky.

In 1995 there was an average of 50 murders a day and a housebreaking every two minutes. In South Africa in 1996 unemployment amongst black South Africans was estimated at 40 per cent; the average monthly wage for a black South African was R301, or about £42 ($65). The average for whites was R5,000, or about £700 ($1,085). This widespread poverty—and inequality of wealth—will not be much ameliorated over the next decade; the incidence of economically-motivated crime may well increase.

You can minimize the risk of becoming a victim of crime by thinking carefully about how you behave. The potentially most dangerous place you are likely to visit is Johannesburg. It's always been a tough place. Other cities, such as Durban, are also experiencing a surge in crime. Even in Johannesburg you should be able to steer clear of trouble, providing you practice the following principles, which hold good for whatever part of the country you might be in:—

• don't walk alone in either downtown Joburg or the city's suburbs at night. Try to avoid downtown Joburg even by day, as mugging is now common. In other cities try to avoid walking alone at night in deserted areas.

- don't be shy of taking advice from either the staff at your hotel or other locals as to what places or what sort of behaviour should be avoided.
- don't visit poor areas, particularly black townships, unless in a group led by an experienced guide from a reputable tour operator, or in the company of people you know and trust.
- don't carry large sums of cash either during the day or at night when you go into high-risk areas.
- don't leave cash and valuables in your hotel room or car; use a hotel deposit box.
- if challenged by a mugger, don't resist; try to stay calm and breath slowly and deeply (it will help your self-control) and be completely passive
- if driving in high-risk areas, lock all doors and don't pick up hitchhikers; at night in cities be particularly vigilant at traffic lights and other junctions where traffic has to stop. Avoid driving in rural areas at night, as much to avoid the risk of a serious accident due to bad lighting as anything else.
- don't hitchhike.
- car hijacking by armed groups in Johannesburg, even during the day, is now relatively common. Don't resist or protest—the hijackers may shoot you. If hiring a car, consider renting the least flashy vehicle your self-esteem permits. Car thefts in 1996 were running at about 100,000 a year; about 10 per cent were by hijackings at gun or knife-point.
- blend into the local scene as much as you can by not being an ostentatious tourist; remember that casual dress is perfectly acceptable in all but the most formal situations. Ask yourself before you go out: 'What do I have about me that makes me look worthwhile mugging?' Then leave it behind or if you must take it, use a tatty, poor-looking bag.
- if you intend going to Eastern Cape province, where lawlessness has reached serious levels in some areas, try to stick to the main roads, go in a group or organized tour, stay to heavily-used coast roads as much as possible, and make sure that you have done all you can to avoid a vehicle breakdown.
- finally, cheer yourself up by remembering that Johannesburg, the most dangerous place you are likely to find yourself in, is probably the least interesting place you will see during your time in the country. So don't waste too much time there unless you have to.

Two important telephone numbers are the **Police Flying Squad**—10–111—and the **Ambulance Service**—10–177. Both are nationwide numbers. Local counselling organizations include **Lifeline** (similar to the Samaritans), numbers for which can be found in local telephone directories.

PLANNING

It may seem obvious, but a little bit of planning in advance of your trip will pay enormous dividends. South Africa is a very easy place to visit as an independent traveller; all you need to do is a little preliminary research and you can customize for yourself a perfect trip.

Part of your planning should be to prioritize what places you wish to visit. It's a vast country and to see it all properly would take several months. Large areas— such as the huge expanses of farmland and cultivated forestry of the eastern Orange Free State, with the occasional small town looking exactly like the one you passed 50 kilometres back—don't really warrant a visit.

This is a personal suggestion where to visit if you have a week, two weeks, three weeks and one month:

ONE WEEK

Cape Town; the Cape peninsula; the winelands of Stellenbosch, Paarl and Franschhoek; and a drive to one of the nearby seaside areas such as Hermanus.

TWO WEEKS

As above, then fly to the Kruger Park, to spend a few days there either on a private game reserve or in one of the several rest camps run by the Kruger Park itself, then driving to the Blyde River Canyon area west of the Kruger Park, before returning to Johannesburg for final departure. If you find yourself with a day or two in Johannesburg, spend it by driving the short distance north to Pretoria, which has a much more interesting range of museums and monuments, and little or none of the tense street atmosphere.

THREE WEEKS

As above, with the difference being to drive from the Blyde River Canyon area to Nelspruit, then fly either to Durban or Richard's Bay, spending the third week exploring the north KwaZulu-Natal coast.

ONE MONTH

As above, with the final week being spent driving from Durban to Pietermaritzburg, Howick and Estcourt, leaving the main route back north to Johannesburg to venture into and stay over a night or two in the Drakensberg mountains, which form the eastern border of Lesotho.

POST AND COMMUNICATIONS

Post offices are usually open from 08.00–16.30 during the week, 08.00–12.00 on Saturday. Smaller ones close for lunch from 13.00–14.00. Most large hotels can arrange mail and fax services.

The telephone system is almost completely automatic; direct dialling to all parts of the world is very easy. Post offices have telephones for both local and international calls. Be careful when using hotel telephones; very high surcharges are levied. If possible take a designated telephone card from your own country, to minimize your expenses. Inside South Africa, for **international enquiries** call 1025; for **local enquiries**, 1023.

Cellular telephones can be hired from a variety of local firms on a daily, weekly or monthly basis; check local newspapers and the Yellow Pages for details.

QUANTITY OR QUALITY?

It might have something to do with the sheer size of the place, or maybe it's some compensatory mechanism which only a psychoanalyst could unravel. Whatever the cause, white middle-class South Africa can feel like a different dimension, where quantity is more highly prized than quality. This intangible can most graphically be felt in the ostentatious consumerism that grips that highly influential sector of society. The size of your house, your salary, the cubic capacity of your car, the number of times you have the caterers round to entertain your guests—all these things matter to many—not all, of course—white middle-class South Africans.

RAILWAYS

• SPOORNET

The railway network, **Spoornet**, was recently semi-privatized, resulting in the closing of many passenger services on smaller routes. Passenger travel is now largely restricted to main destinations on so-called 'name trains', all of which operate a first, second and third-class service. First class is very comfortable, second less so and third—which used to be for non-whites only—is quite spartan.

Passenger services are quite attractive for overseas tourists, who are entitled to a 25 per cent discount on first-class fares (except on the Blue Train), provided that their visit does not exceed three months. Local suburban trains operate in the main industrial conurbations around Cape Town, Durban, Johannesburg and elsewhere—but do not use them; they can be exceptionally dangerous places for travellers who stick out like a sore thumb.

The name trains are all reliable, safe services, offering a cheaper—though much slower—alternative to flying or car hire. They normally have dining cars—adequate if not great cuisine—and sleeping berths; first and second-class coupés have two or three bunks respectively; first and second-class compartments have four or six bunks respectively.

Spoornet now also operates a very useful rail travel pass system, giving considerable cost reductions, only for foreign tourists. Called a **Spoor Pass**, it permits the holder to travel on a given number of days during a specified period. They are available for first or second class travel and include overnight accommodation. The options available are: the SP05, giving five days travel in 21 days; the SP08, giving eight days travel in one month; the SP12, giving 12 days travel in one month; or the SP16, giving 16 days travel in two months.

The disadvantages of the Spoor Pass are that it must be purchased before arriving in South Africa; it does not guarantee a reservation (reservations for the name trains can be made up to three months in advance); and it is not valid for the Blue Train, the Spoornet train for which there is the heaviest demand. For further information concerning the Spoor Pass, contact Tourlink Ltd, PO Box 169, Cresta 2194, South Africa; telephone (011) 404 2617/8, or fax (011) 402 7299.

For **Spoornet train reservations**—which you must make at least 24 hours in advance—either call in at the networks' offices in all the major cities, located at the railway stations, or telephone one of the following major Spoornet centres (bookings can be made by telephone with the use of a credit card):

Johannesburg:	.......(011) 773 2944	Bloemfontein:	......(051) 408 2941
Pretoria:	.................(012) 315 2401	Kimberley:	...........(0531) 88 2631
Durban:	.................(031) 361 7621	East London:	.......(0431) 44 2719
Cape Town:	...........(021) 405 3871		

Among Spoornet's name trains, the most famous is the **Blue Train**, a luxury service travelling the 1,600 kilometres between Pretoria—calling in at Johannesburg—and Cape Town. Its accommodation ranges from The Suite, a luxury compartment for two with en-suite facilities, costing R6,585 (the price being the same for either one or two people, including meals, drinks and bedding), to compartments with communal toilets and showers, priced at R1,910 per person. A compartment with private shower and toilet costs R2,645 per person. Travellers in the lower-priced compartments have to pay extra for meals and drinks. Fares for children aged between two and nine are slightly reduced. The train leaves Pretoria in the early morning, arriving in Cape Town the middle of the following day. On the south-north route it leaves Cape Town late morning, arriving in Pretoria early afternoon the following day. It is also possible to take your car on the Blue Train, which between Johannesburg and Cape Town has a motorcar truck attached.

The Blue Train is very popular; you should make a reservation well in advance of your trip to South Africa. **Group reservations** for parties of 10 or more for the Blue Train can be made by contacting The Manager, Blue Train Reservations, PO Box 2671, Joubert Park 2044, South Africa: telephone (011) 773 7631, fax (011)

773 7643. For **individual reservations** you should telephone one of the four Blue Train offices: Johannesburg (011) 774 4496; Pretoria (012) 315 2436; Cape Town (021) 218 2672; or Durban, (031) 361 7550.

Spoornet operates other mainline trains, including:

Algoa: departs Johannesburg on Sundays, Tuesdays and Thursdays, for Port Elizabeth; and departs Port Elizabeth on Mondays, Wednesdays and Fridays for Johannesburg. This train also stops at a number of other stations including Germiston, Vereeniging, Sasolburg, Bloemfontein, Cradock, and Alicedale. One-way journey time is 19 hours and will use up one day of a Spoor Pass.

Amatola: departs Johannesburg daily (except Saturday) for East London, returning from East London to Johannesburg every day (except Saturday). This train also stops at other stations including Bloemfontein, Bethulie, Queenstown, Cathcart, Toise, Stutterheim, and Berlin. One-way journey time is 20 hours and will use up one day of a Spoor Pass.

Bosvelder: departs Johannesburg daily for Messina, returning daily to Johannesburg from Messina. Among the other stations this train also stops at are Pretoria, Nylstroom, Potgietersrus, Pietersburg, Louis Trichardt, and Mopane. One-way journey time is 15 hours and will use up one day of a Spoor Pass.

Bulawayo: departs Johannesburg on Tuesdays for Bulawayo, returning to Johannesburg on Thursdays. This train also stops at other stations including Pretoria, Potgietersrus, Pietersburg, Louis Trichardt, Messina, Bannockburn, Somashula, and Shangani. One-way journey time is 25 hours and will use up two days of a Spoor Pass.

Diamond Express: departs Bloemfontein for Pretoria every day except Saturday, and from Pretoria to Bloemfontein every day except Saturday. It calls at other stations, including Kimberley, Warrenton, Christiana, Bloemhof, Makwassie, Klerksdorp, Potchefstroom, Oberholzer, Randfontein, Krugersdorp, and Johannesburg. One-way journey time is 15 hours and will use up one day of a Spoor Pass.

Komati: departs Johannesburg for Komatipoort every day, travelling on to Maputo every Sunday, Tuesday and Thursday. It returns from Maputo to Komatipoort on Mondays, Wednesdays and Fridays, from where it operates a daily return service to Johannesburg. Total one-way journey time between Johannesburg and Maputo is almost 30 hours and will therefore use up two days of a Spoor Pass.

Limpopo: departs Johannesburg for Harare on Fridays, returning from Harare to Johannesburg on Sundays. This train also stops at the following stations in both directions: from Johannesburg—Pretoria, Pietersburg, Louis Trichardt, Messina, Customs Halt, Beitbridge, Rutenga, Gweru, Kwekwe, Kadoma, Chegutu, and Norton. One-way journey time is about 26 hours and will therefore use up two days of a Spoor Pass.

Mossel Bay: departs Johannesburg for Mossel Bay on Thursdays, returning from Mossel Bay to Johannesburg on Saturdays. This train also stops at the following stations in both directions: from Johannesburg, Germiston, Vereeniging, Sasolburg, Kroonstad, Henneman, Virginia, Bloemfontein, Trompsburg, Springfontein, Norvalspont, Coleberg, Noupoort, Rosmead, Middelburg, Bethesda Road, Graaff-Reinet, Aberdeen Road, Klipplaat, Willowmore, Oudtshoorn, George, Great Brak River, Little Brak River, and Hartenbos. One-way journey time is about 28 hours and will therefore use up two days of a Spoor Pass.

Southern Cross: departs Cape Town for Port Elizabeth every Friday, returning to Cape Town from Port Elizabeth on Sundays. Other stations this train stops at include Wellington, Wolseley, Worcester, Robertson, Swellendam, George, Oudtshoorn, and Uitenhage. One-way journey time is 24 hours; this trip will use up two days of a Spoor Pass.

Trans Karoo: departs Pretoria for Cape Town on a daily basis, returning from Cape Town to Pretoria also on a daily basis. It also stops at a number of other stations, including Johannesburg, Kimberley, De Aar, Beaufort West, Leeu-Gamka, Matjiesfontein, Worcester, and Wellington. One-way journey time is 28 hours, and requires two days of a Spoor Pass.

Trans Natal: departs Johannesburg daily for Durban, and returns from Durban to Johannesburg also on a daily schedule, calling in at a variety of other stations, including Pietermaritzburg. One-way journey time is almost 14 hours and will use up one day of a Spoor Pass.

Trans Oranje: departs Durban for Cape Town on Thursdays, returning from Cape Town to Durban on Mondays. This train also stops at other stations, including Pietermaritzburg, Estcourt, Colenso, Ladysmith, Harrismith, Bethlehem, Bloemfontein, Kimberley, Modderrivier, Oranjerivier, De Aar, Beaufort West, Worcester, Wolseley, and Wellington. One-way journey time is more than 36 hours; it will use up two days of a Spoor Pass.

• Rovos Rail

For wealthy railway enthusiasts there is an alternative to the Blue Train—**Pride of Africa**, a train run by Rovos Rail, owned and operated by a South African entrepreneur called Rohan Vos. He has built up a fleet of early twentieth-century steam engines and rolling stock, all of which have been carefully restored. For the last few years Rovos Rail has operated several routes, the main one being a leisurely 48-hour journey between Pretoria and Cape Town; that's an overall average speed of about 33 kilometres an hour.

Vos calls The Pride of Africa 'the most luxurious train in the world'; it certainly is an unusual experience. Unlike the Blue Train, which is modern rolling stock pulled by diesel engine, Rovos Rail's carriages are all softly-lit, wood-panelled, carpeted and lavishly appointed, with everything done to encourage the traveller's sense of taking a train journey out of the 1930s. Moreover, for 100 kilometres or so at the start and end of the journey between Pretoria and Cape Town, the train is pulled by steam engine. The steam engine is uncoupled relatively early in the journey because Rovos Rail does not have access to water and coaling facilities en route, but for a brief period you can have authentic steam in your nostrils—and smuts in your eye, should you wish.

Aboard the green-liveried Pride of Africa, you are thoroughly cosseted with three splendid meals a day, accompanied by a wide choice of excellent wines. The rear enclosed observation car, with comfortable sofas and armchairs, allows an all-round view, and has a bar which never seems to close; all drinks are included in the ticket price, as are all meals, cigarettes, postcard stamps and other sundries. There are no telephones, faxes, televisions or radios on board the train (though the train manager does carry a portable telephone for emergencies). The en-suite accommodation is comfortable and spacious, being either 16 or 11 square metres, with air-conditioning, an essential item in the summer, and hot-water bottles for the winter. The beds are wonderfully comfortable, despite the creaking, groaning antiquity of the coaches—after an hour or two such noises just become part of the background. The food is good but do not expect a gourmet's paradise. Service is friendly and attentive, including early morning tea or coffee served at an hour you choose. The route between Pretoria and Cape Town includes a morning stop at Kimberley to visit the Big Hole (the former diamond mine), and on the second and last day of the journey breakfast at Matjiesfontein, an odd little village. Rovos Rail also does an annual Cape Town–Dar Es Salaam and return run.

Fully inclusive prices for the 48-hour Pretoria-Cape Town journey—which is immensely popular, so booking well in advance of your intended travelling date is essential—started at R3,995 for 1996–97. Rovos Rail can be contacted by telephoning (012) 323 6052/4, or by fax on (012) 323 0843.

But whether you take the Blue Train or Pride of Africa, be warned. For most of the rail journey between Pretoria and Cape Town the scenery is repetitious and dull. Until the train passes through a network of tunnels at the Hex River, a couple of hundred kilometres as the crow flies from Cape Town, much of it is through the Karoo, where apart from the occasional sheep, the landscape is visually arid. Once through those tunnels and into the area around Worcester and Paarl, approaching Cape Town itself, the landscape is more attractive, with enormous mountains dwarfing vineyards and small homesteads nestling beside delicate rivers. But that's the final tenth of the journey. In other words, both the Blue Train and Rovos Rail are train experiences rather than an opportunity for observing interesting scenery. The north-eastern Cape has many qualities; visual delight is not one of them.

• Union Limited

A subsidiary of **Transnet** (the holding company of Spoornet) has started trading as Union Limited Steam Railtours and offers genuine steam-train experiences. A six-day trip, using narrow-gauge steam-trains for all but short stints on the first and final days, does a round-trip from Cape Town, along the south coast calling in at Mossel Bay, Knysna and Oudtshoorn before returning to Cape Town. The train has first-class four-berth compartments (taking a maximum of two persons for space and comfort) and two-berth coupés (maximum of one person). Single travellers may be required to share with one other person. Each compartment and coupé has a wash basin and every coach a gas-heated shower. There is no air conditioning. Meals are served in a restored 1933 dining car. A maximum of 80 passengers per tour is permitted, and at present 11 tours are being made each year, so there is likely to be a heavy demand. At R2,200, including all meals, accommodation and tours, it represents good value.

The Union Limited has a few other longer distance steam train tours. These run much more irregularly; it's best to contact the company well in advance of your visit, to see what's available. The address for **The Union Limited** is PO Box 4325, Cape Town 8000; telephone (021) 405 4391, fax (021) 405 4395.

Steam railway enthusiasts can also take a variety of narrow-gauge short trips, through private companies. The Banana Express operates four days a week throughout the year on the KwaZulu-Natal south coast; there are 90 minute round trips from Port Shepstone and full-day excursions. Further information and bookings can be made by telephoning (03931) 76 443. The Outeniqua Choo-Tjoe (telephone 0445 21 361) plies a short distance between George and Knysna along the Garden Route in the Western Cape; the Zululand Express operates a monthly excursion from Durban, slightly inland up the KwaZulu-Natal coast to Hluhluwe—telephone the Hluhluwe Tourism Association (035) 562 0353, fax (035) 562 0351; the Shamwari Express runs between Johannesburg and the Shamwari (private) game reserve, near Grahamstown in the eastern Cape, telephone (042) 851 1196, fax (042) 851 1224.

Rainbow

You will inevitably stumble across the phrase 'rainbow nation,' coined by Archbishop Desmond Tutu. It's become the expression most favoured by those who somehow believe they can wish racial harmony into existence. Used equally by liberals suffering from political vertigo and reactionaries when trying to signify contempt for the new South Africa—the only difference being the latter say it with a curl of the lip.

RIVER RAFTING, KAYAKING AND CANOEING

The South African River Rafters Association in Cape Town can be reached by telephoning (021) 762 2350, and in Durban by telephoning (031) 47 2015.

ROBOTS

Don't be alarmed if, when asking for directions, you are told to 'turn left at the first set of robots' (or variation thereof); it's the local expression for traffic lights.

ROOIBOS

Rooibos tea is unique to South Africa, made from the leaves of the Aspalathus Linearis plant, which grows in the mountainous Cedarberg area of the Cape. With no caffeine and less than half the tannin of ordinary tea, its proponents claim that it's good for everything from insomnia and stomach cramps to nappy rash (when applied directly to the skin).

SATOUR

The South African Tourism Board—Satour—should be your first port of call, even before leaving for your trip. Satour publishes a wide range of brochures packed with useful information, telephone numbers, maps and much else. A list of the addresses, telephone and fax numbers of its overseas and domestic offices is in an appendix to this book on page 311.

SCUBA DIVING AND SNORKELLING

Two points of contact: The South African Underwater Union is in Cape Town, on (021) 930 6549, as is the Sea Fisheries Research Institute, on (021) 439 6160.

SHOPPING

Shopping is one of the country's major pastimes. There are some excellent large chains across the country, such as Woolworth's (for food, clothes and household goods); CNA (books, magazines, newspapers, stationery); Pick 'N Pay (food supermarkets—a particularly good one in Claremont, a Cape Town suburb); Exclusive Books, and Fact and Fiction (bookshops); and OK Bazaar is good for camping/barbecue items. There are also hundreds of 'upmarket' jewellers, department stores, clothes shops and so on. American-style shopping malls have sprung up everywhere.

SPORTING LIFE

A Liverpool club manager once said: 'Some people think football is a matter of life and death. But it's much more serious than that.' He must have been thinking of South Africans, for whom sport is a national quasi-religion. Whatever your choice, there's an organisation ready to help you indulge it. This is a list of telephone numbers—area codes in parentheses—of the national sports bodies.

Acrobatics ....[011] 943 4094	Karate......................[011] 957 2513
Aerobatics ....[011] 805 0366	Karting ....[011] 466 2440
Aikido ....[011] 794 1317	Kendo......................[011] 887 3016
Athletics...................[011] 403 3673	Kung Fu...................[011] 953 5572
Archery ....[011] 315 0373	Lifesaving.................[031] 239 251
Badminton ....[012] 312 6087	Motorsport...............[011] 466 2440
Basketball.................[011] 862 2874	Mountaineering ....[021] 45 3412
Baseball ....[021] 797 4817	Mountain biking.......[011] 964 2301
BMX cycling.............[031] 705 4969	Polo.........................[031] 22 1266
Board sailing ....[031] 29 5761	Roller skating...........[012] 57 2229
Bodybuilding............[016] 81 4077	Rugby......................[021] 685 3038
Bowling....................[011] 788 0005	Shooting/small bore ..[0461] 31 8456
Boxing (amateur)......[012] 379 4913	Shooting/pistol.........[012] 323 6653
Bridge......................[011] 337 4030	Soccer/amateur.........[011] 494 3522
Canoeing..................[0331] 46 0984	Soccer/professional ...[011] 494 4520
Comrades Marathon .[0331] 94 3511	Snooker/Billiards.......[051] 48 8622
Cricket ....[011] 880 2810	Sports for
Darts/Men ....[021] 593 1190	physically disabled..[011] 616 7576
Darts/Women ....[011] 434 3060	Sports for
Equestrian events......[011] 702 1657	mentally disabled....[0431] 41 2222
Fencing....................[021] 761 4967	Surfing/amateur ....[021] 644606
Golf/Men..................[011] 442 3723	Surfing/professional ..[021] 782 2833
Golf/Women.............[016] 23 1936	Swimming.................[011] 880 4328
Golf/Senior...............[011] 887 2895	Squash......................[011] 442 8056
Golf/Professional.......[011] 485 2327	Table tennis..............[041] 55 1811
Gymnastics ....[011] 782 5269	Tennis.......................[011] 402 3580
Gymkhana................[04924] 22221	Tenpin bowling.........[011] 867 3700
Handball...................[011] 782 8817	Triathlon ....[011] 802 7980
Hiking......................[011] 886 6524	Volleyball ....[011] 613 5671
Hockey.....................[011] 485 1108	Weightlifting.............[021] 96 4704
Judo.........................[012] 312 8107	Wrestling..................[016] 32 3616
Jujitsu......................[011] 849 1441	Yacht racing ....[021] 439 1147
Jukskei ....[011] 888 5133	

TAXIS

There are two forms of taxi; the microbus type which has evolved to serve the needs of black South Africans travelling between townships and their place of work in former white-only areas, and the type of taxi familiar the world over, a saloon car with a meter and for-hire illuminated plate.

There is only one rule as far as the first is concerned; don't use them. The risks (accidents, muggings and simple confusion about routes and destinations) make their cheap charges not worth the trouble. This might seem an unpleasant perpetuation of racial divisions, but my advice is not to try to mount your own single-handed social revolution in this sphere. There are plenty of other ways to do that—by simply being polite, for example.

The other type of taxi poses no problem except cost; it's the most expensive way of getting about. These taxis do not trawl the streets plying for trade, but sit at fixed taxi ranks, waiting for you to find them. Hotel porters can call taxis, and the Yellow Pages also list established firms. Make sure that the meter is set at zero before your journey starts.

TERRE'BLANCHE

Once upon a time there used to be a significant political figure called Eugene Terre'Blanche, who led a small but very noisy white racist, right-wing Afrikaner movement called the Afrikaner Weerstandsbeweging, or AWB for short. His threats of mass mayhem if the ANC came to power scared the pants off many people, including most outside observers. After the 1994 democratic election, he soon disappeared from the political scene, a spent volcano. Nevertheless, you may come across people who wonder aloud: 'Whatever happened to Eugene Terre'Blanche?' You can impress them by quoting one of his famous sayings, such as: 'I don't fit into little red sports cars' or 'Liberalism, Communism, Mohammedanism threaten to rob the Afrikaner of the legacy of Blood River.' (See the chapter on HISTORY beginning on page 74).

TIME

South Africa is always two hours ahead of Greenwich Mean Time; seven hours ahead of US Eastern Standard Time; and eight hours behind Australian Eastern Standard Time. There are no different time zones in South Africa.

TIPPING

As ever, this is a contentious issue. If you come from a culture where tipping is second-nature, you will feel at home. Generally 10 per cent in restaurants, if you are happy with things—but watch out for a service charge which might be already included in the total bill. A similar amount is also ample for taxis. In hotels, R2 per bag for porters is sufficient. One of the changes ushered in by the collapse of apartheid is that doormen at some hotels—The Royal, in Durban, for example—are not averse to asking for a tip, should you forget to give one. Don't be intimidated.

Tourist Information
One of the delights of South African travel is the publicity association and/or tourist information bureau. Throughout the country, from the largest city to smallest town, you will easily find these offices, run by dedicated women (the vast majority of them are run by women) who arm you with brochures, accommodation suggestions, advice and guidance concerning your visit to their area. These offices are a marvel and cannot be praised too highly. A full list of the addresses and telephone numbers of these invaluable outposts can be found in a separate appendix. If you know exactly where you are going, you should call/fax them in advance; they have the best local knowledge for good-value accommodation, for example.

Toyi-toyi
As Tokyo Sexwale, first president of Gauteng province, once said: 'It takes two to tango, but more to toyi-toyi.' The toyi-toyi is a form of dance, but one without formal pattern or style. Wherever a bunch of jubilant, angry, happy, victorious, aggressive, peaceful—or otherwise emotionally stirred—black South Africans gather, they are likely to start swinging, swaying, chanting and lifting their legs and dancing in a moving and sometimes frightening rhythmic mass. It's powerful, it's stirring, it speaks volumes, even when you do not understand it.

Truth and Reconciliation Commission
This is one of those aspects of the new South Africa that sounds fine and dandy in principle but which may well go a little sour in practice.

Set up in 1995 under the chairmanship of Archbishop Desmond Tutu, the commission was given the task of determining individual responsibility for human rights' abuses under apartheid. By the end of 1997 the commission should have heard representations from those who considered themselves victims, or relatives of victims, of the apartheid era. Three sub-committees were set up to examine gross abuses of human rights, decide on the granting of an amnesty to those perpetrators of abuses who make a full and frank confession of their crimes, and to determine the appropriate level of reparations to be paid to victims.

It's too early to tell what will happen, but it is at least theoretically possible that someone who confesses even very serious crimes (such as murder) committed in the name of apartheid might be amnestied, whereas someone who committed the same crime but does not confess might later find themselves subject to prosecution. It's not clear how that kind of paradox will be resolved. It will also be interesting to see how the Commission determines what amount of cash is to be paid out of state funds to victims; will there be a sliding scale, so much for mental torture, so much for physical?

There is a need for some form of washing of the huge pile of dirty linen created by apartheid; it's just that the Commission might find that precious little truth—and scant reconciliation—emerges after its two years of work. Still, at least it provides lots of jobs. In February 1996 the Commission advertised for 170 functionaries (all 'remuneration packages' to be 'negotiable') to assist its deliberations.

ULULATION
Be it a funeral, a political demonstration, a football match or any public gathering, a group of women is likely to get together and start ululating—a relatively high-pitched warbling sound, the significance of which radically alters, depending on the context.

UYS, PIETER-DIRK
In the truly dark days of apartheid, one man kept up a continual sniping campaign using a weapon that even the racist government could not silence—satire. Pieter-Dirk Uys has long staged one-man shows in which he impersonates South African public figures, and plays a few fictional stereotypes too, getting under his country's skin. Savage, hilarious, clever, Uys is still going strong in the new South Africa, one of the few individual voices not to have lost his critical edge; the title of his new show in 1996 was You ANC Nothing Yet. If you have the chance to see him perform, pay whatever it costs.

VAT
There is a myth that foreign visitors are able to reclaim all the Value Added Tax they have incurred while visiting South Africa. Like all myths, it has a basis in fact, but unravelling the fact from the fantasy isn't all that simple. Maybe things will improve, but at the moment if you want to reclaim VAT when you leave, it's a bureaucratic chore. To get your full entitlement you must plan ahead carefully. Here's how to do it.

VAT at the rate of 14 per cent is levied on most items and services, including hotel accommodation and transport, and is normally included in the marked price of whatever it is you are buying. Non-resident foreign visitors—except those from Botswana, Lesotho, Namibia and Swaziland—on a temporary visit are entitled to claim back the VAT they have incurred; a company called VAT Refund

Administrators has set up a business whereby such visitors can retrieve slightly less than 12.5 per cent of the VAT they have incurred. Look for a small, multi-lingual explanatory leaflet called Vat Refund Information for Foreign Tourists which can be picked up either on entry or departure from the country.

But be warned. This leaflet does not explain that there are many types of products on which you cannot reclaim VAT. It states that 'no goods consumed or services rendered in South Africa qualify for a VAT refund'—so you cannot claim VAT back on a bottle of wine you have bought but already consumed, nor on hotel or taxi bills.

Furthermore, it makes no mention of a whole host of items—such as antiquities, paintings, or trophies—which also are excluded from the VAT refund process. And at Johannesburg International Airport the VAT Refund Administrators' staff failed to produce for me a list of those excluded products. This is completely unsatisfactory; the average tourist can have no real idea what is and what is not allowed unless a complete list is provided at the port of entry.

And finally, the reclaiming process itself is inordinately bureaucratic, hamstrung with a number of conditions which you may not be made aware of until you attempt to make your claim—by which time it's too late to meet those conditions. The leaflet says the conditions that must be met are the following:

1. All items on which a VAT refund is to be claimed, together with an original (photocopies are not acceptable) tax invoice for those items, must be presented for examination to customs officers on leaving the country; they will endorse the tax invoices with an official stamp.

2. You must produce a passport which indicates you are not a resident of South Africa or the other four countries excluded from the scheme.

3. More important, the tax invoice for the item on which you want to reclaim VAT must carry the following very detailed and precise information—when you make your purchases, ask the retailer to prepare you a tax invoice with this information clearly indicated on the invoice:

    • the words 'tax invoice' must appear in a prominent position
    • the amount of VAT charged must be specified, or a statement to the effect that VAT is included in the cost of the item purchased
    • there must be a tax invoice number
    • the date of issue of the tax invoice
    • the seller's VAT registration number
    • the cost of the goods in Rands
    • the seller's name and address
    • a full description of the goods purchased
    • your own (the buyer's) name

If you leave South Africa from either Johannesburg, Cape Town or Durban International Airports, or the Beit Bridge border post with Zimbabwe, and you satisfy the above requirements, you will be issued with a VAT refund cheque, which you can immediately cash and exchange for foreign currency. If you leave from other airports or via a seaport, you will be asked to send your customs official endorsed tax invoices, together with a copy of your passport and your postal address in your country of residence, to PO Box 9478, Johannesburg 2000, South Africa, and a cheque will be sent to you. Specify what currency you want it in, in order to avoid currency exchange charges in your home country. If you leave the country via other border posts, you won't be able to claim a refund.

There are further catches. There is a maximum refund of R3,000, except where a form called VAT 263 has been issued to you, in which case the maximum refund is R10,000. You are unlikely to encounter the form VAT 263, as it is a specialized form issued by the South African Inland Revenue only to vendors who regularly make supplies to tourists.

Those leaving South Africa via Beit Bridge and who are exporting goods worth more than R2,000 must also have a form called F178, obtainable from a commercial bank. In addition, this type of tourist must also obtain another form, called DA 550, from a customs official at the Beit Bridge border post.

You may also find yourself—as I did in 1996—producing what seems to be a perfectly valid, officially endorsed, information-packed tax invoice, only to be told by the refund staff that 'this seller's VAT registration number does not appear on my computer screen, therefore you cannot claim VAT back on this particular item.'

These irritations are compounded by the fact that, at the busiest departure point, Johannesburg International Airport, the queue for VAT refunds can be as long as two hours. If leaving from there you should allow a couple of hours to complete the whole business.

VISAS & PASSPORTS

All travellers to South Africa must be in possession of a valid passport. Visas used to be much more complicated (due to apartheid) but are now a little more straightforward, although journalists and clergy—an odd coupling of normally unassociated professions—are still singled out for special attention in this area. Visas can be obtained free of charge from South Africa's diplomatic representatives (embassies and high commissions) in the country concerned. There can be a lengthy wait and you should apply well in advance of departure. On arrival, you may have to satisfy an immigration officer that you have sufficient funds to support you during your stay, and you may be asked to show evidence of a return ticket.

The following requirements were valid in 1996. As changes are inevitable, it is advisable to consult the local South African embassy or high commission in advance of making your travel plans.

Citizens of the following countries do not need visas for holiday or business visits or for transits unless they have been specifically advised that their visa exemption status has been withdrawn: Andorra; Argentina; Australia; Austria; Bahrain; Belgium; Bolivia; Botswana; Brazil; Canada; Cape Verde; Chile; Denmark; Finland; France; Germany; Greece; Iceland; Israel; Italy; Japan; Lesotho; Liechtenstein; Luxembourg; Monaco; Namibia; Netherlands; New Zealand; Norway; Paraguay; Portugal; Ireland; Singapore; Spain; Swaziland; Sweden; Switzerland; UK; US; Uruguay.

For visitors from Costa Rica, Ecuador and St Helena, visas are required for holiday and business trips longer than 90 days.

Citizens of the following countries are required to have visas for holiday and business trips greater than 30 days: Barbados; Belize; Benin; Comoros Islands; Congo; Cyprus; Czech Republic; El Salvador; Egypt; French Guiana; Gabon; Guatemala; Guyana; Honduras; Hong Kong; Hungary; Ivory Coast; Jordan; Kenya; Kuwait; Madagascar; Malawi; Malaysia; Mali; Malta; Mauritius; Mexico; Morocco; Nicaragua; Oman; Panama; Peru; Poland; Qatar; Saudi Arabia; Senegal; Seychelles; Slovakian Republic; South Korea; Surinam; Thailand; Tunisia; Turkey; United Arab Emirates; Venezuela; Zambia; and all other South and Central American countries (except Colombia).

Passport holders of all countries not mentioned in the above lists do require visas. Visa applicants from countries where South Africa is not represented may send their applications direct to the Director-General for Home Affairs, Private Bag X114, Pretoria 0001.

In addition, all visitors 'intending to be professionally active in South Africa, that is, journalists, clergymen and other religious workers, performing artists, lecturers, sportsmen (or participants in any amateur sporting event), as well as those contemplating any employment must apply for visas, work or entry permits. In addition, journalists, clergymen and other religious workers also require visas or entry permits for holiday visits,' (to quote the relevant official South African statement on the matter).

Even if you have obtained the correct visa, you may well find—as I did, in 1996—that on arrival at Johannesburg International Airport an immigration official lops several weeks off the visa, telling you to 're-apply for an extension locally'. It's very annoying and time-wasting—but not worth trying to argue.

The following is a list of telephone numbers of embassies and consulates in Johannesburg (telephone code 011) and Pretoria (telephone code 012):-

Argentina: ....012 43 3524 / 011 339 2382
Australia:................................012 342 3740
Austria ....012 46 2483 / 011 403 1850
Belgium:................................012 44 3201 / 011 403 1963
Brazil:...................................012 43 5559/5550
Canada: 012 342 6923
Chile: 012 342 1511/1636
China, People's Republic of: 012 342 4194
Denmark:..............................012 322 0595 / 011 804 3374
Finland:.................................012 343 0275/6
France:..................................012 43 5564 / 011 331 3478
Germany: 011 725 1519
Greece:..................................012 43 7351 / 011 484 1769
Hong Kong: 011 337 8940
Hungary:................................012 43 3020
Iceland: 011 433 3560
India:....................................012 342 5310 / 011 482 8487
Indonesia: 012 342 3355
Ireland:..................................012 342 5062 / 011 836 5869
Israel: 012 421 2222
Italy:.....................................012 43 5541 / 011 728 1392
Japan: 012 342 2100
Korea:...................................012 46 2508/9
Luxembourg: 011 403 3852
Malaysia: 012 342 5988
Mexico: 012 342 5190
Netherlands: 012 344 3910/5
New Zealand:..........................011 337 8940
Norway: 012 323 4790-3
Poland:..................................012 43 2631
Portugal: ....012 341 2340 / 011 336 3820
Russia:...................................012 43 2731/2 / 011 344 4812
Singapore: 011 883 1422
Spain: 012 344 3875
Sri Lanka:...............................011 337 8940
Sweden:..................................012 21 1050
Switzerland: ....012 43 6728 / 011 442 7500
Taiwan: 011 403 3281
Thailand:................................012 342 4600 / 011 880 3999
UK:.......................................012 43 3121 / 011 337 8940
USA: ....012 342 1048 / 011 331 1681
Zimbabwe: ....012 342 5152 / 011 838 2156

Winnie

Many outsiders find it difficult to understand why Nelson Mandela's second wife continued to exercise considerable influence over a sizeable minority of South African black political activists, despite being kicked out of the government of national unity in April 1995—where she was deputy minister of arts, science and culture—for a variety of sound reasons. There is a simple explanation, which should not be forgotten, no matter how embarrassing the upper echelons of the ANC found her in the euphoric days following Nelson Mandela's release from jail in 1990.

It's that during some of the darkest days of apartheid she came to symbolize for many black South Africans all that they were struggling for. She was for a long time the living manifestation of the integrity and courage of her incarcerated husband. And following his release, she vocalized some of the genuine grievances felt by many young black radicals, upset at what they saw as the slowness of socio-economic change. Nelson Mandela sought and obtained a divorce from Winnie in March 1996. But when he has gone from the scene, Winnie Mandela may still be a force to be reckoned with.

Wreck Diving

For detailed information telephone the National Monuments Council in Cape Town, on (021) 462 1502, or fax (021) 462 4509.

X-Rated

South African sexual censorship is now much more relaxed than under apartheid, when female nipples would be airbrushed out of magazine photographs and anything more explicit was a complete taboo. Sun City and the other Sun hotels in the former 'independent' homelands were designed partly to give white South Africans the thrill of soft-porn movies and the chance to rub shoulders—if not more—with people from other races. Those hotels have lost that raison d'etre, now that strip and sex shows, hard porn videos, escort agencies, heterosexual and gay massage services are on tap almost everywhere; just check out the classified ads in any major newspaper. Superficially, the old state-enforced sexual repressions of white, Afrikaner, Calvinist, apartheid-ridden South Africa are disappearing. Underneath that skin-deep liberalism, South Africans of all colours are as neurotic as anyone else.

Yellow Pages

The electronic Yellow Pages service, which can be dialled from any telephone using the number 10 118, is an excellent service. Once connected, you immediately join a queue and an electronic voice counts down in seconds how long you will have to wait for an operator, and keeps you updated on what position you occupy in the queue.

YOUTH HOSTELLING

In 1996 the South African Youth Hostels Association (SAYHA) became a member of the International Youth Hostels Federation. SAYHA trades under the name Hostelling International South Africa, or HISA. HISA has a vast range of brochures, information and good practical advice on budget-priced travel and accommodation, and publishes a regular newsletter called Hostel Update News. There is a vast array of hostels all across the country.

HISA's head office is at 101 Boston House, 46 Strand Street, Cape Town 8001. For further details on HISA's services, write to HISA, PO Box 4402, Cape Town 8000; telephone (021) 419 1853 or fax (021) 216 937.

ZOOS

Many private game reserves ban young children; and you might drive round the (child-friendly) national parks without seeing anything wilder than another tourist. So it's probably a good idea to keep a zoo or two, or other semi-domesticated wildlife arena, up your sleeve.

Johannesburg Zoological Gardens are very good, with more than 300 species of mammals, birds, and reptiles, and are open daily between 08.30–17.30. The National Zoological Gardens in Pretoria are also recommended; telephone (012) 328 3265 for opening times and special events. In Durban, there is a children's animal farm on Battery Beach Road, telephone (031) 321 674. Near Cape Town there is a large zoo at Tygerberg; take the N1 from Cape Town, leave it at exit 39 (on R304) and look for signs to the zoo, which is on Klipheuwel Road, telephone (021) 884 4494, open daily 09.00–17.00.

Languages

There are 11 official languages—Afrikaans, English, Ndebele, Pedi, Sotho, Swati, Tsonga, Tswana, Venda, Xhosa and Zulu, which is by far the most widely-spoken. English will get you by, though a grasp of one of the more widely spoken black African languages is a tremendous asset. Tonality (words of different meaning but otherwise identical, distinguished by tone only) plays a crucial part of Zulu and some other indigenous languages. So do 'clicks', a highly evolved, complicated process of placing the tongue on various parts of the teeth, soft and hard palates and gums—a feature again of Zulu and other local languages—to produce different sounds and meanings.

Language has always been a contentious issue. In modern times Afrikaners have always seen defence of their language, Afrikaans, as a quasi-political issue. Equally, for many black South Africans, Afrikaans has long been seen as a potent symbol of repression. At various times since 1948 the government has tried to force Afrikaans as a medium of schoolroom instruction on an equal basis with English. The struggle against that came to a head on June 1976 in Soweto. A protest march by black schoolchildren and students was met with extreme force by armed police; in the consequent nationwide clashes—which sporadically continued for the next two years—hundreds of young people died. Rarely has language been the spark for such a massive social uprising. Afrikaans is not a popular language with black South Africans, though is very commonly-used among not only the Afrikaner but also the Coloured community.

South African English has words and phrases unique to itself; here is a brief list, including words which have crossed over from being purely Afrikaans.

> bakkie: a pick-up truck
> bazaar: general store
> braaivleis or braai: a barbecue
> boerwors: spicy sausages—lots of different varieties
> buck: antelope—lots of different species
> cafe: small corner shop—not a place to get an expresso
> dagga: marijuana
> dam: reservoir
> howzit?: a generalized form of greeting
> izit?: emphatic expression meaning 'really?'
> jol: derived from 'jolly', meaning party
> just now: meaning 'soon'

koppie: small hill
kak: excrement
lekker: nice, pretty, handsome, cute
mealie: maize corn
rooinek: red-neck (derogative word for a British person)
shame: meaning 'what a pity'
shebeen: black township drinking den
sjambok: large whip
takkie: athletic shoe
township: formerly official, now customarily, blacks-only residential area

Afrikaans

Afrikaans is a relatively straightforward language; English-speakers will probably be surprised how much passive understanding they rapidly acquire. It's a phonetic language; all letters are pronounced. Use a guttural emphasis and roll the letter r, as in Germanic languages.

AFRIKAANS ALPHABET
This is the same as in English.

Only three letters—b, d and g—vary in sound, depending on their position in a word.

The letter b sounds the same as in English, except at the end of a word, when it sounds like the letter p (klub is pronounced klup).

The letter d is again as in English, but when occurring at the end of a word sounds like the English letter t.

The letter g sounds likes ch (as in the English loch) when at the end of a word, such as dag (day). When g is preceded by either an r or an l it sounds like the g in the English word go.

The letters c, q, x and z are seldom used.
Other consonants are pronounced in the following way:
J: like Y in yes
K: used instead of a 'hard' C
V: like F in English (fish/vis)
W: like V in English

Vowels and Dipthongs are rather trickier, though there are some basic rules.

a: short;	like U in nun—eg *man, bank, kan*	
a: long;	like A in father—eg *vader*	
e: short;	like E in pen—eg *hen*	
e: long;	like EE in beer—eg *seer* (sore)	
e: weak;	like E in water—eg *terug* (backwards)	
i: short;	shorter than E in water—eg *dit* (this, it)	
i: long;	like I in ambition—eg *ambisie*	
o: short;	like 'aw' in law—eg *kok* (cook)	
o: long;	like 'oo' in moor—eg *boom* (tree)	
u: short;	like 'y' in abyss—eg *bus*	
u: long;	like U in French—eg *muur* (wall)	
y: short;	like 'ay' in bay—eg *my*	
ô: long;	like 'aw' in saw—eg *môre* (morning)	

Useful Basic Vocabulary

English	Afrikaans
A	
aeroplane	vliegtuig
am	vm
apples	appels
automobile	motor
avenue	laan
B	
baby	baba
bad	sleg
bath	bad
bay	baai
bed	bed
beef	biefstuk
beer	bier
book	boek
breach	strand
bread	brood
brother	broer
building	gebou
butter	botter

English	Afrikaans
C	
cabbage	kool
cat	kat
chair	stoel
cheap	goedkoop
cheese	kaas
cherries	kersies
chicken	hoender
city centre	middestad
city	stad
coffee	koffie
cucumber	komkommer
D	
daily	daagliks
daughter	dogter
dog	hond
E	
eggs	eiers
emergency	nood
enquiries	navrae

ENGLISH	AFRIKAANS
entrance	ingang
exit	uitgang
expensive	duur

F

father	pa
fish	vis
flower	blom
ford	drift
Friday	Vrydag
from	van
fruit	vrugte

G

good day	goeiendag
good evening	goeienaand
good	goed
grapes	druiwe

H

house	huis
how much/many?	hoeveel?
husband	eggenoot

I

information	inligting

J

jam	konfyt

L

lamb	skaap
left	links
lemons	suurlemoene
lettuce	kropslaai

M

madam	mevrou
meat	vleis
meat, dried and salted	biltong
milk	melk
Monday	Maandag
mother	ma
mountain	berg
my	my

ENGLISH	AFRIKAANS

N

name	naam
narrow-minded	verkrampt
next	volgende
no	nee

O

onions	uie
oranges	lemoene
overseas	oersese

P

peaches	perskes
pepper	peper
pharmacy	apteek
pineapple	pynappels
plain	veld
please	asseblief
pm	nm
point	punt
pork	vark
potatoes	aartappels
progressive	verligte
pumpkin	pampoen

R

return	retoer
right	regs
river	riviere
road	pad
road	weg
room	kamer

S

salt	sout
Saturday	Saturdag
single	enkel
sir	meneer
sister	suster
son	seun
soon/in a moment	nou-nou
station	stasie

ENGLISH	AFRIKAANS	ENGLISH	AFRIKAANS
strawberries	aarbeie	Tuesday	Dinsdag
street	straat	**U**	
sugar	suiker	umbrella	sambreel
Sunday	Sondag	**V**	
swimming pool	swembad	veal	kalfsvleis
T		vegetables	groente
table	tafel	**W**	
telephone	telefoon	Wednesday	Woensday
thank you	dankie	week	week
the	die	when?	wanneer?
Thursday	Donderdag	where?	waar?
ticket	kaartjie	why?	waarom?
to	na	wife	vrou
today	vandag	wine	wyn
tomatoes	tamaties	**Y**	
tomorrow	môre	year	jaar
town	dorp	yes	ya
train	trein	yesterday	gister
tree	boom		

Abuse

Unless you wish to cause offence do not use the words bantu, kaffir or native; while they all have innocuous origins (bantu once simply meant 'people' and kaffir derives from the Arabic word for 'infidel' or 'unbeliever') all have semantic significance far removed from those roots and today are regarded as terms of abuse for anyone who does not have a white complexion.

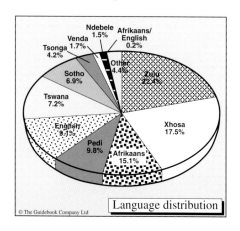

Language distribution

© The Guidebook Company Ltd

ONE NATION, MANY PEOPLES

*I*n the eyes of the law there is now only one type of person in South Africa—a South African. Potentially, it's political dynamite to start unpicking that morally estimable dogma. But as in the eyes of everyone else you are also an Afrikaner, or a Shangaan, or a Xhosa, or a Zulu— just as if you are British you are also Welsh, Scottish or English, or even Cornish or Lancastrian—then we may as well recognise this fact and learn to live with it. It needn't be racist to be curious about what a person's background is, and given South Africa's interesting diversity of cultures it would be a pity to let political correctness get in the way of knowledge and understanding.

Moreover, some terms that were regarded with absolute abhorrence under apartheid—perhaps the best example being 'Coloured', to describe someone of mixed race— are now making a comeback, re-invented as badges of political power. Many Zulus, for instance, have such pride in their origins that they will regard themselves as Zulus first, South Africans second. And while what follows tries to place the various nations within a geographical setting, it's obviously the case that people from all the different language groups and cultures may today be found in all parts of the country—along with Portuguese, Greek, Italian, east European and other immigrants, from all over the world.

Among the indigenous black peoples of South Africa there has

(Above) *From Savage Tribes (1822), "A Kaffir Chief"*

developed over centuries a very sophisticated spirituality, normally deeply embedded in the natural elements that surround their lives. Most of these cultures embrace the notion of a creator or paramount being, omniscient and omnipotent. In addition, there is often a belief in a variety of lesser spirits of the earth, air, water and of ancestors. While this complex metaphysics has largely died away in urban areas, it's very vigorous in many rural parts of the country. So too are the ritual functionaries, such as priests, diviners, prophets, rainmakers and creators of *muti*, or medicine. Such leading figures in a community generally hold their position by reason of inheritance, or perhaps age; one of the important tasks of such people is the preservation of the community's history by means of oral folk-tales and myths about the group's origins. Witchcraft is still widely practised and given great credence, though it is not necessarily of the sinister black type so beloved of horror movies. And onto all this has been grafted Christianity, of a vibrantly evangelical kind. Throughout the country you will find men and women wearing metal badges (a star, or a number, or similar) borne on a small piece of generally dark-green cloth. This signifies their membership of one of the many Zionist Christian churches, the Zionist element having nothing to do with a rabidly pro-Israeli political attitude, but simply being an expression of faith in Christ.

The original inhabitants, the nomadic **San** (also known as Bushmen) were all but wiped out by or integrated into the people known as Khoikhoi, who swept down from the north (see HISTORY). Today, as few as 30,000 San remain, scattered in the north-east of South Africa and neighbouring countries. In turn, the Khoikhoi gradually integrated into other tribes—the British, the Boer, and other African tribes—in and around the Cape.

(Above) *Piet Joubert a leading Boer general*
in the 1899–1902 war against the British

In the eastern Cape, the former Transkei and Ciskei 'homelands', the predominant tribe has long been the **Xhosa**. The Xhosa are in fact a widely diverse people comprising many smaller groupings. In the 19th century they fought the longest and most bitter struggle against British incursions into their territories; very early on some of their number, such as Tiyo Soga, were also adroit enough to try to beat the British not by arms but by acquiring education in the United States and Britain, and returning to take up political agitation on behalf of their people. That tradition, of placing high emphasis upon academic achievement and using it to lever political influence, has meant that the eastern Cape has throughout this century been an African nationalist nerve-centre. Many contemporary well-known ANC leaders, including Nelson Mandela, come from a Xhosa background.

In the rural areas many Xhosa still practise a traditional lifestyle, living in huts within a *kraal*—a larger or smaller homestead settlement, usually fenced off as protection against wild animals—and continuing a hierarchical structure, in which a chief or headman has considerable authority. It's still common among Xhosa, as many other African communities, for a man to pay a dowry—known as *lobola*—to his bride's family upon marriage. A mixture of powerful evangelical Christianity, reverence for ancestors, and belief in spirits all have a part to play in the spiritual side of Xhosa life, as for many other indigenous peoples. Travelling through the eastern Cape's rural areas at the end of spring, you may still come across young males dressed in tall straw hats, with their bodies and faces

(Above) Enoch Mgijima, the self-proclaimed prophet who led his unarmed followers at the Bulhoek massacre on 24 May 1921

painted a ghostly white. This signifies that they are undergoing a traditional, gruelling and for them vital series of tests, culminating in circumcision, the whole experience marking their transition to manhood. Modern capitalism has, in a strange and contradictory manner, come to

impinge on the initiation rites of many young black South Africans. For much of this century, to go and work in the gold mines around the Rand—perhaps an even more gruelling experience—has also been regarded as a test of manhood.

Another major group is the **Ndebele**, now divided into the Southern and Northern Ndebele. Their history is believed to have started some four centuries ago, when a group of Nguni people migrated to the northern parts of the Transvaal, eventually settling around Pretoria and spreading eastwards into what is today Mpumalanga. The Ndebele are well-known for their love of ornate, geometrically-patterned, brightly-hued decoration, of their house exteriors in particular, but also personal objects.

Of the Nguni people, there are today four very intermingled but identifiably distinct groups: the Northern Sotho speaking (the two largest nations being the **Pedi** and **Tswana**); the Lobedu; and the Southern Sotho speakers, or Basotho. The Pedi successfully fought several wars against the Voortrekkers in the 19th century, managing to retain their independence until in 1879 a combined British-Swazi army crushed them and imprisoned their king, Sekhukhune, in a campaign in the Leolu mountains in eastern Transvaal. While many have joined urban society, there are still numerous rural communities, where land is communally owned.

The Tswana are a collection of as many as 59 separate clans, widely-

(Above) *Zionist church service in Johannesburg*

spread across the Northern Cape and North-West provinces, where they have been present for more than 1,000 years. One of the early ANC leaders, Sol Plaatje, came from the Rolong tribe, part of the Tswana nation. The settled, cattle-farming Tswana were forced into the rural 'homeland' of Boputhatswana in the late 1970s, an apartheid-created 'state' of seven small patches of scattered, unconnected land whose capital, Mmabatho, is a thriving if ugly town.

The Lobedu are a small off-shoot of the Karanga people of Zimbabwe, who in the 16th century headed south under a princess and settled in the warm and fertile valley of the Molototsi River, east of Duiwelskloof. The princess—who became a queen—took the name Modjadji, and withdrew from public life, cultivating a myth that she could conjure up rains. The novelist Rider Haggard based his famous story She on Modjadji the Rain Queen; her successors have perpetuated both the myth and have continued to take the same name. Her small band of followers were left alone by the more belligerent tribes, such as Swazis and Zulus, who held her in great esteem for her supposed powers.

Mojadji's status is perhaps enhanced by the position of her capital, on a hillside amid a strange 305-hectare forest of cycads, known as Mojadji cycads, some of which grow as high as 13 metres. This particular cycad dates from perhaps 60 million years ago, and the area occupied by Mojadji has the world's greatest concentration of this rare plant. You

(Above) Zulu women in KwaZulu-Natal

may visit the forest but should first obtain a permit from the magistrate in Kgapane, five kilometres north of Duiwelskloof, telephone (0152) 328 3002; (maps to find the forest can be obtained from any of the publicity associations in the region). You are unlikely to see the contemporary Mojadji; she receives only very special visitors, but you can purchase a cycad plant at a garden centre close to the protected forest; the centre will also give you a permit for the possession of this highly-protected plant.

The Southern Sotho now mainly live in Lesotho, the independent land-locked kingdom situated in the middle of the eastern half of South Africa. Lesotho has long been under the political and economic dominance of South Africa, and today is a fairly miserable place to visit—collapsed infrastructure, badly-eroded land through over-grazing, and impoverished people, though much of the countryside has its own dramatic mountainous beauty. Basotho culture is centred around horse-ownership and horse-riding, essential for such a mountainous region.

The **Shangaan** (sometimes also known as Tsonga) have their own particular language and live primarily in two areas; the eastern parts of Mpumalanga and northern KwaZulu-Natal. A branch of a much larger, Mozambican group, the Shangaan are closely related to the Zulu people but have throughout the centuries staunchly retained their sense of separate identity. In the private game reserves of the Kruger Park you may well find that your tracker comes from the Shangaan people.

In the Northern province, particularly around the town of Thohoyandou, may be found people from another highly distinctive language group, the **Venda**, numerically the smallest black group within the country. Unconquered by Boer, British or other African peoples, the Venda have retained much of their unique culture. Cattle-owning is a definition of wealth and status, and government is by chief and council of elders. They have strong belief in the sacred meanings of lakes, rivers, and trees, and many ritual ceremonies are performed to appease the minor deities. Perhaps the most important of these spirits is the Python God, reputed to inhabit Lake Fundudzi, deep in the interior to the north-west of Thohoyandou, and held to be influential over fertility, both of the land and of its people. The Python God once required the sacrifice of a virgin; ritual murder is still practised among some of the Venda, and witch-burning in the area is a relatively common, though illegal, phenomenon; as many as 300 alleged witches were burned by villagers in 1995 alone. Visitors to the area need not be alarmed for their own safety, however; such practises are contained within Vendan life.

One of the most spine-tingling ceremonies, which can if you are fortunate be observed, is the the Domba, a dance of virgin girls who link up closely in a single, snaking file, moving and swaying in a fashion which imitates the movements of the python. Part final initiation into womanhood, part propitiation to the Python God, the Domba is accompanied by rhythmic drumming; it's simultaneously blood-stirring and blood-curdling.

The **Zulu** nation is one of Africa's giants; Zulu-speakers now form the largest ethnic group of the country, largely within KwaZulu-Natal. There is a continuing political/cultural struggle being waged within South Africa by the Inkatha Freedom Party (IFP) against the ANC-dominated national government; the IFP is a major political force but refused to participate in drawing up the country's new constitution in 1996, a step which inevitably and perhaps deliberately contains the seed of future conflict. There is a strong current in the IFP leadership which hopes to see a secession of KwaZulu-Natal from the overall country, an aspiration which the ANC will not countenance.

Historically the Zulu nation has been South Africa's leading black belligerent, fighting lengthy and often successful wars to fend off Boer and British invasions, and to acquire the land of neighbouring African nations. Culturally, Zulu craftwork is highly creative and brightly colourful. Most rural communities live in traditional rondavels—clay huts with woven-grass roofs. Cattle-wealth is an important indication of social status, and lobola is practised. *Sangomas,* or witch doctors, still cater for both the physical and spiritual welfare of many Zulus, intermingled with modern medical methods.

Within KwaZulu-Natal, particularly Durban, there is a large and vibrant **Indian** community, comprising both Hindu and Moslem believers. Around one million people, mostly Tamil and Gujarati speakers, belong to this group, whose ancestors were shipped into the old Natal state in the late 19th century to work as sugar-cane cutters. They have often occupied an uncomfortable position within South African society, being shunned both by whites and blacks. Many Indians quickly became successful entrepreneurs, and today a large portion of senior ANC figures come from this section of the community.

In a comparable fashion, the **Coloured**, predominantly Afrikaans-speaking sections of South African society, to be found largely in and around the Cape, have frequently been politically squeezed by the white-vs-black conflict, looked down upon by both. Paradoxically, that attitude has forged a vibrant and proud sense of identity amongst Coloured people, who no longer accept that enforced, artificial and reprehensible sense of inferiority. From being a pejorative term used by white racists, 'coloured' today is becoming for some a badge of honour; and why not?

It's difficult to speak of South Africa's whites without immediately succumbing to stereotypes of one kind or another. The racialism with which both **Boer** and **British** historically have imbued the country has been the cause of inordinate suffering, for them as well as the black African societies they pillaged. What saves their communities from complete condemnation is the fact that many Afrikaans and English-speakers have resolutely opposed the xenophobia of their compatriots. Afrikaners can now claim an African identity, many of them tracing their roots back many generations to the earliest Dutch, French Huguenot and German settlers. The terms Afrikaner and Boer—often used as though they are interchangeable—imply slightly different things: Afrikaner may simply mean an Afrikaans-speaker, or is used as a marker of someone who is not of British, English-speaking ancestry; Boer, on the other hand, is an Afrikaans word literally meaning 'farmer', but it also connotes a rather

Johannesburg: no barriers in schools anymore

deeper, more complex attitude of feeling ethnically separate and sometimes of racial intolerance.

Perhaps the weakest claim of all to be South African is that of the
English-speaking, British-descended community. English is widely-
spoken but rarely the dominant language anywhere in South Africa.
British-descended South Africans like to portray themselves as the most
enlightened section of the society, though a cursory glance at the history
books reveals this to be a myth. English-speakers for long dominated the
political and economic life of the country, though that altered considerably following the 1948 election, when Afrikaners wrested from them
much of their accumulated power.

Will all these different groups finally weld themselves into a single
nation, a nation that feels itself to be South African rather than anything
else? To a large extent that has already happened, and the signs generally
are encouraging. The only cloud on the horizon is KwaZulu-Natal; and of
that turbulent region, little except guesswork can be offered at this stage.

History

Homo erectus to Homo bellicus:
Stone Age–16th Century

In some parts of South Africa the soil has a startling orange-red hue, as if it had been long-steeped in blood. The country's history, which can be seen as successive waves of racially-inspired warfare to acquire and control land, is indeed bloody.

There is considerable evidence of early Stone Age habitation. In 1924 in Taung (in the northern Cape) was discovered the fossilized skull of a pre-human primate, *Australopithecus africanus*, dating back as far as two and a half million years. A second, similarly dated skull was later found at Sterkfontein, near Krugersdorp. In 1948 another excavation, at Swartkrans, close to the Sterkfontein site, revealed skulls of the more advanced *Homo erectus*, the first human ancestor to have used fire, who is thought to have lived about one million years ago. Evidence of modern man, *Homo sapiens*, is sparse; few South African sites are reliably dated earlier than 20,000 years; such remains bear great similarity to those left by the San people.

The San were hunter-gatherers, whose communities spread wide across southern Africa and lingered on long after whites first arrived in the late 15th century. It is estimated that some 30,000 descendants of the San still live in South Africa, Botswana and Namibia, though most have now acquired modern lifestyles. In March 1996 Regopstaan Kruiper, who was believed to be the oldest survivor of the San to resist integration into modern society, died aged 96.

The lives of the San were rudely interrupted some 2,000 years ago, when a pastoral revolution began to spread across southern Africa, with cattle and sheep farming being taken up by some of southern Africa's indigenous peoples, the Khoikhoi (called 'Hottentots' by the earliest Dutch settlers). The Khoikhoi—the name is believed to have meant 'men of men'—regarded themselves as superior to the San, who (unlike the Khoikhoi) still practised common ownership of property and food. The Khoikhoi developed the notion of social hierarchy, based on individual ownership of livestock. They migrated south from what is now Botswana, throughout the Cape region, and soon clashed with the nomadic San over land; their domesticated grazing animals denuded the land of pasture vital to the wild game hunted by the San. The two groups battled over centuries, the Khoikhoi forming into increasingly strong fighting units to defend themselves and their herds, while the San either fled to less hospitable regions (such as the Kalahari desert) unsuitable for grazing, or—

eventually—joined forces with and integrated themselves—often in subordinate social roles, such as servants or herdsmen—into the communities of their ancient enemies, with whom they eventually began to intermarry. A further community thus came into being, the Khoisan.

The Khoikhoi bartered their cattle and sheep for items they placed great store by, primarily metals—copper, for decoration, and iron, for tools and weapons— and *dagga*, or *Cannabis sativa*, which they would either chew or boil in water and drink the infusion, or, after the arrival of whites, smoke in pipes. Much of such trade was conducted with related groups of Sotho, Nguni and Tswana-speaking pastoralists, known generically as Bantu-speaking people, who brought the early Iron Age (250AD–1100AD) to South Africa. These peoples spread as far south as what is now KwaZulu-Natal and into the eastern Cape. Early Iron Age remains— such as the pottery fragments, since reassembled into their original, human-like heads, found at Lydenburg, and dated about 500AD—have been unearthed in various spots in the country. Late Iron Age remains have also been found, such as a golden rhinoceros dating from about 1200AD, and excavated from a grave on Mapungubwe Hill.

Cape of Good Hope and Ill Winds: 1487–1652

In August 1487 the navigator and explorer Bartolomeu Dias left Portugal, sailing in two small caravels and a store ship. To him goes the dubious honour of being the first white face to have set eyes on the coast of South Africa, putting in at Mossel Bay on a voyage which took him down the west coast of Africa, and up round the very tip of the continent.

The first contact between white and black augured ill; the Khoikhoi stoned the sailors who put in for fresh water, and for their impudence one of their number was killed by a crossbow. Dias named the cape the Cape of Good Hope—Cabo da Boa Esperança—though it was anything but that for him; he died off the same Cape in a storm during a subsequent voyage in 1500.

A further Portugese expedition, under Vasco da Gama, sailed south in July 1497, putting in again at Mossel Bay and other points of the south coast, again with blood shed, both his sailors' and that of the Khoikhoi. He continued up the east coast, naming the rich green land he saw Terra do Natal, on Christmas Day 1498. In 1503 another Portugese sailor, Antonio de Saldanha, sailed by error into Table Bay, where he climbed Table Mountain. In March 1510 Francisco de Almeida, viceroy of Portugese India, put into Table Bay on his way home to Portugal. There he led an attack of 150 soldiers on a Khoikhoi settlement. For his trouble, he and

e HOOP.

'*Cobo de Goede Hoop*' *from* Historische Reizen door d'oosteresche Deelen van Asia.
Amsterdam, Nicolaas ten Hoorn, 1711

57 of his men died near the mouth of Salt River.

For the Portugese, this land was more trouble than it was worth; violent inhabitants, treacherous winds, perilous rocks—all deterred them from any thought of settlement.

The Company of Dutchmen: 1652–1679

By the end of the 16th century rounding the Cape of Good Hope was still a hazardous voyage, but no longer unfamiliar to Portugese, English and Dutch sailors. Trade between visitors and Khoikhoi coastal-dwellers increased, and the initial mutual distrust and small-scale scrapping had somewhat abated.

But not until 25 March 1647 did the first permanent settlement arise, and then only by virtue of some of those dangerous rocks around Table Bay that have been the death of many sailors. A vessel called the *Haerlem*, belonging to the powerful syndicate of Dutch merchants and traders, the Dutch East India Company, ran aground. The fleet commander ordered an accompanying merchant, Leendert Jansz, to remain ashore and salvage what he could, and to await the return of another fleet. Jansz and 58 other settlers built a small fort of sand and wrecked timber between what is today Milnerton and Bloubergstrand, just outside Cape Town. They survived by hunting and trading with the Khoikhoi, and even explored Robben Island, before being picked up more than a year later. Back in Holland, Jansz gave his opinion on the suitability of the area as a permanent staging post.

In December 1651 Jan van Riebeeck, a more senior member of the Dutch East India Company, was tasked with returning to Table Bay, to establish a permanent Company settlement. Sailing in the *Drommedaris*, along with two other vessels, the *Reijger* and *De Goede Hoop*, Riebeeck landed in Table Bay on 6 April 1652. He was instructed to maintain good relations with the Khoikhoi, though he quickly built a fort in order to defend himself should the need arise. By the time Riebeeck left in 1662 to take up the governorship of Malacca, the settler population of Cape Town (as it rapidly became known) had increased from an original 90 to 463, including 113 imported slaves; the Company strictly forbade enslavement of local people, though eventually the edges between strict enslavement and enforced servitude became very blurred. Slaves were imported by the Dutch from their colonies, and by 1795 it was estimated there were more than 20,000 working in the Cape.

Initially it seems the Dutch East India Company had no intention that their settlement should be either permanent or exclusive. Other maritime nations put into Cape Town without hindrance, though little attempt was made to explore the interior. A feeble attempt to force the Dutch out was staged in 1659 by some elements of the Khoikhoi, and for a decade from the early 1660s various Khoikhoi clans cattle-raided one another in order to profit from trading with the Dutch. Gradually, due to a combination of smallpox epidemics and the expanding ambitions of the earliest Dutch settlers—some of whom became 'free burghers' and who struck out into the interior, independent of the Dutch East India Company—the Khoikhoi found themselves if not slaves, then certainly regarded as trespassers.

Calvinist Croppers: 1679–1800

In 1679 a new Dutch East India Company commander arrived to take charge of Cape Town. Simon van der Stel's brief was to expand the colony's domain, already well underway thanks to the series of inconclusive skirmishes between Dutch troops and Khoikhoi farmers. The numbers of free burghers increased significantly, and quite extensive farming land had been 'given' to them—including 60 freehold grants in the area which become known as Stellenbosch, the colony's second established town—by the Company, which hoped the new farmers would become sufficiently productive to supply the many vessels now calling at Cape Town for revictualling.

The Company had, however, refused to recognize any land rights on the part of the Khoikhoi, who in any case had no concept of individual land ownership, regarding it as communal property, unlike livestock. Land rights were also granted to those immigrants the Dutch favoured, such as more than 200 French Huguenots, who, fleeing religious persecution in France, arrived in the new Cape colony in 1688. They settled in Franschhoek, close to Cape Town, and put their valuable wine-making skills to work.

But instead of settling to till the soil, numerous free burghers preferred to emulate the itinerant Khoikhoi, becoming 'trek-boers' or travelling farmers, grazing their livestock, hunting for game, and subjugating local black inhabitants when it took their fancy. Good grazing land was scarce—and clashes between trekboers and Khoikhoi became inevitable. By 1717 there was such pressure on suitable land for grazing that the Company halted all immigration—except the importation of slaves from west Africa and the Dutch-controlled East Indies.

The Company attempted to regulate all commercial activity in the Cape, leading many of the relatively unskilled yet determinedly independent-minded Dutch settlers to trek ever further into the interior to escape the Company's onerous restrictions. Under pressure from both the Company and such trekboers, by 1740 the only Khoikhoi left in the western parts of the Cape were servants and labourers. Deeper in the interior, the trekboers—whose Calvinist belief in predestination, of being 'chosen' for salvation by God, no doubt assisted their natural inclination to enforce their wishes upon a recalcitrant and, to them, self-evidently 'inferior' and 'heathen' people—used their superior weapons and ruthlessness to enslave the Khoikhoi, San and Khoisan, in all but name.

In the second half of the 18th century the fortunes of the Dutch began to wane, and the Dutch East India Company's small outpost in South Africa had become an administrative nightmare. Independent trekboers, the ancestors of today's Afrikaners, had, by 1795, pushed the colony's boundary as far east as the Great Fish River, relentlessly exploiting the Khoikhoi and San as they went.

At the Great Fish River they came up against a more formidable opponent, the Xhosa people. When it suited them, the trekboers petitioned the governor of the Cape for assistance and troops to defend land they claimed as their own; yet their allegiance to the Cape authorities did not stretch as far as obeying its strictures against slavery. Clashes soon erupted between trekboers and Xhosa over land in the eastern Cape, with the First Frontier War, which culminated in 1781 with the slaughter of unrecorded numbers of Xhosa who refused to remove themselves east of the Great Fish River.

What followed, in broad terms, was a series of confusing trekboer vs Xhosa conflicts, all bloodily inconclusive and contributing to a thorough, lasting distrust between white and black. This bleak pattern was further complicated when, in 1796, a British force wrested control of Cape Town from the Dutch in order, it was said, to prevent this important port from being taken by the French, with whom the British were then at war. The British returned the Cape colony to Holland in 1801, only to re-take it in 1806, when the Napoleonic wars broke out. Britain finally took permanent control in August 1814.

Britain Waives the Rules: 1800–1867

By 1806, the Cape colony consisted of about 22,000 settlers, 25,000 imported slaves, and an indeterminate number of Khoisan. The British moved relatively fast to turn a Dutch outpost into a fully-fledged member of the infant British empire. The importation of slaves was banned in 1807, though slavery itself was not banned by Britain until 1833. In 1809 the first British governor, the Earl of Caledon, issued a 'Hottentot Proclamation,' the import of which rang down through succeeding years; it compelled every Khoisan to have a fixed and registered 'place of abode' and to have a certificate issued by a local *landdrost* (or magistrate, generally Dutch) in order to travel from one district to another. The loathed pass laws were born.

Caledon's successor in September 1811 was Sir John Cradock, a career soldier who was determined to stamp out Xhosa resistance to the new authorities. His tool for crushing the Xhosa was a 34-year-old lieutenant-colonel, John Graham, founder of the all-Khoikhoi Cape Regiment, and whose name lives on today in the city of Grahamstown in the eastern Cape. Together with Boer 'commandos' (mounted and well-armed militia), the British levies conducted a widespread massacre of the Xhosa in 1812; between then and 1858 a series of wars between British and Xhosa took place, with first one and then the other seeming to gain an upper hand, but always with the Xhosa being almost imperceptibly pushed backwards, further east, with the Cape colony extending its geographical reach into their territory.

In 1820 a group of 4,000 British settlers from economically depressed areas were tempted by the offer of free passage and land to migrate to the eastern Cape. As many as 90,000 applications were made for the chance to flee unemployment and poverty in England, but those that arrived in Algoa Bay on 9 April 1820 found little to please them. Forbidden to own slaves, forbidden to travel freely (both measures designed to keep an uneasy peace with the neighbouring Xhosa), their misery was made worse by the discovery that the land they had been promised was infertile. By 1824, most had moved to other parts of the Cape; those that remained turned Grahamstown into a thriving commercial centre, very British in tone. Their presence also reinforced a developing split in the country, between English-speaking, urbanised manufacturers and traders, and the Dutch-speaking, farming, relatively nomadic Boers.

Gradually, the British forces began to subdue the Xhosa. A new colony, British Kaffraria, was established in 1848. Colonel Harry Smith, who became the Cape colony governor in 1847, told defeated Xhosa chiefs in 1848 that their territory would be divided up into 'counties, towns and villages bearing English names. You shall all learn to speak English at the schools which I shall establish...You may no longer be naked and wicked barbarians, which you will ever be unless you labour and become industrious.' No finer definition of the British imperial ethic can be imagined.

The final nail in the coffin of the Xhosa as an independent nation was, ironically, hammered home by an adolescent Xhosa girl, Nongqawuse. She claimed to have been told by tribal ancestors that the Xhosa must kill all their cattle. She persuaded the independent Xhosa paramount chief, Sarhili, of her views; 15 months after the cattle-killing began, the starving, morally-abject Xhosa were effectively finished as a threat to British hegemony.

But throughout the 19th century British authority—over both the Dutch farmers, by now simply known as Boers, and the various indigenous black tribes, who often were at odds with one another as well as with the Boers—was vigorously and often violently challenged. In the case of the Boers, the resistance to British rule

A contemporary view of the Zulu victory against British troops at Isandlwhana, 22 January 1879

ultimately resulted in a nationwide war, and the deaths of many thousands of British troops, Boers—and black South Africans.

A crucial development, of lasting significance even today, took place in the first two decades of the new century, far beyond the control of the country's new imperial authorities. In 1815 Senzangakona, the leader of the then little-known and relatively unimportant Zulu chiefdom, died, and was replaced by Shaka, then aged about 30. When he took over, the Zulu army is estimated to have been no more than 500 strong; he quickly quadrupled that, and, when Dingiswayo, chief of the much larger Mthethwa clan was murdered in 1818, Shaka was his natural successor. His first act was to execute everyone he regarded capable of challenging his bid for the throne.

Shaka instilled strict discipline into his much-enlarged army, by requiring all his soldiers to be celibate; by training them to march long distances at rapid speeds; and by introducing new battle tactics and superior skills at close-quarter fighting, with a shorter stabbing spear. He embarked on a series of successful wars of conquest over neighbouring tribes in the region now called KwaZulu-Natal, steadily building a large, Zulu, kingdom.

Traditional historians have termed this period the *Mfecane* (Zulu for 'crushing'), in which Shaka's predatory nation-building was held responsible for depopulating vast areas of the country. This interpretation of the period and its events admirably suited the Afrikaner view of history, which has claimed that Boer trekkers of the mid-19th century moved into undisputed, empty territory over which no indigenous peoples held sway. More recently, some historians have argued that the *Mfecane* did not occur. They argue instead that while Shaka was indeed intent on subjugating neighbours, other factors were responsible for the vast movements of black peoples and other upheavals, including serious droughts, the impact of white slave-rading, the spread of firearms via white traders, and a more diffuse struggle for dominance conducted between many different clans, tribes and groups.

Whether or not the *Mfecane* took place, Shaka was responsible for creating not only an important power within the fledgling South Africa; his lasting bequest was the proud sense of nationhood still possessed by Zulus today. In 1828 he too was murdered, by his half brother Dingane, abetted by another brother, Mhlangane, and a senior tribal official, Mbhopa.

Contemporaneous with the growth of the Zulu nation under Shaka and the struggle between black tribes in Transvaal and Natal was a growing Boer dissatisfaction at British rule. The Boers, who had acquired their own sense of developing identity, regarded themselves as pioneer settlers in a hostile environment, though much of the hostility they had provoked themselves, through their unwillingness to deal equably with the black peoples they encountered. One considerable antago-

An elderly Zulu with his traditional weapons

nism they felt towards the British concerned the Cape administration's Ordinance 50 of 1828. It granted (in theory) that 'Hottentots and other free persons of colour' would have equality before the law, something utterly antipathetical for the Boers, who happily practised slavery. Slavery was abolished in 1833; the Emancipation Act gave slave owners not more than a third of a slave's market value in compensation. Moreover that compensation was paid in England, which meant that the Boers had to deal with foreign agents who charged a large fee for their services. British failure to prevent Xhosa raiding parties from invading 'their' land was the final straw for the Boers.

Between 1835 and 1837 several prominent Boer leaders—Louis Trichardt, Hans van Rensburg, Hendrik Potgieter, Gert Maritz and Piet Retief—led thousands of disgruntled Boer farmers and their families in ox-drawn wagons on a series of expeditions far north into what became known as Transvaal, and east into Natal. Their common aim was to escape British rule by forming their own, independent and self-governing republics. Many were to die, from malaria and other tropical diseases, or in battle with tribes they encountered. These 'Voortrekkers' (literally 'front trekkers') who initiated the Great Trek have entered the folklore of Afrikaner culture, revered as heroes and heroines, despite their practice of enslaving the children of black groups they defeated in battle. This fierce sense of independence engendered by their struggles to flee British rule and to dominate black African society sowed the seeds of the later bloody clashes that were to erupt between Boer and Brit, and Afrikaner and black South African much later in the 19th and 20th centuries.

Perhaps the most important catalyst for Boer-African relations occurred on 16 December 1838, in the battle of Blood River. On 6 February 1838 Piet Retief visited the new Zulu king, Dingane, at his capital, Mgundgundlovu (Zulu for 'the place of the great elephant') near present-day Ulundi in KwaZulu-Natal. It is claimed by some historians that Dingane agreed to sign over to the trekkers a vast portion of territory, in exchange for cattle and rifles. Retief and a small party were restrained and stoned to death, and a few days later the Zulus attacked Retief's followers, encamped in a *laager* (a circular formation of waggons) at a place now called Weenen ('weeping' in Afrikaans), killing as many as 500 of them. In November the same year Andries Pretorius took over as commandant-general in Natal and prepared his revenge against what was seen as Dingane's treachery. On 16 December, Pretorius' trekkers formed an immense *laager* of 57 waggons, with three cannons, on the banks of the Ncome River, a tributary of the Thukela, some 50 kilometres from present-day Dundee, in the KwaZulu-Natal Midlands. At dawn, 10,000 Zulus attacked the 468 trekkers, who fought them off with much superior weaponry, killing 3,000 Zulus; just three trekkers were wounded, none killed. Such was the slaughter on that day that the Ncome was thereafter called Blood River. On the site of the battle today there are bronze replicas of the 57 waggons, formed in a *laager*; it is a sinister place.

The considerable defeat inflicted on the Zulus threw their nation into a civil war, resulting in the usurpation of Dingane by his half-brother, Mpande—who in a superbly grotesque gesture installed Pretorius as king of the Zulus.

Pretorius' new republic, called Natal, lasted only five years; in 1843 the British annexed Natal, and the Boers trekked once more, this time north, into what became the Orange Free State and, yet further north, Transvaal. In 1842 Boer trekkers declared a republic at Alleman's Drift, on the Orange River. In 1852 the Transvaal

Boers were granted independence from the British under the terms of the Sand River Convention—one of the terms being that they would not practice slavery in their new republic, a codicil that was immediately ignored.

In 1854 a convention at Bloemfontein established the Boer republic of the Orange Free State, and by 1860 various small Boer statelets north of the Vaal River had incorporated themselves into what was called the South African Republic (SAR), which existed until 1902. In the infant Boer republics life was often harsh and violent; with guns now in the possession not only of the Boers but also Africans, it was never entirely clear who had the upper hand. Indeed, in some remote areas Boer farmers even paid taxes to African chiefs in exchange for physical protection from rival African groups. Boer and African societies found themselves increasingly inter-dependent for trade in arms, food and other essentials, though the coexistence was often uneasy and occasionally flared into outright conflict.

All this independent Boer activity took place while, as it were, the British had their hands full defeating the Xhosa in the eastern Cape and, after 1843, administering their new colony of Natal, where labour shortages were becoming so severe that in 1860 the first batch of indentured Indian labourers were imported; between 1860 and 1911 some 152,000 Indians arrived, more than 50 per cent of them staying on after their indentures had been worked out.

Diamonds are Trumps: 1867–1886

The picking up of a 21.25 carat diamond in 1867 at De Kalk farm, near Hopetown, on the south bank of the Orange River, by two small children, was to have momentous implications for the country's future. It spurred individuals to a hasty scramble to find more and by 1871 the richest seam had been located, at Colesberg Kopje, which eventually became the deepest man-made hole in the world, at Kimberley.

Colesberg Kopje was situated in Griqualand West, inhabited by the Griqua people, who had lived there for some 70 years. It was also an area claimed by both the Orange Free State and the South African Republic. A court of arbitration presided over by Robert Keate, the British lieutenant-governor of Natal, found in favour of the Griqua, who were thereupon persuaded to ask for British protection. Griqualand West became a Crown Colony in 1871, and was formally annexed to the Cape in 1880. Another Boer grievance against the British was born; not only were they deprived of riches they considered theirs, but black workers were tempted in huge numbers to leave their farms for the better pay to be had by working as labourers in the diamond fields.

Migrant workers head off to the mines in the late 19th century

The population of Kimberley exploded; by 1873 there were 50,000 people, half of them white, busily digging for diamonds. Kimberley rapidly acquired the character of a wild-west town, where law was enforced by those with the greatest muscle. Early entrepreneurs such as the Oxford University-educated Cecil Rhodes and the London cockney Barney Barnato made fabulous fortunes not so much by digging diamonds as by amalgamating and controlling smaller exploration companies and selling shares in them. Rhodes in particular was an astute and unscrupulous financier, who grasped the importance of monopolizing mineral production in order to regulate otherwise wildly fluctuating prices and, by extension, the value of shares in his De Beers Consolidated Mines company.

In January 1877 the British marched with a small force of mounted police into the South African Republic, on the spurious grounds that the Boers were unable peacefully to coexist with their African neighbours. On 12 April, the Republic was proclaimed a British colony. In fact, the British parliament's passage the same year of the South Africa Act—which formally unified the various southern African colonies and the Orange Free State into a single unit, obedient to the British Crown—was little more than an effort to ensure that growing British imperial interests in the region would not be interfered with by independent, anti-British Boers.

But the British forces on the ground were already over-extended. In January 1879 British troops invaded the hitherto independent Zululand. They immediately suffered a humiliating defeat at Isandlwana, with almost 1,200 troops slaughtered; British mythology prefers to recall the (admittedly courageous) defence of Rorke's Drift by a handful of troops. Despite the setbacks, the British forces eventually crushed the Zulu armies and divided King Cetshwayo's kingdom into 13 lesser chiefdoms. Cetshwayo was initially exiled and in 1882 even permitted to have lunch with Queen Victoria in England. He was allowed to return to Zululand in January 1883; Zululand was eventually annexed directly by the Colony of Natal in 1897. Other minors wars in other parts of the British-controlled territories sparked up and were bloodily defeated in the late 1870s and early 1880s. British control was at best patchy.

Boer responses to enforced integration into the British empire were at first diplomatic. Paul Kruger, who was born in the Cape Colony on 10 October 1825 and whose family had been one of the first to trek away from the British in 1835, headed two delegations to London in 1877 and 1878. His brief was to ask the British government to respect the Sand River Convention of 1852, which had ceded Boer independence. The failure of those commissions meant that by 1880 Boer frustrations spilled over into direct action.

On 16 December 1880—a symbolic date for them—Transvaal Boers at Paardekraal declared themselves once more independent and a brief war broke out with Britain. Kruger (whose political ideology was a mish-mash of Biblical texts and sheer stubborness) joined with two other Boer leaders, Piet Joubert and Marthinus Wessel Pretorius to lead the renewed South African Republic. Boer commandos first defeated a sizeable British force just 50 kilometres from the British stronghold of Pretoria, then inflicted a couple more costly defeats, before utterly routing 400 British troops at Majuba Hill on 27 February 1881. A convention was held at Pretoria on 31 August 1881—and the Transvaal became a self-governing state. In 1883 Kruger became president of the republic, established as the pre-eminent Boer political leader.

Gold-diggers and Gunshots: 1886–1899

Various gold strikes had been made in the eastern Transvaal in the 1870s but not until 1886 was the greatest discovery made, on the Witwatersrand, situated between Pretoria and Johannesburg.

For the Boer leaders of the Transvaal the discovery of gold was a double-edged sword; their perpetually semi-bankrupt administration would find the injection of wealth very useful, but the price to be paid was a massive influx of rowdy, lawless and godless immigrants, interested in only one thing—money. These foreign for-tune-hunters were despisingly called *uitlanders* ('foreigners') by the Boers, who grudgingly accepted their presence, denied them the vote but nevertheless taxed mining revenues, the cash from which was used to stockpile German-manufactured armaments.

Some *uitlanders* however were more acceptable than others, not least some of the class of super-rich entrepreneurs who came to be known as the Randlords, such as Sammy Marks, who did his best to maintain good relations with both British and Boer leaders. Marks, Rhodes and others rapidly muscled into the gold-mining busi-ness, exercising almost as much political as commercial clout.

Rhodes became prime minister of the Cape Colony in 1894, from which posi-tion he ensured that his commercial interests—which he saw as indistinguishable from those of the expanding British empire—were suitably protected. One of his first measures was the passage of the Glen Grey Act. The Act severely curtailed the amount of land which could legally be owned by Africans, and imposed an annual tax on all Africans who could not prove they had been in 'bona fide' employment for at least three months in a year. Rhodes was explicit about the purpose of the Act; it was to force more Africans off the land and into employment in (white-owned) commerce, particularly the diamond and gold mines, where the demand for cheap labour was almost insatiable. This was little more than a mirroring of how the Boer

Transvaal Republic sought to force Africans off the land and into servitude for white farmers; there, any African working for a white farmer was exempt from paying tax, while a sliding scale of levies was imposed on all others.

By 1896 greater Johannesburg had almost 51,000 white inhabitants, just over 10 per cent of them being citizens of the South African Republic, the rest disenfranchised *uitlanders*. In Britain, the Colonial Office under the empire-chasing Joseph Chamberlain had been encouraged by Rhodes to believe

Paul Kruger, Boer leader

that the *uitlanders* were suffering at the hands of cruel Boer politicians. At the end of December 1895 Chamberlain and Rhodes were instrumental in launching a farcical raid, led by Leander Starr Jameson, from the Bechuanaland Protectorate north of the South African Republic, the aim of which was to overthrow the SAR's president, Paul Kruger. The Jameson Raid failed and Rhodes resigned as Cape prime minister, but British politicians—and public sentiment, whipped up by exaggerated newspaper reports—determined that the riches of the Rand were not to be left in the hands of the Boers.

Alfred Milner—Lord Milner—was despatched from Britain in 1897 to become the new governor of the Cape Colony. Milner's mission was to bring into the British empire, by hook or by crook, a united South Africa, in which the independent Boer Republics were subsumed within the colony. Negotiations between Milner and

Kruger over extending the franchise to embrace the *uitlanders* were merely a pretext for Milner. The talks collapsed; the British moved troops in force to the Cape's borders with the South African Republic; Kruger demanded their removal; Milner refused.

On 11 October 1899 the SAR and the OFS declared themselves at war with Britain. Next day, the first shots were fired by Boer commandos against a British troop train—and the British suffered the first of many humiliations in a protracted, miserable war. The British troops surrendered to what they considered was a disordered rabble unable even to afford a proper uniform. The rabble was to humble the might of the British empire for three years.

A Bitter End: War Without Victory: 1899–1948

The Second South African War, as it has come to be known, lasted until 31 May 1902. It was a David and Goliath struggle, fought between vastly unequal opponents. Some 450,000 British and empire troops (22,000 of whom were to die), well armed and trained, led by eminent and experienced generals, outnumbered the Boer commandos by five-to-one.

The Boer farmers had little experience of conventional warfare and none on such a scale as this. Highly individualistic, they often would return home to see their families in the midst of a campaign or even a battle. Their commanders were democratically elected from among their own ranks. Towards the end of the bitter conflict 31,000 of them were in exile, 136,000 of their wives and children were incarcerated in 50 concentration camps inside the country; their homes razed to the ground, and their livestock killed. Their African workers were also rounded up and imprisoned in camps. Some 28,000 Boers are believed to have died in the camps, while at least 14,000 Africans succumbed to disease and illnesses associated with malnutrition. Africans were drawn into the war on both sides, about 100,000 of them being employed by the British forces, mostly as non-combatants, though a large number bore arms.

But the Boers had three advantages. They quickly learned the arts of guerilla warfare—swift movement, concealed ambushes, rapid withdrawal in the face of overwhelming odds, and refusal to engage in close combat. They also knew the country very well; where the ordinary, heavily encumbered British soldier encountered hardship, the Boer found a friend. Finally, they were not burdened—as were the British forces—by some of the most staggeringly incompetent military leaders ever to march against an enemy.

On the Boer side, the war brought to public prominence men who proved themselves not only capable military leaders, such as Koos de la Rey, Piet Joubert, and Christiaan de Wet, but also those who, besides being adroit fighters were additionally to have major impact on the civilian political life of the future Union of South Africa, such as Louis Botha and Jan Smuts. On the British side, no-one emerged with much glory.

Many battles were fought, with many defeats inflicted on the British, with the Boers (futilely) laying seige to Ladysmith, Mafeking and Kimberley. Gradually the overwhelmingly superior number of British troops, plus their ruthless scorched earth and concentration camp policies, brought about a split in the Boers. In 1901 some decided to sue for peace. They were derisively called *hensoppers* (handsuppers) by those determined never to give in, the *bittereinders* (bitterenders). On 31 May 1902 even the *bittereinders* threw in the towel. Exhausted and resentful,

The Boer general Louis Botha during the 1899–1902 war

the Treaty of Vereeniging forced them to give up their republics and recognize British sovereignty. Kruger left for self-imposed exile in Europe, where he died in 1904. Britain set about rebuilding the economy of the country, and eventually ceded in 1906 a modicum of self-government to the former Boer republics of the Transvaal and Orange Free State. In 1910 a Union of South Africa was declared, with Louis Botha as its first prime minister.

The hopes of black Africans that British victory would put them on a more equal legal and political footing with whites proved illusory; despite persisting Boer-Briton rivalry, the two white communities concurred in regarding black South Africans as inferior, fit only to be exploited as disenfranchised labourers.

CASUALTIES OF WAR

Rooineks [1], said Oom Schalk Lourens, are queer. For instance, there was that day when my nephew Hannes and I had dealings with a couple of Englishmen near Dewetsdorp. [...] Hannes and I were lying behind a rock watching the road. Hannes spent odd moments like that in what he called a useful way. He would file the points of his Mauser [2] cartridges on a piece of flat stone until the lead showed through the steel, in that way making them into dum-dum bullets.

I often spoke to my nephew Hannes about that.

'Hannes,' I used to say. 'That is a sin. The Lord is looking at you.'

'That's all right,' said Hannes. 'The Lord knows that this is the Boer War, and in war-time he will always forgive a little foolishness like this, especially as the English are so many.'

Anyway, as we lay behind that rock we saw, far down the road, two horsemen come galloping up. We remained perfectly still and let them approach to within four hundred paces. They were English officers. They were mounted on first-rate horses and their uniforms looked very fine and smart. They were the most stylish-looking

A Boer family from the 1899–1902 war

men I had seen for some time, and I felt quite ashamed of my own ragged trousers and veldskoens[3]. I was glad that I was behind a rock and they couldn't see me. Especially as my jacket was also torn all the way down the back, as a result of my having had three days before to get through a barbed-wire fence rather quickly. I just got through in time, too. The veld-kornet[4], who was a fat man and couldn't run so fast, was about twenty yards behind me. And he remained on the wire with a bullet through him. All through the Boer War I was pleased that I was thin and never troubled with corns.

Hannes and I fired just about the same time. One of the officers fell off his horse. He struck the road with his shoulders and rolled over twice, kicking up the red dust as he turned. Then the other soldier did a queer thing. He drew up his horse and got off. He gave just one look in our direction. Then he led his horse up to where the other man was twisting and struggling on the ground. It took him a little while to lift him on to his horse, for it is no easy matter to pick up a man like that when he is helpless. And he did all this slowly and calmly, as though he was not concerned about the fact that the men who had just shot his friend were lying only a few hundred yards away. He managed in some way to support the wounded man across the saddle, and walked on beside the horse. After going a few yards he stopped and seemed to remember something. He turned round and waved at the spot where he imagined we were hiding, as though inviting us to shoot. During all that time I had simply lain watching him, astonished at his coolness.

But when he waved his hand I thrust another cartridge into the breech of my Martini and aimed. I aimed very carefully and was just on the point of pulling the trigger when Hannes put his hand on the barrel and pushed up my rifle.

'Don't shoot, Oom Schalk,' he said. 'That's a brave man.'

I looked at Hannes in surprise. His face was very white. I said nothing, and allowed my rifle to sink down on to the grass, but I couldn't understand what had come over my nephew. It seemed that not only was that Englishman queer, but that Hannes was also queer. That's all nonsense not killing a man just because he's brave. If he's a brave man and he's fighting on the wrong side, that's all the more reason to shoot him.

I was with my nephew Hannes for another few months after that. Then one day, in a skirmish near the Vaal River, Hannes with a few dozen other burghers was cut *off from the commando and had to surrender. That was the last I ever saw of him. I heard later on that, after taking him prisoner, the English searched Hannes and* found dum-dum bullets in his possession. They shot him for that. I was very much grieved when I heard of Hannes' death. He had always been full of life and high spirits. Perhaps Hannes was right in saying that the Lord didn't mind about a little foolishness like dum-dum bullets. But the mistake he made was in forgetting that the English did mind.

I was in the veld until they made peace. Then we laid down our rifles and went home. What I knew my farm by was the hole under the koppie where I quarried slate-stones for the threshing-floor. That was about all that remained as I left it. Everything else was gone. My home was burnt down. My lands were laid waste. My cattle and sheep were slaughtered. Even the stones I had piled for the kraals were pulled down. My wife came out of the concentration camp and we went together to look at our old farm. My wife had gone into the concentration camp with our two children, but she came out alone. And when I saw her again and noticed the way she had changed, I knew that I, who had been through all the fighting, had not seen the Boer War.

Herman Charles Bosman: from Bosman at his Best

1) ROOINEK: Afrikaans word literally meaning 'redneck'. A derogatory term for the British, whose unprotected necks would turn red in the unaccustomed sunshine. 2) MAUSER: German-made rifle. 3) VELDSKOENS: type of crude shoe. 4) VELD-KORNET: junior officer on the Boers' side.

(Above) *A Boer commando unit carries a wounded comrade in the 1899–1902 war*

Between 1910 and 1948 the political life of South Africa consisted largely of a series of white liberal and educated middle-class black pleas to the British parliament to prevent the passage of legislation that would materially affect the property-owning and voting rights of non-white South Africans. These pleas, without fail, fell entirely on deaf ears. Successive British governments were indifferent to the entrenchment of racialism in this—as in other—parts of the empire.

The response of black South African teachers, journalists, religious ministers and similarly highly-educated professional people, was to establish the South African Native National Congress (SANNC) in 1912; in 1923 it changed its name to the African National Congress. The 1913 Land Act was the most devastating piece of legislation, preventing blacks from ownership of land in all but 7.5 per cent (amended in 1936 to 13 per cent) of the country, inside so-called reserves. The rest was declared solely for white ownership. Despite this crude racism, when war broke out in Europe in August 1914, the SANNC was swept up in a spirit of patriotism and offered to raise 5,000 troops to serve in German South West Africa (now Namibia). Jan Smuts, then South Africa's minister of defence, declined; it was, he said, a war between people of 'European descent'. Nevertheless, such was the demand for labour that 83,000 black South Africans eventually served in non-combatant roles in Europe.

In the early part of the 20th century, there were two fundamentally opposed forces at work inside South Africa, both seeking to wring or force concessions from the dominant British hierarchy. On one side were the slowly developing, openly activist black movements, spearheaded by the ANC and, from 1928, aided by the Communist Party of South Africa (CPSA), the only white-dominated political organization to permit non-white members. Smuts, who had become prime minister in 1919 following the death of Louis Botha, demonstrated his willingness to crush ruthlessly even the most absurd black rebellion. On 24 May 1921 he sanctioned the use of armed police to slaughter members of an obscure Christian sect—the Israelites—occupying supposedly 'white' land at Bulhoek, near Queenstown in the eastern Cape. Led by the self-proclaimed prophet Enoch Mgijima, they prophesied the imminence of Judgement Day and refused to leave the land. One hundred and eighty three died in the massacre.

On the other side there was a resurgence in Afrikaner nationalism. In 1918 the Afrikaner Broederbond (Afrikaner Brotherhood) was formed, aimed at the promotion of the Afrikaans language and the insertion of Afrikaner influence in all walks of life. In 1921 it became a clandestine, highly secretive organization. Over decades it became enormously powerful, such that (particularly after 1948) membership of it was a passport to political, commercial and military success.

The Broederbond's hand was considerably strengthened in the general election of 1924, when the relatively new Nationalist Party, under Barry Hertzog, came to power. Afrikaans was recognized as an official language for the first time in 1925. The move by Afrikaners to recover the political initiative was further strengthened by a US-funded investigation in 1929–32 into white poverty in South Africa. This calculated that out of a total white population of 1.8 million in 1931, more than 300,000—mostly Afrikaners—were living in dire poverty. The study neglected to consider how many black South Africans were in the same condition.

A 1924 Afrikaner nationalist cartoon. showing the breakdown of imperialism by the pro-british government

In 1934 Hertzog and Smuts formed the United South African National Party, and established a so-called Fusion Government, while the more extreme Afrikaner nationalist, Daniel Malan, broke to form the 'Purified' National Party. In 1936, Hertzog succeeded in passing legislation that abolished the (very limited) voting rights of Africans in the Cape; similar abolition of Coloured voting rights was to happen 20 years later.

As the world slipped towards another war, opposition to the political emasculation of non-white South Africans all but fell apart. In 1939 prime minister Hertzog opposed South Africa's entry in World War II and evinced considerable sympathy for Nazi Germany, as did many of his

Rural poverty among whites, in the 1930s.

Afrikaner compatriots. Smuts, however, backed the British and, as the new prime minister, carried the bulk of his party—and the country—into the war on the side of the British empire. Many Afrikaners opposed to the British joined the Ossewabrandweg ('Ox-wagon sentinels'), a quasi-fascist movement that carried out acts of sabotage against the South African war effort.

By the late 1940s such was the serious poverty in the African rural reserves that many people flocked into white-only urban areas. In the general election of 1948 D F Malan's Herenigde (Reunited) National Party (HNP) campaigned on a platform of apartheid, complete racial separation—and won a small but crucial victory. Malan formed the first exclusively Afrikaner government. In 1951 the HNP adopted the name, National Party.

White was Might: 1948–1964

Malan's administration set about a programme of 'Afrikanerization'—systematically purging the military and public services of senior and middle-ranking (white) figures identified as being opposed to Afrikaner domination, replacing them with faithful Broederbonders. Simultaneously, various key pieces of legislation—such as the 1949 Prohibition of Mixed Marriages Act—were passed, putting the apartheid programme in place. In 1950 sexual relations between white and non-whites were banned. The activities of the CPSA were curtailed; the ANC reeled from the legislative onslaught introduced by the NP government.

In 1952 a protest campaign was planned by the ANC, trades unionists and leaders of the Coloured People's Congress. Out of that a Congress of the People was scheduled for 25–26 June 1955, to be held in Kliptown, near Soweto. Almost 3,000 delegates attended to acclaim a 10 point Freedom Charter, an incendiary document as far as the white authorities were concerned. The security forces arrested all those who attended the Congress. In December 1956 156 leading anti-apartheid activists were charged with treason; all were eventually acquitted.

On 21 March 1960, demonstrators were gunned down by police in the Transvaal township of Sharpeville; 69 died. In October 1961, shortly after the NP achieved their fifth successive election victory with a massive majority, the ANC initiated an armed struggle. Its first bombs exploded in Port Elizabeth on 15 and 16 December; some 200 more followed over the next 18 months. An ANC leader, Nelson Mandela, was arrested in Natal on 5 August 1962 and sentenced to life imprisonment. Arrests of other senior ANC figures soon followed. By 1964, the head had apparently been lopped from the anti-apartheid movement.

Radical onslaught: 1964–1989

Under Hendrik Verwoerd, the deeply sinister Afrikaner who was prime minister between 1958 and 1966, apartheid was crystallized and systematized as never before. His brand of racism had a veneer of subtlety, arguing that black South Africans were to be placed in virtual internal exile not because they were inferior to whites, but because they were not really South African at all.

Aftermath of the Sharpeville massacre, 21 March 1960

This specious nonsense fooled neither black South Africans nor international public opinion—for which Verwoerd cared little. In 1961 he had the satisfaction of declaring South Africa to be a republic, following a 1960 referendum which narrowly voted (by 52 per cent in a whites-only poll in which nine per cent abstained) in support of the country's withdrawal from the Commonwealth. Verwoerd was assassinated on 6 September 1966 by Dimitri Tsafendas, who after a swift trial was declared insane, an opinion many black South Africans probably did not share.

Verwoerd's successor was a rather more crude proponent of apartheid, John Vorster, who as minister of justice had been responsible for some of the most repressive measures taken against anti-apartheid protesters. Vorster will go down in history for many nasty, absurd actions. He it was who said in 1975: 'Anyone who wants to talk to me on the basis that Mandela is the leader of black South Africa can forget it.' But by September 1978 Vorster's government was embroiled in financial scandals involving misuse of government funds, siphoned off into the department of information for pro-government propaganda purposes. Vorster resigned as prime minister in late 1978 for 'health reasons' and became state president; he died, unmourned by all except his closest family, in 1983.

After Vorster came P W (Pieter Willem) Botha. He too believed that power must remain in white hands, but attempted to present a softer image to the rest of the world, hinting that the days of extreme apartheid *might* be over. He created a tri-cameral parliament (following another whites-only referendum, in November 1983) in which Coloured and Indian representatives could sit—though many Coloured and Indian people, as well as hardline Afrikaners, bitterly opposed such a development, albeit from vastly different perspectives. In August 1983 a significant new anti-apartheid force, the ANC-aligned United Democratic Front (UDF) was brought into being, primarily to oppose the new tri-cameral parliament, which it regarded as an odious attempt to placate only Coloured and Indian disenfranchised South Africans; a year later the UDF claimed the support of some 3 million people, from all communities, white, black, coloured, Indian. 1985 saw the launch of COSATU, the Congress of South African Trade Unions, a non-racial umbrella federation grouping together more than 500,000 workers.

These encouraging developments, along with some mild reforms (such as repeal of legislation banning mixed-race marriages and sexual intercourse, and the abolition of the pass laws) in 1986 were overshadowed by increasing violence across the country, much of it the result of clashes between UDF/ANC supporters and supporters of Inkatha, the largely Zulu movement under the control of chief Mangosuthu Buthelezi.

Buthelezi had been a member of the ANC before it was banned in 1960, but had come in for intense ANC criticism for accepting the leadership of the KwaZulu 'homeland' from the government. Inkatha (which later was re-christened the Inkatha Freedom Party, or IFP) came to be regarded by most ANC sympathizers as essentially a Zulu nationalist organization, more interested in building its own regional powerbase within white-ruled South Africa than in seeing the country united under one democratically elected government.

Botha declared a state of emergency in 36 districts across the country on 20 July 1985; within a few months more than 14,000 people had been arrested. The ANC called upon its activists to render townships 'ungovernable'. The level of political and criminal violence rose dramatically; townships became confusing, dangerous and lawless places, where a casual word to the wrong person could result in a political or a personal enemy being hacked to death or 'necklaced'—the practice of slipping a rubber tyre over a person and setting it alight. In June 1986, just before the tenth anniversary of the Soweto uprising, Botha's government imposed a nationwide state of emergency.

That same year foreign multinationals began to close down their South African operations, as the ANC's call for international sanctions began to bite. The so-called independent homelands began to fall apart, as their corrupt black administrations also came under increasing pressure from disaffected youth. By now, South Africa was almost utterly isolated from the international community, which shunned it. Still president Botha was unable to yield on the essential issues—the release of Nelson Mandela and the unbanning of the ANC.

A Tricky Endgame: 1989–1996 and Beyond

Fate intervened. On 18 January 1989 Botha suffered a stroke, and relinquished leadership of the NP but without giving up the office of head of state, the presidency. Following rancorous internal elections, F W (Frederik Willem) de Klerk became

Chief Mangosuthu Buthelezi, dressed for business

NP party leader. By the end of August 1989 the senior figures of the NP conspired to make it clear to Botha that he could not stay on as president. He felt himself—not unjustly—to have been stabbed in the back, and grudgingly resigned in favour of de Klerk. De Klerk then succeeded in winning for the NP a general election, though with its parliamentary majority reduced from 80 to 20 seats.

De Klerk from the outset seemed determined to deal with the ANC. After his election victory he swiftly released from prison several of its most prominent figures, in October 1989, when he gave expression to a sentiment that only a few years previously would have been regarded as heretical weakness. He said then: 'Most South Africans are tired of confrontation and wish to speak to one another about the road of prosperity and justice for all.'

On 13 December 1989 he met with Nelson Mandela; on 2 February 1990 he announced in parliament in Cape Town the unbanning of the ANC, the PAC and the CPSA, the lifting of a host of restrictions on the media and other entities. He also announced the immediate, unconditional release of Nelson Mandela, who walked free from jail on Sunday 11 February 1990.

After much wrangling between the various political forces in the country, it was agreed to stage South Africa's first democratic elections in April 1994, under an interim constitution. Despite persisting ANC/IFP strife and attempts by white extremists to intimidate voters, the elections took place in a remarkably calm, reasonable atmosphere. But it must be said that many observers judged the elections to be only as free and fair as was possible in such turbulent circumstances. A large ANC majority was anticipated, but the ANC did less well than some predicted, taking 62.6 per cent of the national vote and 252 of the 400 seats in the national assembly. It failed to get a majority in two provinces—Western Cape (where the NP formed the majority) and KwaZulu-Natal (where the IFP dominated). On 10 May 1994 Nelson Mandela became president, and F W de Klerk one of two deputy presidents.

Had the ANC taken two-thirds of the national vote in 1994 it would have been able to write a new, permanent constitution without consulting the other parties. Its failure to do so created space for considerable bickering over the future constitution between the ANC, the NP, and the IFP, now the three leading political forces in the country. A new, wide-ranging constitution was passed just before its deadline in May 1996. Almost immediately afterwards, F W de Klerk withdrew his National Party from the goverment of national unity, and went into open opposition against the

ANC. In fact, the ANC in power has proved itself to be astonishingly pragmatic, quietly ignoring many of the more radical demands contained in its 1955 Freedom Charter, much to the dissatisfaction of more radical groups within the country, and to the surprised contentment of the international financial community.

Saint or sinner? The last Nationalist Party head of state, F W de Klerk

By 1996 there were many contradictory signs as to the country's future. The NP was internally divided. The IFP, still under the sway of Buthelezi, controlled KwaZulu-Natal province, and vigorously opposed ANC policies. Violent clashes between the ANC and the IFP were still an almost daily occurrence, particularly in KwaZulu-Natal, while ANC and IFP leaders paid lip service to the need for peace. In the decade 1986–96, an estimated 15,000 people were killed in politically-motivated clashes—mainly between the IFP and the ANC—in the KwaZulu-Natal region. By 1996 some of the most senior ANC figures privately spoke of the impossibility of dealing with the IFP while Buthelezi was still in control. Ominously, Mandela said on 21 March 1996— the 36th anniversary of the Sharpeville massacre—while addressing an audience in Newcastle, in KwaZulu-Natal: 'There is a war between Africans in this province.'

The clock relentlessly ticks on towards 1999, the date set for fresh national elections and Nelson Mandela's planned retirement from political life. By 1996 Mandela had approved as the future leader of the ANC Thabo Mbeki, a man of stature and intelligence—but lacking Mandela's credibility and unifying prestige. There was far to go before the bloodletting would finally cease.

CULTURE

Today's South Africa has a lively arts scene. Be it music, painting, sculpture, cinema, theatre, dance or literature, all modes of creative expression are flourishing, with many internationally-recognised artists achieving fine work.

San rock paintings, Cedarberg mountains

In sport too, the cessation of apartheid seems to have given fresh impetus to the country's national teams, particularly in cricket, football and rugby. In 1995 the world rugby championship was played in South Africa, the final victors; in 1996 the country's cricket team gave a resounding thrashing to England in South Africa; and (again in early 1996) South Africa's football squad, known locally as Bafana Bafana (The Boys! The Boys!) won the African nation's soccer competition. It's almost as if the newly-liberated country has been engaged in a mass orgy of sporting celebration.

The country's first inhabitants, the San, were also its first artists, decorating their caves with murals of the creatures and objects they saw around them. More than 3,000 sites of such rock painting have been identified, some as old as 30,000 years. The last-known San rock painter was shot by a white farmer in 1850 in the Drakensberg.

A tradition of western-style painting began to develop with relatively early adventurers such as Thomas Baines (1820–75), many of whose paintings of early frontier wars and peoples can be seen in various galleries in the country; the Museum Africa in Johannesburg has a particularly good collection of his and the work of other early colonialist painters. Other important painters who span the late 19th and early 20th centuries are the landscape specialists Frans Oerder, Pieter Wenning, and the more stylised, less naturalistic Jacob Pierneef. Later painters, such as Terence MacCaw and Walter Battiss, broke completely from naturalism. Among sculptors, Anton van Wouw, active in the first half of the 20th

(Above) The Owl House at Nieu Bethesda

century, is widely recognised as the country's leading exponent, although many rate equally highly the reclusive Helen Martins, who produced a great deal of naif work, much of which can still be seen in her old house in Nieu Bethesda.

The black sculptor Sydney Kumalo, who died in 1990, and the painter and sculptor George Pemba have also gained international recognition; black township painting and sculpture is now very popular and commands high prices. Of contemporary artists, William Kentridge—whose work crosses barriers, going into film and theatre—is perhaps the best-known internationally. There's much going on, with myriad art festivals, galleries and exhibitions all across the country. South African photographers, such as David Goldblatt, have also gained deserved international recognition.

Street life in Soweto

The music scene is equally vibrant. South Africa is well-plugged into all the latest trends, but jazz and rock are particularly popular. In black African culture music has long been an important mode of expression not just through instruments but the whole body, where movement, voice and instrument fuse. The rhythms and sounds of African music led naturally to jazz, which, being adopted and transformed in the US, fed back into South African townships and was re-formed into a unique style, known as *marabi*; the African Jazz Pioneers were perhaps the best exponents of the genre. Some of the country's best contemporary musicians, such as Hugh Masakela and 'Dollar' Brand (now known as Abdullah Ibrahim), originate from that tradition.

But perhaps it is in the field of literature, in the 20th century, where

Harmony is breaking out all over

South Africans have been most outstanding. Many local writers found their driving compulsion—inspiration is hardly an appropriate word—from the distorted race relations they grew up within. In a parallel fashion to the stimulus many east European and Soviet artists found from the repressive atmosphere of communism, apartheid provoked writers—black and white—to do much of their best work.

Novelist, critic and essayist Nadime Gordimer won the Nobel Prize for Literature in 1991, the first South African to do so. Other famous fiction writers include Charles Bosman, Alan Paton, and more recently Breyten Breytenbach, André Brink, J M Coetzee, and the immensely popular Wilbur Smith. Other prose writers, such as Eugene Marais (*The Soul of the Ape* and *The Soul of the White Ant*) and Laurens van der Post (*The Lost World of the Kalahari*) have established reputations for fine observation of the natural world; Marais was also a founder of lyrical Afrikaans poetry. Another interesting 20th-century Afrikaans writer was Louis Leipoldt, who besides poetry wrote lastingly absorbing histories of wine and indigenous cookery: 'Zebra flesh I should without hesitation deem the tenderest, most savoury, and best flavoured of all game meat, especially when the animal is young.'

Black writers too have shone, particularly in the field of journalism and essays. Sol Plaatje, in the first decades of the 20th century, wrote some powerful analyses of the destruction of black society, but it was really in the 1950s, with *Drum* magazine, that writers such as Lewis Nkosi, Can Themba and Blake Modisane began to pour out a mass of pacy, stylish journalism.

But it must be said that, for most South Africans, sport, not the arts, is the favourite recreational pastime. South African athletes were unwelcome outside their country for many years under apartheid, during the cultural boycott. Now that boycott is over, the country's sportsmen and women are grabbing honours all over the place. Sports which once were racially divided have, as if by magic, become popular across the divide. Thus many black South Africans now turn out to cheer the Springboks (the national rugby team) and the national cricket eleven—unimaginable a few years ago. Meanwhile, whites who once looked down on soccer as purely a black sport are now showing a greater interest in the sport. Some South African soccer teams have wonderfully outlandish names, such as the Orlando Pirates, the Mamelodi Sundowns, the Moroka Swallows and the Kaizer Chiefs.

It's not just a game—it's a religion

Long distance road-running is also a very big sport, dominated by the annual 90-kilometre Comrades Marathon between Durban and Pietermaritzburg; more than 14,000 runners take part in this gruelling slog. World-class facilities for every kind of activity exist in almost every city, such as Johannesburg's Standard Bank Arena for tennis, or (outside the same city) the Kyalami Formula One race-track. South African golf courses are the best the world can offer, and horse-racing events are enormously popular.

Finally, there is one huge sporting topic on the minds of almost all South Africans—Cape Town may well be the site of the 2004 Olympic Games. There are two key dates in 1997 concerning the city's bid to host the games. In February 1997 the International Olympic Committee is due to select four cities (from the 11 contenders) as a shortlist. In September 1997 the IOC will choose the winner.

Cape Town is a strongly-favoured candidate, as much for political reasons—the ending of apartheid, and the sense that it's time for Africa to stage them—as anything else. While those behind the bid are naturally very gung-ho about the games, many others see the expenditure of R1bn of government money as unlikely to lead to any lasting benefit for Cape Town and the surrounding areas. It's a tricky subject, with the sceptics being in a clear minority. But, as Ian Phimister, a University of Cape Town professor of history, puts it—in today's South Africa, where many people still exist in dire poverty, yet the whole nation seems fixated on the latest sporting triumph, 'there are lots of circuses but not much bread.'

Flora and Fauna

South Africa promotes itself to visitors as 'a world in one country'—a corny slogan, but nonetheless accurate. Few countries have quite such geographical variety; even fewer have such an abundant, various animal and plant-life; fewer still have done anything like as much to conserve and protect the natural environment. Throughout this century successive governments have steadily turned the country into a patchwork quilt of conservation areas and nature reserves, repairing where possible the depredations wrought by the mindless mass hunting of previous eras.

It might even be argued that, paradoxically, apartheid inadvertently assisted South Africa in its conservation policies; the lengthy cultural isolation of the country meant that it dropped off the tourist map, in turn inhibiting growth of the kind of mass-market tourism that has been so damaging to other parts of the world. Today, South Africans from all sides of the community are highly sensitive to the need to protect and conserve their wildlife. Unlike much of Africa, there is every reason to be optimistic South Africa will continue to be a responsible guardian of its many thousands of indigenous species.

Just how much natural riches are we talking about? The country is vastly, disproportionately, blessed by Nature. It's got less than one per cent of the world's land mass, yet has 4.6 per cent of the world's reptile species, 5.8 per cent of its mammals, eight per cent of its birds, and 10 per cent of its higher plants. Moreover, many of these species—a third of the plants and reptiles, 15 per cent of the mammals and six per cent of the birds—are found *nowhere* else in the world. More than 50,000 species of insect have been identified in the country; spiders, termites, moths, butterflies, beetles, ants—the teeming mass of insect-life alone is enough for a lifetime's exploration.

You will often hear/see the word *veld* (pronounced 'felt'). This Afrikaans word—used by all language speakers—is the generic term for all types of open country in South Africa. There are various types of veld—high, low, middle, as well as bushveld, thornveld and grassveld, all depending on local characteristics such as climate, elevation and cultivation. But the country is generally divided into the highveld, the lowveld and the middleveld.

The lowveld is the name given to the region where the altitude above sea level is approximately 150–600 metres.It stretches down from the eastern border of the country, through parts of Swaziland and into northern KwaZulu-Natal. The soil tends to be rich, porous and prone to erosion through water run-off.

The middleveld is the term applied to the vast area of land north of Pretoria and ranging far and wide into the whole of the Cape, where the altitude above sea level is generally between 600 and 1,200 metres. The landscape is characterized by individual mountains and kopjes (rugged, smaller hills). In parts of Northern Province and Mpumalanga this area is also heavily marked by bushveld.

The highveld is that part of the country comprising the high-plateau bounded on the east and south by the Great Escarpment, consisting of the Drakensberg, the Lesotho Highlands, and the Cape range of mountains. To the north and west the boundaries are less clearly defined. Altitude is between 1,200 and 1,850 metres above sea level, though in Lesotho this can reach as high as 3,350 metres. The soil tends to be poor quality and very prone to water and wind erosion.

Flora

South Africa is home to 24,000 different plant species, almost 10 per cent of the world's flowering plants—more than in the US, a country seven times bigger. The Cape peninsula, an area the size of the relatively tiny Isle of Wight in the UK, was declared a National Park in early 1996; it has more native plants than the *whole* of Britain. Indeed, the Cape is home to one of the world's six so-called 'Floral Kingdoms'. Moreover, it's the only one of those six which is entirely contained within one country; the other five spread across continents.

The country broadly divides into six ecological regions or biomes: **Fynbos, Succulent Karoo, Forest, Savanna, Nama-Karoo** and **Grassland**.

The Cape floral kingdom is primarily composed of *fynbos*, an Afrikaans word meaning 'fine bush'—evergreen plants with small, hard leaves. It's a vegetation very similar to that found in the Mediterranean. South African *fynbos* is made up of three groups of plants—proteas, heathers and restios. Altogether there are more than 8,500 different types of *fynbos*, with over 6,000 being endemic to South Africa. The *fynbos* region stretches from Nieuwoudtville—which is about 250 kilometres directly north of Cape Town—to Port Elizabeth—almost 800 kilometres east of Cape Town on the southern coast. Since the 1970 Mountain Catchment Areas Act, approximately 1.4 million hectares of (state-owned and private) land have been brought into protected catchment areas, resulting in the conservation of almost half of the mountain *fynbos* ecosystems and more than 90 per cent of all mountain *fynbos* species. Perhaps the most famous example of *fynbos* is the protea, a national emblem; there are whole forests of proteas in some parts of the Cape and Drakensberg regions.

In Namaqualand, that ill-defined region in the furthest north-west of the country, there is a four-week annual flower show over which man has no control. This is the *Succulent Karoo* region, where, from the beginning of August to late September, depending when the winter rains fall, the desert is transformed into a carpet of colour. Orange, pink, yellow and white mesembryantheums (succulent daisies), aloes, lilies, flowering herbs—hundreds of different species all burst into life and decorate the otherwise drab desert. By October the flowers have usually all disappeared; annual rainfall in this area is rarely more than 20 centimetres. The best time of the day to see the flowers is from 11.00–16.00, when the sun is at full strength.

Even if you cannot visit Namaqualand for the flowering season there is nevertheless much else to see. In the mountainous desert of the Richtersveld to the north, you can spot on granite *koppies* (small hills) strange-looking succulent plants called *Pachypodium namaquanum* (elephant's trunk), also known in Afrikaans as *halfmens*, or half-humans. Tall, slender, with knobbly trunks, they have at the top a small bush of leaves, supposedly resembling a human head. Many of them are believed to be centuries old; each ring of spines supposedly represents a year of growth. In this region you can also spot the slow-growing *aloe dichotoma*, known in Afrikaans as the *kokerboom* or quiver tree, the bark of which was once used by San tribesmen to make quivers to carry their poisoned arrows. To the south and east, the Nama-Karoo biome, which covers a vast area known as the Great Karoo in Northern Cape province, is perhaps the country's least interesting area for plant-life. Cold winters and hot summers, plus little rainfall, produces mostly low shrubland and hardy grasses, such as feather grass and ostrich grass.

In a semi-arid country such as this, indigenous *Forest* is rare, though between Mossel Bay and Algoa Bay, and particularly around Knysna and the Tsitsikamma area (in the south-east of Western Cape province), there are dense rainforests, with *podocarpus* (yellowwood, reaching heights of 40 metres), stinkwood, *Olea capensis* (ironwood), *Xymalos monospora* (lemonwood) and many other types of tree, as well as a host of creepers and ferns. There are vast expanses of forests in the east of the Orange Free State and down into KwaZulu-Natal, but these are largely artificially-created pinewood plantations, imported trees to provide timber and pulp. Some rainforest vegetation can be found along the coast of KwaZulu-Natal, where further north it turns into mangrove swamps.

The *Savanna* biome, comprising mixed grassland and trees, is generally known as the *bushveld*, and covers much of the inland coastal areas of KwaZulu-Natal, large swathes of Mpumalanga and Northern provinces, as well as part of Northern Cape and North-West provinces. In the Kalahari (Northern Cape), the *Acacia erioloba* (camel thorn) and *Tarchonanthus camphoratus* (camphor bush) are common; in Northern province you will find *Adansonia digitata*, the baobab tree, with its distinctive convex, thick trunk, often several metres in diameter. The baobab has large white flowers and a gourd-like fruit with edible pulp known as monkey bread—for obvious reasons. In other parts of the bushveld you can see the *Acacia nigrescens*, or knob-thorn tree, with long sharp spikes on its trunk and wild fig trees. There is

also the *Colophospermum mopane*, or mopane tree, the leaves of which are much loved by elephants; a fat spotted caterpillar, the mopane worm, lives on this tree, and is a highly prized, nutty-tasting delicacy for local inhabitants—either dried or roasted immediately on capture. The marula tree is also quite common; folklore has it that elephants get drunk on the fermenting, plum-like, mango-flavoured marula fruit. That's a myth, but it's certainly true that you can buy a locally-produced a marula-flavoured cream liqueur.

The *Grassland* biome, which spreads across much of the highveld—a plateau rising to above 1,800 metres on its eastern side—covers much of northern KwaZulu-Natal, the Free State, Gauteng and up into Mpumalanga. It's an area of summer rainfall and cold winters, and dominated by two main types of grass, 'sweet' (on the western side) and 'sour' (to the east), the terms referring to the value of the grass as fodder. About 10 per cent of the world's identified species of grass—there are some 10,000 different species—are to be found in this area, which has little or no indigenous forest.

Fauna

There is such a diversity of animal life in South Africa that you could spend several years in exploration. Most tourists will hope to see the 'big five'—buffalo, elephant, leopard, lion and rhino—but there are so many fascinating mammals, amphibians, reptiles, birds, insects and fish that no-one should return home disappointed. What you see and how you see it is all a question of careful planning. Remember that all these creatures are *wild* animals; do not get out of your vehicle, both for your sake and theirs, unless you are accompanied by an expert ranger or you have stopped at a designated rest or viewing area. Even harmless-looking baboons can cause severe damage—they have canines larger than those of the lion.

The densest concentrations of game are to be found in the bushveld of Eastern Cape, KwaZulu-Natal, the Kalahari and Mpumalanga. Game can be very elusive; spotting one of the Kruger Park's 8,000 elephants can be a matter of luck. After all, they traverse an area the size of Belgium, and after a period of heavy rain, when the bush is dense and high, seeing *anything* can be very difficult.

Within these regions, the only places to see game (apart from some of the local zoos) are in the National or provincial parks or private games reserves (see the National Parks appendix for details, page 300). No longer do massive herds of buffalo or antelopes wander nomadically through huge empty plains, as in some parts of Africa. But the parks alone account for 3.2 million hectares, a vast area of land bigger than many medium-sized countries.

What should you hope to see? It depends on the time of year you visit; late autumn and winter (May to September), when the bush is lower and the larger animals are less easily able to find water, is a good time. But all year you stand a good chance of seeing antelope of all kinds particularly (the very common) impala, known to rangers in the Kruger Park as 'bush-burger' because it's a predator's version of a quick and easy take-away meal. Herds of zebra, giraffe, kudu, and wildebeest can normally be spotted without too much trouble in the larger parks, such as the Kruger, as can wandering groups of baboons. You might also spot white rhino (distinguished from the scarcer black rhino by its square lower lip), warthog, jackal, caracal, brown and spotted hyena, civet and—if you are very lucky—the wild dog, now an endangered species.

People fear the lumbering, bulky **rhino**, which can weigh as much as five tons, but they are myopic and generally move peacefully off if they become nervous. Considerably more dangerous are **crocodiles** and **hippopotamuses**, both of which should be approached only with the greatest caution. Crocodiles swiftly seize and drag their prey beneath the water, to drown it; hippos are very territorial, can move over short distances at speeds of up to 30 kilometres an hour, and will effortlessly crush those unwary enough to invade their space. Equally aggressive is the **Cape buffalo**, which occur in large numbers, particularly in the Kruger Park; solitary rogue bulls and nursing females are the most likely to charge.

Cheetahs are also now quite scarce, but at **Hoedspruit** (in eastern Mpumalanga) there is a very interesting **Cheetah Project**, for research and breeding of this carnivore. You may visit the project (08.30–16.00 Monday–Saturday, no reservation, 08.30–16.00 Sunday, prior reservation required, telephone either 012 804 1711 or 015282 and ask for 4321/5241).

Lions can be seen in the Kruger Park and the Kalahari Gemsbok Park. A large male, recognised by the distinguishing mane, may weigh up to 180 kilogrammes; the female, who does almost all the killing, is smaller and maneless. They spend much of the day lying under bushes or in the shelter of rocks, and are most active in the very early morning, after dawn. They are territorial; a small pride of a few males and a dozen females will regard an area up to 400 square kilometres as theirs.

Leopards are to be found in almost all the game reserves, and small numbers also live in the country's more mountainous regions. Solitary animals, they often can be found lying spread-eagled in a tree. At night, when they have made a kill, they frequently drag their prey up a favourite tree, where they can consume it at leisure. Unlike the other large cats, leopards enjoy meat which has turned putrid; they will feast on a rotten impala carcase with great gusto.

The greatest numbers of African **elephant**, (larger than the Asian and with wider, flatter ears), are found in the Kruger Park, though groups are scattered

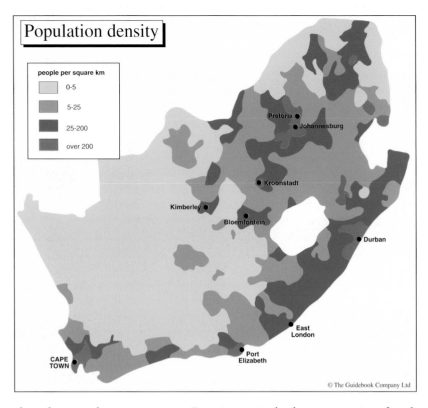

through some other game reserves. Gregarious animals, they are sometimes found in herds as large as 50, though individuals do roam around too. Constantly on the move in search of fodder and water—the average daily food intake of a full-grown bull, weighing as much as 6.5 tonnes, is about 250 kilogrammes—you can often see where an elephant has been, either by enormous dung droppings or the peculiar sight of a tree which has been pushed over, its roots unearthed, as though some huge force has just plucked it from the ground.

Among other animals you should be on the watch for are the **bat-eared fox** (identifiable by its long legs and huge ears); the **Cape Hunting** or **wild dog**, about the size of a large domestic dog—scarce, but it can be recognised by its unusual yellow and black splotchy patched, and white-tipped tail; **hyenas**, which have astonishingly powerful jaws, enabling it to crush and digest the largest of bones, will probably be heard more than seen—at night they are frequently given to emitting a howl which rises to a pitched scream; the **pangolin** or scaly ant-eater, which thrives on the large termite mounds dotted around everywhere; and, if you are extremely lucky, the shy but very fierce honey badger, a small omnivore recognisable by a broad creamy-white stripe running from its head down its back—honeybadgers have even been known to attack buffalo.

The smaller amphibians and reptiles are more difficult to find, partly because they

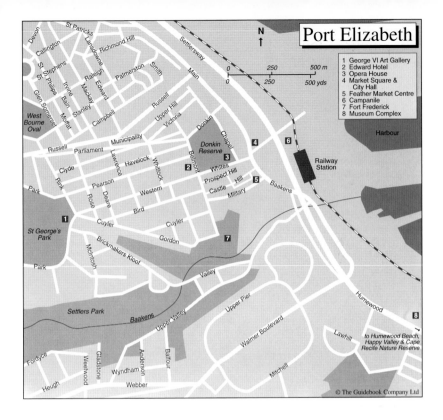

Port Elizabeth

1 George VI Art Gallery
2 Edward Hotel
3 Opera House
4 Market Square &
  City Hall
5 Feather Market Centre
6 Campanile
7 Fort Frederick
8 Museum Complex

Harbour

0 ____ 250 ____ 500 m
0 ____ 250 ____ 500 yds

St Patricks
Dexon
Callington
Lansdowne
Richmond Hill
Settlersway
Main
St Stephens
Raleigh
Edward
Palmerston
Smith
Irvine
Mackay
Campbell
Upper Hill
Victoria
Donkin
Chapel
Glen Somerset
Bain
Moffat
Stanley
Russell
West Bourne Oval
Russell
Parliament
Municipality
Lawrence
Havelock
Whitlock
Donkin Reserve
Belmont
Railway Station
Clyde
Rink
Pearson
Deare
Western
Whites
Prospect Hill
Castle
Military
Baakens
Park
Rose
Bird
Cuyler
Cuyler
Gordon
St George's Park
Brickmakers Kloof
McIntosh
Park
Valley
Settlers Park
Baakens
Upper Valley
Upper Pier
Humewood
Fordyce
Weetwood
Gladstone
Anderson
Balfour
Walmer Boulevard
Lawhill
to Humewood Beach,
Happy Valley & Cape
Recife Nature Reserve
Heugh
Wyndham
Webber
Mitchell

© The Guidebook Company Ltd

are primarily nocturnal creatures. South Africa is believed to have about 120 different amphibian species, and there are 12 species of land **tortoise**, the highest number in a single country. **Chameleons** can be found, as well as several types of lizard including the **Nile monitor**. There are about 130 different species of snake, only 14 of which have potentially fatal bites, though no-one would wish to tangle with the very large **rock python**, nor encounter the highly toxic **black mamba**. Its cousin, the **green mamba**, is also poisonous, but its venom is less rapidly-acting. The **boomslang**, which likes to hang around in trees, is reckoned by some to be the deadliest of African snakes; but it has small fangs set far back in the jaw, and must chew to inject its venom.

Ornithologists will find South Africa a rich paradise, wherein are some 900 bird species. On the coasts there are **cormorants**, **gulls**, **gannets**, **oystercatchers**, **petrels**, **plovers**, **terns**, and **Jackass penguins**. Inland, in the savanna bushveld, many different types of **eagle**, **kestrel**, **falcons**, **hornbills**, **shrikes**, **bustards**, **kingfishers**, **weavers**, **whydahs** and **bee-eaters** have a natural habitat. If you are lucky you might spot a rare **honeybuzzard**, or, near an animal carcase, one of the four types of **vulture** most commonly found in Southern Africa. It is of course imperative to go armed with one of the best field guides (see Selected Further Reading, page 319) and a good pair of lightweight binoculars.

Nor should we forget the ostrich, the world's biggest bird. Just don't get too close without supervision—it can deliver a nasty kick, (see Special Topic OSTRICHES, page 262).

Provinces Part One

South Africa is divided into nine provinces, each with quite different qualities; some are worth spending more time on than others. Some are densely packed, others almost empty and unexplored. High-octane nightlife, remote beautiful beaches, spectacular scenery, close encounters with unique wildlife—South Africa has it all. **Hotels**, **Places to Eat** and **National Park** details are listed separately.

Eastern Cape

In the 19th century this region was the site of many bitter, small-scale conflicts between the Xhosa, Boer farmers and British settlers. In recent years it has unfortunately experienced some of the worst political unrest and violent crime in the country. If driving alone in the coastal areas make sure your vehicle is roadworthy and equipped for emergency breakdowns; take a mobile telephone if possible.

Its cities are not worth spending much time in, but the coastal region north of East London—called the **Wild Coast**—has some idyllic hideaways, while inland are some of the country's best nature reserves and walking trails.

PORT ELIZABETH

The industrial coastal city of PE (as locals call it) is the country's fifth biggest, on Algoa Bay, some 780 kilometres on the south coast east of Cape Town on the N2; the airport is four kilometres from the city and the railway station is on Station Street, in the city centre. The local telephone prefix is 041.

Founded in 1820, Sir Rufus Donkin, the acting Cape governor, named it after his wife, who had died in India. Local tourist promoters valiantly tout PE as the 'Friendly City', which it certainly is, but that's scant compensation for the relative lack of historical or visual attractions. PE today has a very built-up feel—an ugly motorway system slices the town itself from the port—and is not one of the country's high spots. It should not detain you long; an hour is ample for the main city sights.

Among its steep hills overlooking the harbour PE has some pleasant, centrally-positioned parks, including: the 54-hectare **Settlers**, (through which flows the Baakens River), with lots of indigenous plants and birds; St George's, which contains in its 73 hectares a collection of rare orchids in the Edward Pearson Conservatory, a swimming-pool and steam baths, the **Mannville Open-Air Theatre**, (annual productions of Shakespeare), the **George VI Gallery**, a collection of minor 19th and 20th-century English art and South African paintings—in this park on the first Sunday of each month contemporary artists sell their work—and the country's oldest cricket ground; and the **Donkin Reserve** where apart from an 1861 lighthouse, you can find the PE publicity association. The association has maps for the **Donkin Heritage Trail**, a 5-kilometre walk through the historical parts of the city, including Donkin Street, which has some interesting late-Victorian terraces.

Other attractive spots are around **City Hall** (built 1858–62) and **Market Square**, both on Main Street. Nearby is the **Feather Market Centre** (built 1885 in the heyday of the ostrich feather boom) which today is a concert hall and conference centre; guided tours are available (telephone 041 555 5514). **Fort Frederick** (open daily between sunrise and sunset), on Belmont Terrace, dates from 1799 and is a large square stone building, built by the British to defend themselves against Xhosa attacks—though it never came under fire. The best view in the city is from the **Campanile** (telephone 041 561 056) at the harbour entrance. There are 204 steps to the top of this monument to the 1820 settlers; it houses 23 bells.

Family fun things are mostly on the sea-front where—apart from the beaches—there is on Humewood Beach the **Museum Complex**, which houses an Oceanarium and Aquarium, a snake park and bird house. The museum is dedicated largely to early Settler history; all open daily (telephone 041 561 054). **Happy Valley**—also by Humewood Beach—is a small family amusement park with scenes from nursery rhymes and fairy tales. A short drive south of PE on the coast is the **Cape Recife Nature Reserve**, 350 hectares of dunes with many marine birds.

PE NIGHTLIFE

The **Opera House** (telephone 562 256) and the open-air **Mannville Theatre** (telephone 559 711) stage good productions.

SPORTS GROUNDS

St George's Park for cricket (telephone 551 646); for Eastern Cape **rugby** on Bibury Avenue, Linkside, telephone 551 325.

AROUND PE

About 70 kilometres north of PE on the R335 is the **Addo Elephant National Park**; further on is the **Zuurberg National Park** (*See* NATIONAL PARK APPENDIX, *page 300*).

Twenty five kilometres west of PE off the N2 is **Van Staden's Wild Flower Reserve**, with 500 hectares of fynbos, proteas and other wild flowers.

The **Tsitsikamma National Park** (see National Park appendix, see page xxx) is about 150 kilometres west of PE, off the N2.

Jeffrey's Bay, about 70 kilometres west of PE, is surf-city. Beyond Jeffrey's Bay is another, slightly less-developed resort area, **St Francis Bay**.

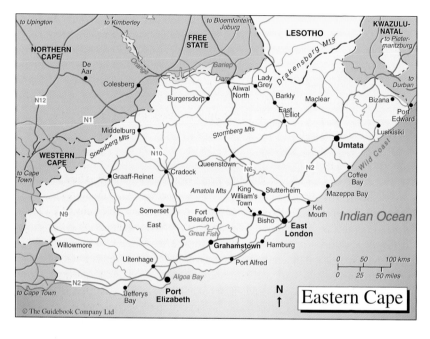

to Upington

to Kimberley

to Bloemfontein
Joburg

KWAZULU-
NATAL
to Pieter-
maritzburg

NORTHERN
CAPE

FREE
STATE

LESOTHO

De
Aar

Colesberg

Gariep
Dam

Lady
Grey

Drakensberg Mts

to
Durban

N12

Burgersdorp

Aliwal
North

Barkly

Maclear

Bizana

Port
Edward

N1

Orange

East
Elliot

Middelburg

Stormberg Mts

Lusikisiki

Sneeuberg Mts

N10

Umtata

Wild Coast

WESTERN
CAPE

Queenstown

N6

N2

to Cape
Town

Graaff-Reinet

Cradock

Coffee
Bay

N9

Somerset

Amatola Mts

King
William's
Town

Stutterheim

Mazeppa Bay

East

Fort
Beaufort

Bisho

Kei
Mouth

Indian Ocean

Great Fish

East
London

Willowmore

Grahamstown

Hamburg

Uitenhage

Port Alfred

0   50   100 kms

N2

Algoa Bay

0   25   50 miles

to Cape Town

Jefferys
Bay

Port
Elizabeth

N
↑

Eastern Cape

© The Guidebook Company Ltd

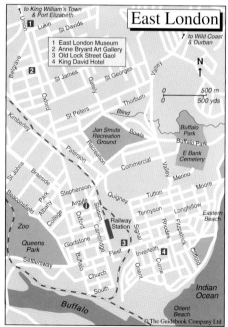

to King William's Town
& Port Elizabeth

Union

1

Lukin

St Davids

East London

to Wild Coast
& Durban

1 East London Museum
2 Anne Bryant Art Gallery
3 Old Lock Street Gaol
4 King David Hotel

Belgrave

2

St James

Gately

St Georges

Valley

N
↑

Oxford

St Peters

Thorburn

Blind

0   500 m

0   500 yds

Kimberley

Jan Smuts
Recreation
Ground

Bowls

Buffalo
Park

Buffalo Park

Recreation

E Bank
Cemetery

St Johns

Braeside

Paterson

Commercial

Valley

Merino

Moore

Park

Stephenson

Tutton

Longfellow

Beaconsfield

Albany

College

Argyle

Quigney

Tennyson

Rhodes

Fitzpatrick

Eastern
Beach

Zoo

Oxford

Station

Cambridge

Railway
Station

Signal

3

Curie

Clifford

Queens
Park

Gladstone

Buffalo

Fleet

Inverleith

4

Settlersway

Church

Orient

South

Indian
Ocean

Buffalo

Orient
Beach

© The Guidebook Company Ltd

The **Shamwari Game Reserve** (an expensive private reserve) is some 90 kilometres north-east of PE, off the N10 near **Alicedale**; it's the only reserve in the eastern Cape where all the 'big five' can be seen. PO Box 7814, Newton Park 6055; telephone (042) 851 1196, fax (042) 851 1224.

The **Baviaanskloof Wilderness Area** is a 200,000 hectare conservation area some 200 kilometres west of PE on the R332; three mountain ranges, two rivers, 58 mammal 293 bird species. Lots of hiking trails and basic overnight accommodation; 32 kilometres north of PE is **Uitenhage**; an ugly industrial outpost to be avoided.

EAST LONDON

Some 1100 kilometres east along the south coast from Cape Town is South Africa's only river port. **East London** is on the N2, with an airport five kilometres from the city centre. The local telephone prefix is **0431**. An unattractive city, it's not an intensely cultivated tourist spot—which has its advantages for those who go there—but there are points of interest.

Eastern and **Orient** beaches are both good for family swimming and dolphin-spotting. Near the centre is **Queen's Park Botanical Garden and Zoo** (open daily 09.00–17.00). At the corner of Oxford Street and St Mark's is the **Anne Bryant** art gallery, a grand Edwardian building with contemporary South African art (open 09.30–17.00 Monday–Friday, half-day Saturday). On the corner of Oxford and Lukin Streets is the East London Museum, a large natural history museum which has a stuffed coelacanth—a prehistoric fish species still around in South African waters—and what's thought to be the only surviving dodo's egg in the world (open 09.30–17.00 Monday–Friday, half day Saturday). Near the air terminal buildings, on Fleet Street, is the **Old Lock Street Gaol**, now a small shopping centre but where the old death cells and original gallows have been preserved.

SPORTS GROUNDS

Buffalo Park is the centre for cricket (telephone 430 814) and the **Basil Kenyon** stadium for rugby (telephone 22 647).

AROUND EAST LONDON

Just outside the city (north-east on the N2) is the **Gonubie Nature Reserve**, a small wetland bird sanctuary.

Some 30 kilometres north of the city on the N6 is the **Mpongo Game Reserve**, with a camp site; it contains some big game, such as elephant, giraffe and white rhino.

Drive up the coast north of East London to **Morgan's Bay** and **Kei Mouth**, two attractive small resorts, with hotels—you have to take the N2 and loop back in on the R349, a total of some 140 kilometres.

ABOUT ACTIVE RESISTANCE

You are either alive and proud or you are dead, and when you are dead, you can't care anyway. And your method of death can itself be a politicising thing. So you die in the riots. For a hell of a lot of them, in fact, there's really nothing to lose—almost literally, given the kind of situations that they come from. So if you can overcome the personal fear of death, which is a highly irrational thing, you know, then you're on the way.

And in interrogation the same sort of thing applies. I was talking to this policeman, and I told him, 'If you want us to make any progress, the best thing is for us to talk. Don't try any form of rough stuff, because it just won't work.' And this is absolutely true also. For I just couldn't see what they could do to me which would make me all of a sudden soften to them. If they talk to me, well I'm bound to be affected by them as human beings. But the moment they adopt rough stuff, they are imprinting in my mind that they are police. And I only understand one form of dealing with the police, and that's to be as unhelpful as possible. So I button up. And I told them this: 'It's up to you.' We had a boxing match the first day I was arrested. Some guy tried to clout me with a club. I went into him like a bull. I think he was under instructions to take it so far and no further, and using open hands so that he doesn't leave any marks on the face. And of course he said [...] 'I will kill you.' He meant to intimidate. And my answer was: 'How long is it going to take you?' Now of course they were observing my reaction. And they could see that I was completely unbothered. If they beat me up, it's to my advantage. I can use it. They just killed somebody in jail—a friend of mine—about ten days before I was arrested. Now it would have been bloody useful evidence for them to assault me. At least it would indicate what kind of possibilities were there, leading to this guy's death. So, I wanted them to go ahead and do what they could do, so that I could use it. I wasn't really afraid that their violence might lead me to make revelations I didn't want to make, because I had nothing to reveal on this particular issue. I was operating from a very good position, and they were in a very weak position. My attitude is, I'm not going to allow them to carry out their programme faithfully. If they want to beat me five times, they can only do so on condition that I allow them to beat me five times. If I react sharply, equally and oppositely, to the first clap, they are not going to be able to systematically count the next four claps, you see. It's a fight. So if they had meant to give me so much of a beating, and not more, my idea is to make them go beyond what they wanted to give me and to give back as much as I can give so that it becomes an uncontrollable thing. You see the one problem this guy had with me: he couldn't really fight with me because it meant he must hit back, like a man. But he was given instructions, you see, on how to hit, and now these instructions were no longer applying because it was a fight. So I said to them, 'Listen, if you guys want to do this your way, you have got to handcuff me and bind my feet together, so that I can't respond. If you allow me to respond, I'm certainly going to respond. And I'm afraid you may have to kill me in the process even if it's not your intention.

Steve Biko: from I Write What I Like: 1978

Steve Biko (following page) is recognized as one of the leading founders of the Black Consciousness movement of the 1970s, which held that black South Africans should not depend on white liberals in order to become free. He died aged 30 in police custody in September 1977.

Some 70 kilometres west of East London on the N2 is **Bisho**, a dull pre-fabricated town built in 1981 to be the capital of the (now defunct) 'homeland' of Ciskei. In what can only be a nod towards political correctness, Bisho has also been made the capital of the Eastern Cape. Nearby is **King William's Town** (telephone prefix 0433), birth and burial place of Steve Biko; it has one of South Africa's best museums, the **Kaffrarian Museum** (09.00–12.45, 14.00–17.00, Monday–Friday), which depicts the depradations suffered by the Xhosa at the hands of Boer and British settlers. Among the thousands of stuffed animals is Huberta, who was the last remaining hippopotamus in the eastern Cape until three hunters shot her in April 1931 as she was bathing in Keiskamma River.

North of King William's Town on the R346 is **Stutterheim**, a 19th-century German mission town, through which passes the N6 highway. An interesting (but lengthy, 35 kilometres, dirt road) detour south of Stutterheim takes you to the grave of **Sandile**, chief of the Gaika, who was killed in June 1878 in the Ninth Frontier War with the British. Buried next to him are two British soldiers.

GRAHAMSTOWN

The presence of Rhodes University, one of South Africa's best universities, gives this small place a more relaxed, intellectual and culturally vibrant feel than many other larger cities in the eastern Cape. The local telephone prefix is **0461**. Some 900 kilometres east from Cape Town on the N2, Grahamstown is a short drive—about 60 kilometres—inland from the seaside resort of **Port Alfred**, and 125 kilometres from PE.

Every July this cathedral city springs into life, hosting a major international arts festival which lasts about two weeks. During that time finding accommodation is almost impossible, unless you have sensibly booked well in advance. Grahamstown is well worth a visit, if only to escape the tense atmosphere currently prevailing in much of the rest of the province.

Originally set up in 1812 as a British army staging post, by 1831 it was the Cape Colony's second largest town. It still has the feel of a small English market town about it; a couple of hours is ample to see all it has. The Anglican cathedral of **St Michael and St George** on **High Street** dominates the centre. It took 128 years to build, from its origin as a parish church in 1824 to the completion of the Lady Chapel in 1952. Crossing High Street is **Somerset Street**, which has several museums, all of which close during weekdays between 13.00–14.00: the **Albany Museum** (on early Settler life, 09.30–17.00 Monday–Friday, 14.00–17.00 Saturday/Sunday); the **National History Museum** (early African cultures, 09.30–17.00 Monday–Friday, 14.00–17.00 Saturday), and the **Institute of Ichthyology** (dedicated to South African fish, 08.30–17.00 Monday–Friday). The **Botanical Gardens** on Lucas Avenue are delightful and have an interesting flea market at weekends.

On Bathurst Street is the **Observatory Museum** which, beside being a wonderful example of Victorian colonial architecture, houses the only camera obscura (through which visitors can observer the activities of the town) in the southern hemisphere (09.30–17.00 Monday–Friday, closed between 13.00–14.00, and Saturday 09.00–13.00).

On Gunfire Hill, a short walk from the centre, is **Fort Selwyn**, built in 1836, alongside the **Settlers Monument**, which has a restaurant and theatre.

AROUND GRAHAMSTOWN

Kenton-on-Sea and **Port Alfred** are two small attractive beach resorts some 60 kilometres south of Grahamstown; there are great beaches in this area, stretching for miles. En route to Port Alfred the small town of **Bathurst** has a popular hotel and pub called the Pig and Whistle, as well as a large conservation area, with hiking trails and a camp site for tents. Nearby is also the **Kowie Nature Reserve** which has an 8 kilometres hiking trail. North-west of the town of **Salem** (en route to Kenton-on-Sea) is the **Thomas Baines Nature Reserve**, with various game including buffalo, bontebok and white rhino. Further out from Grahamstown is the **Great Fish River Reserve**, comprising the **Andries Vosloo**, **Sam Knott** and **Double Drift Nature** (telephone 0401 952 115) reserves.

Further out on the coast is the resort of **Hamburg**, established in 1857 by former soldiers of the British German Legion, at the mouth of the Keiskamma River; an excellent fishing spot.

WILD COAST

The Wild Coast—which derived its name from the amount of shipwrecks it has seen—is one of the most attractive parts of the country, with superb, endless white sand beaches; but it has a major disadvantage for the independent traveller—poor roads. The N2 highway runs about 60 kilometres inland parallel to the coast, but links with the coast only by dirt roads; even the tarred roads in this part of the world are full of potholes. This region was formerly the 'independent' homeland of Transkei—one of the worst dumping-grounds for black South Africans—and was starved of investment; the legacy is dire poverty, poor infrastructure, and violent crime.

Unfortunately if you wish to traverse the northern part of this coast there is no way of avoiding driving either through **Lusikisiki** or **Umtata**, which besides dreadful roads also have a very hostile atmosphere. If continuing up the R61 coastroad into the southern coastal areas of KwaZulu-Natal to get to resorts such as **Margate**, you will also have to drive through **Bizana** (unless making a very large loop back onto the N2), which also has terrible roads and an aggressive feel about it. The advice is to be cautious and drive only in daylight hours.

The advantage of such conditions is that tourism to the area—once a firm favourite of many South Africans—has considerably dropped off; people are deterred by sensationalist reports of crime levels. That's a pity, because the area is almost completely pollution-free, and has abundant, rich wildlife, and seafood which cannot be bettered.

The **Wild Coast Hiking Trail** runs all along the coast and takes experienced hikers almost a month, starting in Port Edward and finishing at Coffee Bay; telephone (0471) 24 322 for details. These days it's vital to do the trail in groups, as crime along the coast is rampant. Among the better places to stop at are (from East London) **Qolora Mouth** (a good hotel here called Kob Inn, telephone 0474 4421), **Wavecrest**, **Mazeppa Bay**, the **Dwesa Nature Reserve**, **The Haven**, and **Coffee Bay**. Ten kilometres south of Coffee Bay is the Hole in the Wall, a massive rock arch standing in the sea. North of Coffee Bay is the **Hluleka Nature Reserve**; nearby is **Umngazi Mouth**, a very peaceful and secluded small resort of thatched bungalows with a restaurant.

Further up the coast you reach the small town of **Port St John's**, at the mouth of the Umzimvubu River. Nearby are two more nature reserves, **Mount Thesiger** and **Silaka**. Further north are more resorts: **Embotyi**, **Port Grosvenor** and the **Mkambati Nature Reserve**. As the Wild Coast ends, the more built-up and less peaceful southern coast of KwaZulu-Natal begins, at **Port Edward**.

EASTERN PROVINCE INLAND

Fort Beaufort, on the Kat River about 90 kilometres north of Grahamstown on the R67, is set amid spectacular mountain scenery. Like many towns in the region, it started out as a British military garrison in 1823. Close by, in the Victorian town of **Alice**, is Fort Hare University, formerly the **Lovedale Mission College**, where among others Tiyo Soga, one of the founders of African nationalism, was educated in the 19th century. It's open to visitors and houses an excellent collection of contemporary South African art in its **De Beers Centenary** gallery.

North of Alice on the R345 is the village of **Hogsback**, focal point of the **Amatola Mountain Range**, in which there is the 105 kilometres **Amatola Hiking Trail**, through the valleys and mountains of the richly forested Amatola Mountains. Reckoned to be the country's toughest trail, it takes very fit hikers six days to complete; basic lodges are available for overnight stops (telephone 0401 92 171). The Amatola Forest Reserve has a vast array of hiking trails; telephone 0401 91 131/2/3. J R R Tolkien walked through the Hogsback in his childhood, and the forest landscape is thought to have inspired him when he wrote *Lord of the Rings*. Hogsback is a beautiful, little-known spot, which gets its name from the rocky ridge running above the village.

About 50 kilometres north of Fort Beaufort (on the R67) is the **Katberg** escarpment, highest point of the Amatola range; various nature trails through yellowwood forests and mountain streams inhabited by a variety of birdlife. The **Mpofu Game Reserve** in the Katberg covers 12,000 hectares; accommodation is available (telephone 040452 1002).

East from Port Elizabeth on the N2, take the N10; about 260 kilometres north of PE is another former British garrison town, established in 1813. **Cradock** has an interesting library and some sulphur medicinal springs, but its greatest attraction lies about 25 kilometres to the west, off the R61, the **Mountain Zebra National Park** (see National Parks' appendix, page 305).

A couple of hundred kilometres north of PE on the R75 is the town of **Graaff-Reinet**, (telephone prefix **0491**) through which passes the N9 highway. It dates from 1786 and has fortunately hardly been touched by modern architects. It's set among some of the highest ranges of hills in the country, including the gloomily forbidding **Valley of Desolation**, easily accessible via a steep 2 kilometres walk from the town. The 16,000 hectare **Karoo Nature Reserve**, which contains species such as the Cape mountain zebra, eland, black wildebeest and mountain reedbuck, encircles the town, which claims to have more than 200 national monuments—including two entire streets, **Stretch's Court** and **Parsonage Street**. You can happily skip most of them, but some you shouldn't.

Reinet House on Parsonage Street (daily, 09.00–17.00) was built in 1812. Now it's rather an ordinary though finely-decorated museum with yellowwood ceilings and stinkwood floors, though the rear courtyard has what is claimed to be the largest grapevine in the world, with a circumference of 2.4 metres, height of 1.5 metres and covering an area of 124 square metres. It still bears fruit. The Drostdy on Church Street, one of the main streets through the town, is now a hotel. It was built in 1806 as the residence of the *landdrost*, or magistrate. Behind the hotel is Stretch's Court, now part of the hotel. Also interesting is the **Residency**, on Parsonage Street, dating from the early 19th century (09.00–17.00, Monday–Friday). It's now a museum of early 19th-century life, with an interesting collection of hunting rifles and muskets.

A trek of 54 kilometres north of Graaff-Reinet takes you to the village of **Nieu Bethesda**, famous for one of its inhabitants, the eccentric artist Helen Martins, who lived there in the 1950s. In the isolated village (accessible only by dirt roads) is her **Owl House**, which is decorated with ornate, primitive sculptures, many of them (unsurprisingly) being owls. Close by is the **Compassberg**, highest peak (2,504 metres) of the **Sneeuberg Mountains**. This is some of the finest mountain scenery in the Great Karoo region.

Back-track from Nieu Bethesda onto the N9 highway to drive north via **Naudesberg** and **Lootsberg** passes, onto Middelburg—a town without any interest whatsoever, except for the bent-wire artefacts being sold on the roadside, unlike anything you will find in curio shops. Other towns (such as Cradock and Aberdeen) in this area are uninteresting; the phrase 'stultifyingly dull' was invented for them. However, one of the finest National Parks, the **Mountain Zebra**, is just off the R61, west of Cradock. (See National Parks appendix, page 305).

Some 100 kilometres north of Stutterheim on the N6 highway lies **Queenstown** (founded 1853), which has little of interest except the odd **Collector's Museum** at 4 Reservoir Street (09.00–17.00, Monday–Friday), with large collections of peculiarly-selected items such as car badges. The town also has an unusual hexagonal open square, with six streets radiating from it, designed to facilitate easy perimeter defence. Beyond lies the rugged **Stormberg** mountain range and the N6 cuts through the magnificent Penhoek Pass.

To the north and north-east of Queenstown lie some of the prettiest parts of the country, in the

The Owl House at Nieu Bethesda

foothills of the **Drakensberg** mountain range. At the far north, where the Eastern Cape joins the Free State, is **Aliwal North**, with a hot springs resort. Further round the southern edge of the Drakensberg are two small towns worth visiting—**Lady Grey**, **Barkly East**, (both on the R58 east of Aliwal North) and the delightful village of **Rhodes** (on the smaller R396).

In Lady Grey, which is dominated by the **Witteberg Mountains**, you can take a strange train ride to Barkly East, which is 1,813 metres above sea level; the gradients are so steep that the train negotiates eight reverses. South of Barkly East on the R58 is a small farm called **Denorbin**, where there are 32 metres of San murals, the longest in South Africa. Continue along the R58, through the magnificent Barkly Pass, and you reach the town of **Elliot**. Turn left at Elliot along the R56 and drive through **Ugie** to **Maclear**, a small trading post; nearby is a strange mountain called Gatberg ('hole mountain'), so called because it has a hole through its peak. At Maclear turn left onto the R396 and eventually you reach the **Naudesnek Pass**, South Africa's highest road pass (2,623 metres), which can be blocked during the winter. A short drive beyond that is Rhodes, with a very comfortable Victorian hotel. In all this region there are many hiking trails; consult the local publicity association for details.

Free State

Officially now simply the **Free State**, (which is how many South Africans have long referred to it anyway), this province was originally the **Orange Free State**; some still call it that, and many road signs and other pieces of officialdom still refer to the OFS. The name change is a rather misconceived attempt to legislate out of existence the supposed Boer/Voortrekker (and therefore extreme racist) connotations of OFS. It's misconceived because, although it was founded by Boer trekkers, it gained the Orange part in 1848, when Sir Harry Smith, then Cape Colony governor, proclaimed it British territory and named it the 'Orange River Sovereignty'. In 1854 when, after having crushed the Ndebele, the Boer trekkers felt strong enough to declare an independent republic, they called it the Orange Free State.

The 'Orange' came about for a very simple reason; the massive, 2,000 kilometres **Orange River**, which bisects the northern half of the country and whose source is high up in the mountains of Lesotho, forms the southern border of the province. Shaped like a kidney bean, with the concave edge forming the border with Lesotho and the Vaal River (a tributary of the Orange) the northern border, the Free State is essentially one vast prairie, with one major city, **Bloemfontein** (the provincial capital), a couple of major industrial centres, some very interesting nature reserves, and a few dozen small, uninteresting clone-like towns, scattered across it like a handful of confetti. It may be the breadbasket of South Africa, but as far as the pressed-for-time traveller is concerned, it's not a province deserving lengthy attention.

BLOEMFONTEIN

Although it largely escaped the political violence of the apartheid era (it's still a place where you can walk around without anxiety), it's long felt like a hard, Afrikaner city, lacking in culture. The horrid architecture doesn't help; the city has few interesting older buildings, and they are swamped by massive concrete blocks. Bloemfontein feels as though it's caught in a time-warp in which Hendrik Verwoerd could pop out at any moment and say the last few years have all been a big mistake. The ANC was born here in 1912, but you'd never believe it—there's nothing to mark the spot, wherever it might be.

Bloemfontein (which literally means 'flower fountain'—a water spring, nothing to do with blossoms) is 402 kilometres south of Johannesburg on the N1 highway. Its airport is 14 kilometres from the city, the **railway station** (telephone 408 2941) is on **Maitland Street** in the centre; the local telephone prefix is **051**. Like many other South African cities, the town centre is laid out on a grid system. The city makes the best of itself, but its sights can essentially be divided into two cate-

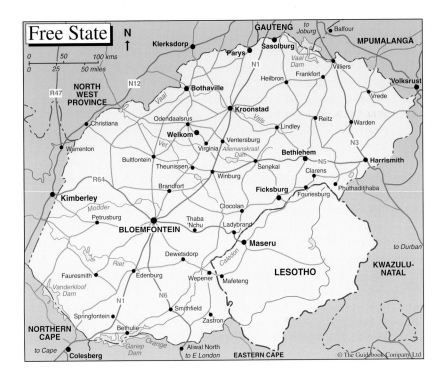

gories—gardens and Boer memorabilia.

Central starting point is **Hoffman Square**, between **Maitland** and **St Andrew's** Streets. Hoffman Square contains the tourist information office (one of the less well-equipped you will encounter). Most of the main monuments are within a 10-minute walking radius of Hoffman Square, including:

Hertzog House, former home of Boer war general, National Party founder, prime minister and thorough-going racist Barry Hertzog. Now a rather dull museum; (**Goddard Street**, 09.00–12.00, 13.00–16.00, Monday–Friday, telephone 477 301).

From there, walk along Goddard and Saltzmann Streets to join St George's where, at the junction with President Brand Street is the **First Raadsaal** (10.15–15.00 Monday–Friday, 14.00–17.00 Saturday–Sunday, telephone 479 610), a one-roomed, thatched, beaten-dung floored building dating from 1849 (the city's oldest building) and originally used not only as the first seat of government of the OFS, but also as the headquarters for the military, the civil service, the school and even as a dance-hall.

A short distance away on President Brand is the **Old Presidency**, built in 1885 (10.00–12.00, 13.00–16.00 Tuesday–Friday, 14.00–17.00 Saturday–Sunday, telephone 480 949). Now a museum to OFS presidents and concert hall.

Further along from the Old Presidency on President Brand is the **National Afrikaans Literary Museum and Research Archive** (08.00–12.00, 13.00–16.00 Monday–Friday, 09.00–12.00 Saturday–Sunday), which stores and displays many manuscripts of the most important writers in Afrikaans, living and dead.

Continue along President Brand, crossing Elizabeth Street, is the **Fourth Raadsaal**, a red-brick 1893 building which housed the final parliament of the OFS until the British forces occupied Bloemfontein in 1900. Its domed tower and doric columns give it an impressive bulk; inside are six busts of former OFS presidents, along with the original parliamentary benches. Visits by appointment only—telephone 478 898. Outside is an equestrian statue of the Boer general Christiaan De Wet, *sjambok* (whip) in hand. Further along President Brand, over Charles Street, is the **City Hall**, another self-important building which boasts some good Italian marble and Burmese teak.

Returning along Charles Street, heading in the direction of Hoffman Square, you will first encounter the **National Museum** on Aliwal Street, a rather dull natural history collection (08.00–17.00 Monday–Saturday, 13.00–18.00 Sunday, telephone 479 609). Further along there is an interesting twin-spired Dutch Reformed Church at the top of **Floreat Mall**. Called the **Mother Church**, it's the only such twin-spired DRC in South Africa, built in 1880; here the presidents of the OFS would take their oath of office.

Outside this small area there are other curiosities. On Church Street, opposite President Brand cemetery (where many of the Boer dead from the Second South African war are buried) is **Queen's Fort** (08.00–16.00 Monday–Friday), built in 1848 by Voortrekkers. Further south along Church Street the road intersects with Monument Street, which, if you turn down it and cross the railway bridge, leads after a very short distance to the **National Women's Memorial** and the adjacent **Military Museum** (09.00–16.30 Monday–Friday, 09.00–17.00 Saturday, 14.00–17.00 Sunday, telephone 47 344). The memorial is dedicated to the Boer women and children who died in British concentration camps; the museum is an impressive collection of materials from the conflict, presented entirely from the Boer point of view.

Along Andries Pretorius Street, heading north-east from the city centre, is a huge **white horse** constructed on the slopes of **Naval Hill**, laid out in the Second South African war by troops from the Wiltshire regiment as a landmark for cavalry coming in from the plains. Two large British naval guns are on the top of the hill.

Out towards that part of the city is a **private museum** dedicated to rugby, owned by a man called Choet Visser; telephone him on 314 124 or 480 181 to arrange a visit.

There are a number of pleasant parks and gardens in and around the city. To the west of the centre is **King's Park**, which has more than 4,000 rose bushes, a small but well-managed zoo, and a small lake; it stages a flea market the first Saturday of each month. Next to this park is **President Swart Park**, with various sporting facilities. Around Naval Hill is the **Franklin Game Reserve**, 200 hectares where various antelope can be found. On the western edge of Naval Hill is **Hamilton Park**, which has a famous orchid house. Some 10 kilometres north-west of the centre up **General Dan Pienaar Drive** is the **National Botanical Garden**, 45 hectares devoted to indigenous flora of the Free State.

NIGHTLIFE
The city has one good theatre, the **Sand Du Plessis** on Markgraaf Street, telephone 477 771.

SOUTH OF BLOEMFONTEIN
Next to the town of **Bethulie**, almost 200 kilometres south-west of Bloemfontein, is a massive 374-square kilometre dam, formerly known as Hendrik Verwoerd Dam but now called **Gariep Dam**. On its western side is a popular, rather bustling holiday resort, but around it are some excellent nature reserves. The **Gariep Dam Nature Reserve**, which joins the dam's shoreline, has a large mixed antelope population, as does the **Oviston Nature Reserve**, on the dam's southern shore. Perhaps best of all is the **Tussen-die-Riviere Reserve**, at the confluence of the Orange and Caledon rivers, about 10 kilometres east of Bethulie. The reserve supports more game and a greater diversity of game, (as well as abundant bird life), than anywhere else in the Free State. It's open for visitors September-April—there are three one-day hikes—but is reserved for hunters during autumn and winter.

EAST OF BLOEMFONTEIN
Sixty kilometres west of Bloemfontein is **Thaba 'Nchu** ('black mountain') which was formerly part of Boputhatswana. Little more than a village, it has nearby the **Maria Moroka Reserve**, which has some rare bird life, including the blue korhaan. Further east along the R64 you reach **Ladybrand**, a small, uninteresting town except for the fact that it's the closest South African staging post to **Maseru**, capital of Lesotho. It's also at the centre of the Eastern Highlands, which form the curving border with Lesotho, all along which are various points where you can stop to see San people rock paintings.

From Ladybrand you can either take the R26 south, to the towns of **Wepener** and (further south) **Zastron**, both of which have good walking trails; Zastron also

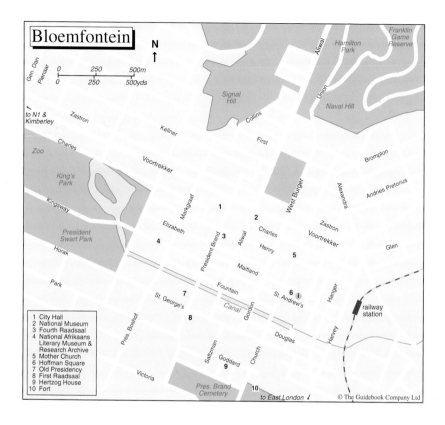

Bloemfontein

N ↑

0 — 250 — 500m
0 — 250 — 500yds

Gen. Dan Pienaar

to N1 & Kimberley
Zastron

Zoo
Charles

King's Park

Kingsway

President Swart Park

Horak

Park

Elizabeth

Markgraaf

St. George's

Pres. Boshof

Victoria

Kellner

Voortrekker

President Brand

Aliwal

Charles

Henry

Maitland

Fountain

Canal

Gordon

Saltzman

Goddard

Church

Pres. Brand Cemetery

Signal Hill

Collins

First

West Burger

Douglas

Harvey

Signal Hill

Naval Hill

Union

Aliwal

Hamilton Park

Franklin Game Reserve

Brompton

Alexandra

Andries Pretorius

Zastron

Voortrekker

Glen

Hanger

railway station

to East London

1 City Hall
2 National Museum
3 Fourth Raadsaal
4 National Afrikaans
   Literary Museum &
   Research Archive
5 Mother Church
6 Hoffman Square
7 Old Presidency
8 First Raadsaal
9 Hertzog House
10 Fort

© The Guidebook Company Ltd

has an unusual phenomenon, the **Eye of Zastron**, a 9 metre-diameter hole in one of the cliffs of the **Aasvoëlberg** ('vulture mountains'). Or you can head north-east along the R26 to **Ficksburg**, a small but pretty town, up to **Fouriesburg**, where there are some interesting small craft shops and cafes. Beyond Fouriesburg, a few kilometres along the R711 heading north at the town of **Clarens**, is the road leading to the **Golden Gate National Park** (see National Parks' appendix, page 302).

On the east side of the Gold Gate park is the large town of **Harrismith**, which bestrides the N3 highway, linking Joburg with Durban. There are a couple of small, overlooked nature reserves close to this otherwise uninteresting town, at the far end of the Highlands route. The private **Mount Everest Game Reserve** (telephone 01436 23 493) has 1,000 hectares of various game and horse-riding facilities; the **Sterkfontein Dam Nature Reserve** is 25 kilometres south of Harrismith.

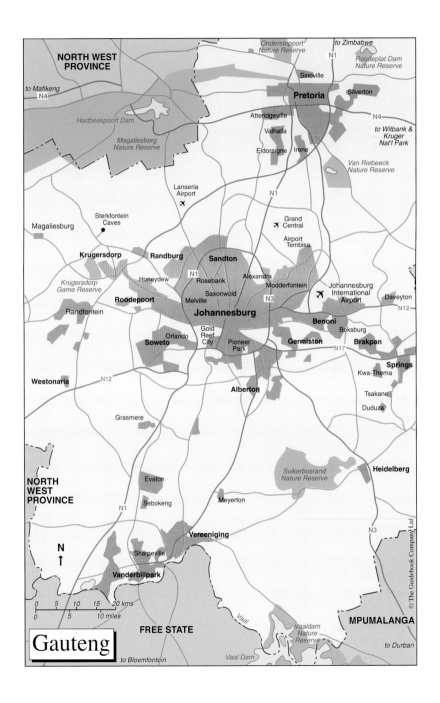

NORTH WEST
PROVINCE

to Mafikeng
N4

Hartbeespoort Dam

Magaliesberg
Nature Reserve

Magaliesburg

Onderstepoort
Nature Reserve

to Zimbabwe
N1

Roodeplat Dam
Nature Reserve

Sinoville

Pretoria

Silverton

Atteridgeville

Valhalla

Eldoraigne   Irene

N4

to Witbank &
Kruger
Nat'l Park

Van Riebeeck
Nature Reserve

Lanseria
Airport

Sterkfontein
Caves

N1

Grand
Central

Airport
Tembisa

Krugersdorp   Randburg   Sandton

Krugersdorp
Game Reserve

Honeydew

N1
Rosebank

Alexandra

Modderfontein

Johannesburg
International
Airport

Daveyton

N12

Roodepoort
Saxonwold
Melville

N3

Randfontein   Johannesburg

Benoni

Boksburg

Orlando
Soweto

Gold
Reef
City

Pioneer
Park

Germiston

Brakpan

N17

Springs

Kwa-Thema

Westonaria   N12

Alberton

Tsakane

Duduza

Grasmere

Suikerbosrand
Nature Reserve

Heidelberg

NORTH
WEST
PROVINCE

Evaton

N1

Sebokeng

Meyerton

N3

Vereeniging

N
↑

Sharpeville

Vanderbijlpark

0   5   10   15   20 kms
0   5   10 miles

© The Guidebook Company Ltd

FREE STATE

to Bloemfontein

Vaal

Vaaldam
Nature
Reserve

Vaal Dam

MPUMALANGA

to Durban

Gauteng

North of Bloemfontein

From Harrismith the choice is either to speed up the N3, diverting left on the R51 at **Villiers** and thence on the R716 to enter the vast **Vaal Dam Nature Reserve**, or to return deeper into the Free State along the R49, heading west towards Bethlehem. If you travel along the R49 to **Bethlehem** and Senekal you will see some of the most over-crowded and impoverished areas of South Africa, as this was formerly the **Qwa-Qwa** 'homeland'; Qwa-Qwa ironically means 'whiter-than-white'—nothing to do with apartheid but a reference to a prominent sandstone hill.

The Vaal Dam is a 300 square-kilometre reservoir where a wide range of water sports can be practised. Unfortunately it's less than 50 kilometres south-east of **Sasolburg**, an industrial monster founded in 1954. Sasol is an acronym for the Afrikaans version of South African Coal, Oil and Gas Corporation. The town has plenty of parks but it's otherwise single-mindedly devoted to producing synthetic fuels.

From within the Free State Sasolburg is also approached by the other main national highway running through the province, the N1, on which between Bloemfontein and Joburg there are some other uninteresting towns, such as (going south) **Parys**, **Kroonstad** (which stages the country's annual national *Jukskei* tournament—*Jukskei* is a nationally-developed, entirely Afrikaaner activity which involves tossing clubs at a peg; startlingly mindless), and, a detour (which you should not take) off the N1 to **Welkom**, which, despite its inviting name, is just the centre of the Free State's gold-mining industry—about 30 per cent of the country's gold is mined in the Free State.

Drive straight past the exits for Welkom and between **Ventersburg** (to the north) and **Winburg** (to the south) off the N1 is the **Willem Pretorius Game Reserve**, a 12,000-hectare public reserve centred on the Allemanskraal Dam, where there is self-catering accommodation, caravan and camping facilities, a restaurant and various activities (telephone 05777 4003). There are white rhino, buffalo, giraffe, various antelope, and large raptors among the 200 bird species.

Gauteng

Gauteng —a Sotho word meaning 'place of gold'—is by far the most densely populated province, whose capital, **Johannesburg** (telephone prefix 011), is the business centre of the country. 'Joburg', as locals refer to it, also exercises inordinate influence over every other aspect of South African life. A 19th-century city built on the back of gold-mining, Joburg is a sophisticated place with little of great historical interest but bursting with night-life, restaurants and entertainments of all kinds.

Gauteng's other major city of this *highveld* region, **Pretoria** (telephone prefix 012), 56 kilometres to the north, is the administrative capital of the country. It's also fast becoming an interesting, less crime-ridden alternative to Joburg for travellers to visit and stay in. Less bustling than Joburg, its less brash past has endowed it with more interesting historical sites than its glitzier southern neighbour.

JOHANNESBURG

Joburg is about 1,500 kilometres north-east of Cape Town; the international airport is some 25 kilometres east of the city centre, and long-distance coaches use the Rotunda Bus Station on the corner of Rissik and Wolmarans Streets, the latter also being the site of the central railway station. There is a 24 hour 'What's On' telephone line—400 2222—for up-to-the-minute information. There is also a dial-a-lift service to link hitchhikers with motorists; telephone (011) 648 8136/648 8602.

The streets of **Central Business District** (CBD) of Joburg are usefully laid out on a grid system, but do not casually stroll these streets, map in hand, looking like an obvious stranger—it's a good way to stand out as an easy mugging/pickpocket victim. Welcome to the mugging capital of South Africa, downtown Joburg. A decade ago the CBD was a thriving, bustling place, where all the country's major businesses had to be. Today, as the district has grown more violent, those businesses are fast relocating to northern suburbs such as **Sandton**, leaving behind them vast empty offices which no-one wants to rent. As (white) businesses leave, (black) entrepreneurs enter; the CBD's streets today are thronged with street traders all selling the same goods—fruit and plastic.

There is little to detain you in the CBD. **The South African Transport Museum** (in the old concourse of the railway station, 07.30–15.45, Monday–Friday, telephone 773 9118) has a unique collection of model trains and other transportation items. The **Johannesburg Art Gallery** (Klein Street, by **Joubert Park**, 10.00–17.00, Tue-Sun, telephone 725 3180) houses a range of South African art. Joubert Park, the city's oldest, is now a fairly crime-plagued area and you should exercise care. The **Soweto Art Gallery** (second floor, Victory House, 34 Harrison Street, 08.00–18.00 Monday–Friday, half-day Saturday, telephone 836 0252), exhibits works from black township artists. The **Standard Bank Gallery** (first floor, corner of Simmonds and Frederick Streets, 08.30–16.30 Monday–Friday, half-day Saturday, telephone 636 6973) features contemporary South African and international art. Those interested in seeing local artists in their studios should contact the **Johannesburg Studio Route** (telephone/ 646 1170).

The **Carlton Centre** (between Commissioner and Main Streets) is worth a visit. A vast shopping precinct, it has a tall revolving tower, the **Carlton Panorama** (open daily 09.00-23.00) on its 50th floor, from which you can see the whole vista of the

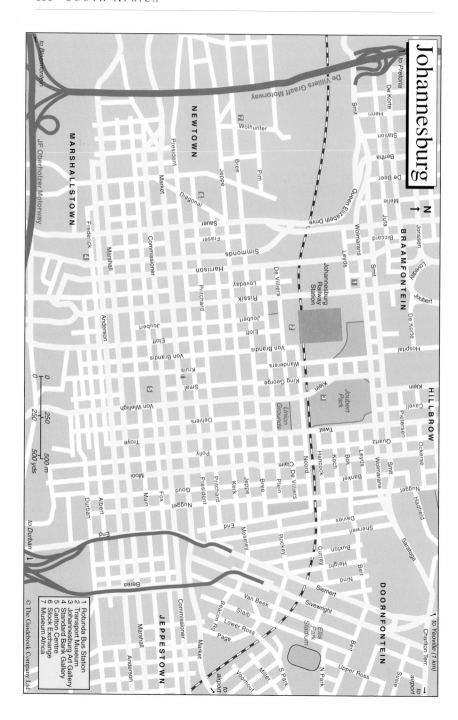

Johannesburg

N →

1 Rotunda Bus Station
2 Transport Museum
3 Johannesburg Art Gallery
4 Standard Bank Gallery
5 Carlton Centre
6 Stock Exchange
7 Museum Africa

© The Guidebook Company Ltd

Rand, its mines, townships and suburbs. At 11 Diagonal Street is a huge, glass-fronted building that is meant to represent the shape of a diamond; it's the **Stock Exchange** (tours at 11.00 and 14.00, Tuesday–Thursday, and 11.00 only on Monday and Friday, telephone 833 6580). It shares Diagonal Street with various *muti* or African magic/herbalist shops; not such an odd conjunction, if you think about it.

Diagonal Street runs along the edge of a nondescript district called Newtown, a five-minute drive or (alarming) half-hour walk from the Carlton centre. In this unprepossessing district is one of the better museums of the country, **Museum Africa** (corner of Bree and Wolhunter Streets, telephone 833 5624, open 09.00–17.00 Tuesday–Sunday); it has lots of African arts, crafts and historically important materials, including a good exhibition of life in black townships. It also has a small but excellent craft shop, with some unusual contemporary work. The **Market Theatre** complex is also here, on Bree Street (with several contemporary art exhibitions, jazz bar, restaurant and cafes as well as the famous theatre itself, home to much impressive anti-apartheid work in the past), telephone 832 1641 for details of activities and performances.

There are various tours that can be taken in and around the city. If you want to visit **Soweto**—and it's a fascinating if occasionally distressing experience—then the best tour is run by **Jimmy's Face to Face Tours**, which picks up at various points in the CBD and northern suburbs. A four-hour tour costs about R100, and two tours a day are available, seven days a week. Telephone 331 6109/6209, or 985 0569, or (mobile) 082 553 1587; fax 331 5388. You should not think about visiting Soweto without an experienced guide. Jimmy's also runs other good tours, including one round **Joburg nightlife**.

The most interesting **gold mine tours** can be arranged via the Chamber of Mines in Hollard Street, (telephone 838 8211); alternatively visit **Gold Reef City**, a rather kitsch theme park 6 kilometres from the CBD, constructed around number 14 shaft of Crown Mines (on Main Reef Road, telephone 496 1400/1600), where among many activities you can see molten gold being poured and take a tour down a mine shaft. The tour only goes down as far as 200 metres; the total depth is almost 4 kilometres, at which point the heat and humidity are similar to those of Durban at the height of summer—in which conditions men (mostly black) were expected to blast and heave rock.

Gold Reef City is an odd place; the casual visitor who knows nothing of the bloody, savage history of South African gold-mining gets no impression of the blood, sweat and toil of black South Africans, nor sees anything of the exploitation they experienced, living in single-sex, badly-equipped compounds. Still, there's not much else to help families while away their time in Joburg, and the daily **gumboot dancing** (performed in the wellington boots every migrant mine-worker was given to wear) is spectacular.

SUBURBS

Joburg's northern suburbs all tend to blur into one another—even though for (white) inhabitants of the city there is a distinct pecking order. At the last count, **Saxonwold** seemed to be regarded the most 'up' upmarket place for the rich to be. It has a large, 54 hectare **Zoo** (Hermann Eckstein Park, off Jan Smuts Avenue, 08.30–17.30 Monday–Friday, telephone 646 2000) which together with the nearby lake is a good place for family outings. There are nocturnal tours available. Also in the zoo grounds is the **National Museum of Military History** (20 Erlsworld Way, 09.00–16.30, Monday–Friday, telephone 646 5513), which has a large collection of militaria and war art.

Close by the zoo in the Roosevelt Park district are the city's delightful **Botanical Gardens**, (in **Jan Van Riebeeck Park**), with a 24-acre rose garden, believed the largest in the world (off Thomas Bowler Street, 07.00–16.00, daily, telephone 782 0517). Next door is the **Emmarentia Dam**, with lots to do for water-sport enthusiasts. In the same park is the **Melville Koppies Nature Reserve** (off Judith Road, Emmarentia, open every third Sunday of the month September–May, telephone 782 7064), where Stone and Iron Age relics have been discovered and preserved. The **Melrose Wild Bird Sanctuary** (in Melrose, a 10-minute drive north from the CBD, telephone 782 7064) is a pleasant spot and has more than 120 different bird species.

Most of Joburg's northern suburbs are nothing more than the happy-hunting grounds of white wealth, but its useful to be familiar with some of them. **Sandton** is one of the plushest northern suburbs, home to only the very wealthy (although **Alexandra**, one of the most deprived townships in the province, is just a stone's throw away). Sandton has had a bad press among white liberals and black radicals, as being a heartless place fit only for the wealthy and snobbish. That's changing, very fast. It now has a very large and useful shopping centre, good for stocking up at before going on long journeys. Another good shopping and entertainment northern suburb is **Rosebank**, which has (besides all the regular chains) good bookshops and an excellent music store, the CD Warehouse.

Other suburbs worth knowing: **Melville** (north-west of the CBD) is good for restaurants and night-life; **Yeoville**, **Bellvue** and **Observatory** (north-east of the CBD) have some interesting cafes, bars, restaurants and shops; **Braamfontein** is home to the University of the Witwatersrand ('Wits'); **Hillbrow** (just north of the CBD) used to be the place for the arty crowd to hang out, its racial barriers having been eroded over the years—it's now dangerous to wander about in, full of drug addicts, pimps, petty criminals and homeless people, though its admirers (there still are some) regard its particular no-holds-barred ambience with affection.

FURTHER OUT

There's not much of interest in most of the bigger outlying urban areas around Joburg proper. The east Rand is littered with industrial suburbs such as **Germiston**, **Boksburg**, **Benoni** and **Springs**, while the north-western area round **Randburg** is pretty much just a commuter-belt. To the south-west is **Soweto**—which is fascinating but highly dangerous for the unaccompanied, easily-lost, obvious tourist. South-east of Joburg is the **Suikerbosrand Nature Reserve**, more than 13,000 hectares of grassland and ridges, with several hiking trails and camps; telephone (0151) 2181.

Far west of Joburg (and close to Magaliesburg, a more attractive place to stay overnight) is **Krugersdorp**, which has a 1,400 hectare game reserve with baboons, lion, rhino, giraffe and zebra. There are swimming pools, a children's play area and accommodation (telephone 953 1770/665 4342). North of Krugersdorp are the famous **Sterkfontein Caves**, where many ancient relics have been discovered (09.00–16.00, Tuesday-Sunday, telephone 965 634), which can be visited only under guided supervision. The caves can be reached by taking the R28 Krugersdorp highway, turn right onto R47, then right again onto the R563.

JOBURG NIGHTLIFE

There are hundreds of cinemas, theatres, clubs and restaurants; local newspapers carry comprehensive, up-to-date listings. Three of the best theatres are the **Alhambra** (telephone 402 6174), the **Civic** (telephone 304 3408), and the **Windybrow** (telephone 720 7094/5), but the **Market** (telephone 832 1641) is perhaps the best for contemporary drama.

SPORTS GROUNDS

The home to rugby is **Ellis Park** (in Doornfontein, telephone 402 2960), for cricket, **Wanderers Stadium** (in Illovo, telephone 788 1008), and for soccer a variety of stadiums around the city. For details of matches contact the National Soccer League on 494 4520. On Baragwanath Road, heading south-west from the city centre towards Soweto is Soccer City, a stadium which holds 130,000 spectators. There are also a host of golf and tennis clubs. For golf, telephone the **Golfline** on 907 1632; for tennis, telephone 402 3580.

STEALING DIGNITY

Naked. Humiliated. Hoping to God time's going to go quickly. Trying to pass off awkwardness with a shrug and wry jokes; big-shot businessmen, professional men, ordinary guys just come for a pass stand around stripped in the waiting-room of the Non-European Affairs Department in Johannesburg each work-day of the week. Hundreds of them, each day.

You want a pass. Right. You go into a structure that looks like a public convenience. It is on the corner of Albert and Polly Streets. You find a blackjack - one of those black-uniformed municipal policemen - sitting on a high stool. He barks at you that you should not be an idiot: can't you see the queue? You join the queue of hundreds of other Africans, and you get counted off.

If you are in a batch that is to see the doctor for a medical certificate, you get a little ticket that permits you to enter the eastern gate to the great building of the city's Non-European Affairs Department. You join another queue that goes in and out of iron railings and right into the building.

Inside you meet white-coated clerks and medical aides who yell you into removing your top clothing, yell you into joining a queue that leads to a green-curtained room, and yell others off from this sacrosanct queue.

In due course you get your turn to step up to the X-ray machine, hug it according to instructions, and your chest gets X-rayed. Then you pass into an inner room where you are curtly told to drop your trousers, all of you in a row.

You might be a dignified businessman, a top-class lawyer, a jeweller, a wood merchant, or anybody. You will find yourself naked. Well, you wanted a permit to work in Johannesburg, didn't you? The official world is not finicky about your embarrassed modesty.

Recently the Non-European Affairs Department issued a new instruction that all Africans who work for themselves, that is, all Africans who don't work for a European, must also be registered. This edict includes some of the elite members of African society: businessmen, doctors, musicians, lawyers, and also those who are still looking for work...

The authorities claim that the humiliation of the mass naked parade is unavoidable. If they tried to give everyone individual attention they wouldn't have time to get through their work.

Pressed further, one official said, 'What's so wrong with this, after all? Why, during the war, old men, young men had to strip all together. They thought nothing of it.'

But, Mr Official, Mr Non-European Affairs Department, Mr Everybody who thinks things like this are OK, we aren't at war. There's no emergency. We're a civilized country, we keep telling the rest of the world.

Can Themba; 'Nude Pass Parade',
from his collection The Will To Die, published 1972.
Themba (1924–68) was one of the period's best South African journalists.

(Above) *A policeman checks the passbook of a black South African in the 1960s*

MINING

DIAMONDS

The discovery of first diamonds—in 1867—and then gold—initially in 1871, then much more significant finds in 1886—had an enormous impact on the embryonic South Africa. The great hole at Kimberley, where white miners crawled like ants in search of diamonds, is today nothing more than the world's largest man-made crater, almost entirely filled with water; the huge heaps of ochre-coloured earth that surround Johannesburg are little more than ugly witness to the heyday of gold mining.

But the greatest change wrought by the diamonds and gold can be seen on every street corner, though it's not immediately obvious. The legacy of South Africa's mineral wealth is the grotesque distortion of the relationship between black and white races. The white capitalists who built the country's greatest economic asset also established a servant-master, slave-boss mentality that is no longer sanctified by government and law, but which is only changing slowly.

In 1867 two children, Erasmus and Louisa Jacobs, found a shiny pebble on their neighbour's farm close to Hopetown, on the Orange River. By various hands it reached a jeweller in Grahamstown, who assayed it as a 21.25 carat diamond. Richard Southey, then Colonial Secretary of the Cape, prophesied: 'This diamond is the rock upon which the future success of South Africa will be built.' By early 1871 digging started at a farm called Vooruitzicht, owned by Johannes and Diederik de Beer. A few months later there was discovered close by an enormously rich pipe of diamondiferous lava at Colesberg Kopje, later named the De Beers New Rush, ultimately known as the Kimberley Mine.

Initially, black Africans were grudgingly permitted to buy diamond digger's licences. But white miners banded together and, under the (normally unproved) allegation of widespread illicit diamond buying (IDB) and theft by blacks, white miners managed to force the suspension of all licences held by blacks, who were required to re-apply for a licence—but only if they managed to obtain signatures of support from five 'respectable' white diggers. The white miners also created a system whereby all blacks on or around the diggings had to be in continual possession of a pass; without it, they were declared to be there illegally, and subject to severe corporal punishment. For black South Africans, the pass system—which after 1948, under apartheid, was introduced for all who wished to enter or work in so-called white areas—came to be one of the most hated instruments of social and economic repression.

In the very early months at Kimberley, immense confusion reigned as individuals scrabbled to lay and protect their claims. The hundreds of individual claims gradually formed themselves into a grid, with an average claim being 9.5 metres square. By 1872 there were some 1,600 owner-diggers; at its peak as many as 30,000 men worked day and night at digging and clearing. A digger who first staked a claim, having paid a licence fee of 10 shillings a month, could sell his rights for whatever he might get; such claims were speculatively traded, sometimes for many thousands of pounds.

On the surface there was a two-metre layer of soil that sometimes contained diamonds. Beneath that, a 20-metre-thick layer of yellowish soil was moderately rich in diamonds. At variable levels, miners would strike a reef of extremely hard rock, which would be removed only with considerable effort. A further layer, called kimberlite and blueish in colour, was the richest in diamonds. The open-cast mine eventually went to a depth of 365 metres, before underground mining took over. At Kimberley, the yield was 10lbs of diamonds for every 70,000 tons of earth extracted.

As the Big Hole grew, so too did Kimberley, becoming a Wild West town where diggers rubbed shoulders with cut-throats, sharp-dealing diamond merchants, prostitutes and assorted other riff-raff. Fights over claims, accidents and casual death, were commonplace; law was made by the rich and those with muscle enough to enforce their own interests. Whites were lured by the thought of riches; blacks by the hope of wages. A pattern was laid for the future—white ownership and urban domination, with black migrant labour from the rural areas and exclusion from any form of influence.

By the middle of 1881 most of the individual miners had amalgamated into joint-stock companies, many of which crashed that same year when the wildly speculative share-price bubble burst. Those that survived became not only extremely wealthy but also exercised enormous influence, both over mining and the political life of the fledgling South Africa.

Cecil Rhodes' De Beers Mining Company quickly gained control of all the dry diggings in the Kimberley area. One of his most notorious initiatives was to develop a closed compound system to house black African mine workers, who were closely guarded on their way to the mines, and intimately searched on their return after the working day.

GOLD

*T*he wealth of diamond entrepreneurs such as Rhodes stood them in good stead when it came to exploiting the gold reefs discovered in 1886 along the 500-kilometre ridge, known as the Witwatersrand ('ridge of white waters'), just to the north of Johannesburg.

The Rand (as it soon became known) was in the then independent Boer state called the South African Republic (SAR), ruled by President Stephanus Johannes Paulus (Paul) Kruger. Most historians accept that an immigrant, George Harrison, was the first to find gold on the Rand, in March 1886 on a farm called Langlaagte. Harrison preferred to try his luck on some alluvial diggings in the eastern Transvaal, and sold his Rand claim for £10.

The early Rand gold diggers soon discovered that while the reef was large and regular, it was very poor quality; vast amounts of earth needed to be sifted to retrieve quite small quantities of gold ore. For every million tons of ore today extracted on the Rand, just seven tons of gold are recovered. To make the Rand's gold mining profitable it was necessary to invest in expensive, large machinery—and keep labourers' wages as low as possible.

To a large extent the legal framework of the SAR as it impinged on black Africans played into the hands of the 'Randlords', as the mighty entrepreneurs such as Rhodes came to be known. Blacks were not allowed to own land in the SAR; they had the legal right only to be labourers or tenants of Boer farmers. The first SAR mining law stated that 'no coloured person may be a (digging) licence holder, or in any way be connected with the working of the gold mines, except as a working man in the service of whites.'

Despite Kruger's suspicions of the hordes of white foreigners (derogatively called *uitlanders*) who flooded in and quickly built up the tin-roofed shanty town of Johannesburg, trailing in their wake a boozy, sleazy, fast-dealing way of life, he and his colleagues saw gold as a means of staving off the imminent bankruptcy of their Boer republic. Gold would be a tolerated evil.

Kruger and the Randlords found common ground in the treatment of black Africans. Boers had traditionally regarded blacks as inferior, and had waged a long struggle to wring land from them and force them to become landless, menial labourers. The Chamber of Mines (established in 1887) needed lots of cheap labour. Thus the Volksraad (Parliament) was only too happy to pass a whole range of laws which made it all but impossible for black Africans to continue sup-

porting themselves by self-sufficient farming. The only alternative for many was to migrate and work on the Rand, housed in appalling compounds, indentured for lengthy periods and subject to criminal charges for breaking their contract. Trade unions were banned; even moving to a mine with better wages became impossible, thanks to a change in the terms of the pass laws restricting black Africans' movements. Black Africans were given only the most poorly-paid tasks on the mines, while white workers enjoyed job reservation, preserving skilled and supervisory roles for them alone.

South Africa is today responsible for some 36 per cent of world gold production; and Paul Kruger has been granted the status of having an exclusive gold coin, the Krugerrand, named after him. Diamonds and gold have brought immense wealth to the country; but they also brought immense suffering. Johannesburg, even today, is known by many black South Africans—with perhaps a touch of rueful irony, given how little they have benefitted from it—as e 'Goli, city of gold.

(Above) *Early gold-mining days on the Rand*

(Top left) Johannesburg at night as seen from Hillbrow; (top right) Shopping is a national pastime; (bottom) it's cool to be warm

(top) *Johannesburg: A funfair on the Rand*; (bottom left) *Soweto: A tiny entrepreneur charges 10 cents to use his trampoline*; (bottom right) *Soweto: Evangelical preachers regularly ride the local trains*

Pretoria

Pretoria, the administrative centre of government (Cape Town is currently South Africa's legislative seat), used to be a very unpleasant place to visit. The 19th-century capital of the first Voortrekker republic, the SAR, it was so closely identified with apartheid repression—many ANC activists convicted of terrorist offences were hanged in the local jail—that the place had an eerie atmosphere.

How remarkably it has changed; even Nelson Mandela is now advertising its attractions (see page 151). Today it's a more relaxing place to visit than Joburg. Its 70,000 jacaranda trees—their lilac-coloured bloom best seen in October—help make it a more beautiful city. The telephone prefix is **012**.

The city centre is again helpfully laid out on a grid system; many of the most important sites are within easy walking distance. **Church Square** (at the intersection of Church and Paul Kruger Streets) is perhaps the best place to start. It's dominated by a huge bronze statue of Paul Kruger by Anton van Wouw, one of South Africa's best sculptors. **Church Street** itself is one of the world's longest, stretching for 43 kilometres. The Square has three buildings dating from the era of Kruger, the **Old Raadsaal** (parliament); the **Palace of Justice**; and the **Reserve Bank**.

From the Square, west along Church Street (between Booth and Potgieter Streets) is **Kruger's House**, a single-storey building with a verandah that opens onto the street (08.30–16.00 Monday-Saturday, 11.00–16.00 Sunday). This was a residence presented to Kruger by a grateful Boer nation in 1884; today it is a charming museum, with many of Kruger's own possessions on open display. In the rear is also Kruger's private railway coach, and a collection of fascinating relics from the Anglo-Boer conflict. Cold drinks available on a serve-yourself, honesty basis.

In the Compol Building on Pretorius Street is the **Police Museum**, an odd exhibition of criminal activity and police response (telephone 353 6771). While on this theme, there is also an interesting **Correctional Service Museum**, the only one of its kind in South Africa, at the Central Prison, on Potgieter Street; displays include illegally manufactured items and the hobbies of prisoners (Tuesday–Friday 09.00–15.00, telephone 314 1766).

South of Church Square on Paul Kruger Street is the **Transvaal Museum of Natural History**, reckoned one of the best in the country. It has an extensive range of exhibits of early man and a good bookshop; (09.00–17.00 Monday–Saturday, 11.00–17.00 Sunday, telephone 322 7632).

Further south down Paul Kruger Street and left onto Jacob Mare Street, opposite Burgers Park, brings you to **Melrose House**, one of the glories of the city (10.00–17.00 Tuesday–Saturday, 10.00–20.00 Thursday, 12.00–17.00 Sunday,

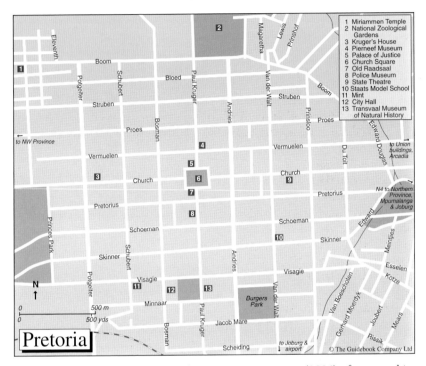

Pretoria

1 Miriammen Temple
2 National Zoological Gardens
3 Kruger's House
4 Pierneef Museum
5 Palace of Justice
6 Church Square
7 Old Raadsaal
8 Police Museum
9 State Theatre
10 Staats Model School
11 Mint
12 City Hall
13 Transvaal Museum of Natural History

© The Guidebook Company Ltd

closed Monday, telephone 322 2805). A Victorian mansion (1886) of great architectural elegance, Melrose House was the site chosen to sign the peace treaty on 31 May 1902 which formally ended the South African War. It's a delightful place to take some refreshments.

On Vermeulen Street, on the northern side of Church Square is the **Pierneef Museum** (08.00–16.00 Monday–Friday, closed weekends, telephone 323 1419), which has an impressive collection of the work of the landscape painter Jacob Pierneef (1886–1957).

On Van der Walt Street is the **Staats Model School**. The young Winston Churchill was imprisoned here in the South African War, and made a spectacular escape. On Schubart Street is South Africa's **Mint** (telephone 325 4813) which can be visited but only with two weeks' notice.

Further out from the centre, in the district known as Asiatic Bazaar, between Sixth and Seventh Streets, is the **Miriammen Temple**, Pretoria's oldest Hindu Temple (always open), built in 1905. There is also an interesting mosque on Queen Street. Along Boom Street, at the corner of Paul Kruger Street, to the north of Church Square, are the **National Zoological Gardens** (08.00–17.30, daily, summer;

08.00–17.00, daily, winter, telephone 328 3268), a zoo where many of the country's wild animals and birds can be seen.

The **Union Buildings**, South Africa's centre of political power, are to the far east of Church Square, in a suburb called Arcadia. They are closed to the public, but the 1913-built sandstone structure is impressive, and the surrounding area makes for a pleasant stroll. Also in Arcadia is the **Pretoria Art Museum** (corner of Schoeman and Wessels Streets, 10.00–17.00 Tuesday–Saturday; 10.00–20.00 Wednesday; 12.00–18.00 Sunday, telephone 344 1807), which has a fine collection of modern and contemporary South African art.

PRETORIA NIGHTLIFE

The **State Theatre** (on Church Street, telephone 322 1665) has seven auditoria for opera, orchestral works, drama, ballet and other shows. There are also many cinemas and clubs; check local newspapers for up-to-date listings.

SPORTS GROUND

The **Loftus Park** stadium of Kirness Street is home to rugby (telephone 344 4011) while for cricket **Centurion Park** on South Street, Verwoerdburg, is pre-eminent (telephone 663 1005).

AROUND PRETORIA

On Monument Hill six kilometres south of the city centre is a grandiose monstrosity called the **Voortrekker Monument** (09.00–16.45 Monday–Saturday, 11.00–16.45 Sunday, telephone 326 6770/323 0682). To get to it take Potgieter Street heading south from the city centre, and follow the very clear signposts. It took 11 years to build and was finished in 1949, a commemoration of the 1838 Great Trek. Forty metres high, with an interior domed-ceiling of 30 metres, it is surrounded by a *laager* of 64 ox-wagons carved into a granite wall. It could have been designed by the Nazi architect Albert Speer, such is its architectural style. Inside is a granite cenotaph cunningly arranged so that at noon each year on 16 December (the anniversary date of the battle of Blood River—*see* HISTORY, *page 84*) the sun's rays can fall upon the inscription *Ons Vir Jou, Suid-Afrika*—'We Are For Thee, South Africa'. It's a very strange building, sombre and entirely self-righteous. You can climb almost to the top via 260 steps.

In the district called New Muckleneuk is an 11-hectare park called the **Austin Roberts Bird** sanctuary, off Boshoff Street, about 10 kilometres from the city centre. There are more than 100 different species of birds, in natural surroundings; (07.00–17.00, weekends and public holidays only, telephone 344 3840).

The **National Botanical Gardens** are on Cussonia Avenue, in Brummeria, about

10 kilometres east of the city centre, in a beautiful 77 hectare estate with thousands of indigenous plants; (08.00–17.00 Monday–Friday, 08.00–18.00 weekends, telephone 804 3200).

On the R101, also called Voortrekkers Road, some 10 kilometres north of the city centre, is the **Wonderboom Nature Reserve**, a 450 hectare reserve which was created in 1949 specifically to protect one tree, an enormous 1,000-year-old, 23-metre-high wild fig tree. Nearby are the remains of a small fort, built for the defence of Pretoria after the 1896 Jameson Raid (see **History**, page 89).

In the small village of Irene, on Nelmapius Road (M31), some 25 kilometres south of Pretoria, is **Doornkloof Farm**, a tin-roofed house that was once the home of former prime minister Jan Smuts (10.00–17.00, Monday–Friday, telephone 677 1176). Near Irene is the **Van Riebeeck Nature Reserve**, with a range of hiking trails.

Of considerable interest is the **Sammy Marks Museum** (exit 11 off the N4 highway, between Pretoria and Witbank; 09.00–16.00 Tuesday–Friday, 10.00–16.00 weekends, telephone 803 6158), former Victorian home of the pioneering entrepreneur Sammy Marks. It's packed with fascinating Marks' family pieces, and there are excellent tour guides who bring it to life. There's also a very attractive garden and good restaurant.

The **Tswaing Eco Museum**, 40 kilometres north-west of Pretoria, is an enormous crater created by the fall of a meteorite. Telephone (01211) 44 171 or (01214) 98 730 before going.

An interesting place to visit is the **Cheetah Research and Breeding Centre** at De Wildt, about 35 kilometres north-west of Pretoria, on R513. You must telephone in advance; PO Box 16, De Wildt 0251, telephone 504 1921 or (01204) 41 921.

Thirty kilometres east of Pretoria, via the N4 highway, is **Cullinan**, an old mining town which grew up around the Premier Diamond Mine. The mine produced some of the world's largest diamonds (including the 3,106 carat *Cullinan*—now part of the Crown Jewels, in London—and the 530 carat *Greater Star of Africa*). To arrange a surface tour (Monday–Friday), telephone (01213) 40 081.

(Above) *"One for all: the many guises of President Mandela. The president lends his face to an advertisement for Pretoria as a tourist destination"* runs the caption

KwaZulu-Natal

This province gets its name from a combination of the old Natal State and the supposed homeland of the Zulu people, KwaZulu, which, under its chief executive officer, Mangosuthu Buthelezi, refused to be pushed by the apartheid regime into a fictitious and artificial 'independence' in the late 1970s. In 1995 there seemed to be uncertainty whether **Pietermaritzburg** or **Ulundi** would eventually be the provincial capital, neither of which is anything like the province's largest city—that status is claimed by **Durban**. (If Ulundi, the traditional 19th century stronghold of the Zulu kings and capital of the former KwaZulu 'homeland' is eventually made KwaZulu-Natal's capital, it will only be for politically-correct reasons; it's small and today has nothing of intrinsic interest.)

The province has a widely varying geography and climate, ranging from coastal humidity and high rainfall, to the temperate, hilly Natal Midlands, through to the high peaks of the Drakensberg. It's an ideal place to see lots of different wildlife.

DURBAN

South Africa's third-biggest city is a major port and commercial centre as well as being an important harbour. **Durban** is named after Sir Benjamin D'Urban, the Cape governor who annexed Natal in 1843. Almost 600 kilometres south of Johannesburg via the N3 highway, or 1,080 kilometres east of Cape Town along the N2 highway, Durban is for many South Africans a favourite sun, sand and shopping holiday resort; the weather and the water stay warm all year round. Its airport is 15 kilometres south of the city centre, the railway station is two kilometres north-west of the city centre on Umgeni Road; the city's telephone prefix is 031.

It's a busy city and finding parking can be difficult; one of the best ways of getting about is by the Mynah shuttle buses, which in the city centre ply routes along West and Smith Streets, and up and down Boscombe, Playfair, Gillespie and Erskine Streets behind North and South beaches.

Like all South African cities, Durban is surrounded by (formal and informal) townships, which you should not enter unless accompanied by an experienced guide. Township tour guides are available; consult the tourist office for expert advice.

Durban spreads across some 300 square kilometres, from the Umgeni River to the far north, along the southern coast and inland up a ridge of hills called Berea, which is also a fashionable suburb and where the University of Natal is situated. The harbour is almost landlocked, the southern part bordered by an 8-kilometre long headland called the **Bluff**, the northern side by a spit called the **Point**. There

Zulu dancers

are six beaches along Durban's sea-front; from the north they are Country Club, Battery, Bay of Plenty, North, South and Addington, with North and South beaches being the most heavily frequented as they are within easy walking distance of the main beach-front hotels.

It's fairly easy to get your bearings in the bustling city centre, which is traversed by some lengthy east-west avenues—**Smith**, **West** and **Pine**, all leading towards the beach area—and across which straddle numerous shorter streets, running in a north-south direction. The downtown centre of Durban is just a couple of blocks behind the beachfront, a six-kilometre stretch of hotels, restaurants, shops, gardens, amusement parks—and beaches—known as the Golden Mile, which stretches all down the beachfront road between **Marine Road** and **Lower Marine Parade**. The Golden Mile has most of the city's more raucous tourist attractions, such as **Seaworld** (bottom of West Street and Lower Marine Parade), an aquarium (09.00–21.00, telephone 374 079) where sharks and other fish are fed in daily shows; and an amusement park with overhead cable-car, called **Funworld** (Marine Parade, open daily, telephone 329 776). On Snell Parade, at the northern end of Marine Road, are various family-oriented entertainments: the Fitzsimons Snake Park, with many more reptiles other than snakes (daily, telephone 376 456); **Waterworld**, a waterpark with all manner of slides and rides (09.00-17.30, daily,

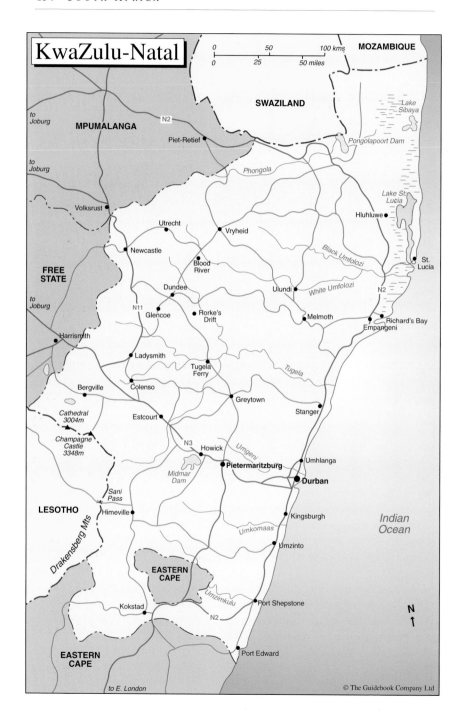

KwaZulu-Natal

0   50   100 kms
0   25   50 miles

MOZAMBIQUE

SWAZILAND

Lake Sibaya

to Joburg

MPUMALANGA

N2

Piet-Retief

Pongolapoort Dam

Phongola

to Joburg

Lake St. Lucia

Volksrust

Utrecht

Vryheid

Hluhluwe

FREE STATE

Newcastle

Blood River

Black Umfolozi

St. Lucia

Dundee

Ulundi

White Umfolozi

N2

to Joburg

N11

Glencoe

Rorke's Drift

Melmoth

Richard's Bay

Harrismith

Empangeni

Ladysmith

Tugela Ferry

Tugela

Bergville

Colenso

Cathedral 3004m

Greytown

Stanger

Champagne Castle 3348m

Estcourt

N3

Howick

Umgeni

Midmar Dam

Pietermaritzburg

Umhlanga

Sani Pass

Durban

LESOTHO

Himeville

Kingsburgh

Indian Ocean

Drakensberg Mts

Umkomaas

Umzinto

EASTERN CAPE

Umzimkulu

Kokstad

Port Shepstone

N2

N

EASTERN CAPE

Port Edward

to E. London

© The Guidebook Company Ltd

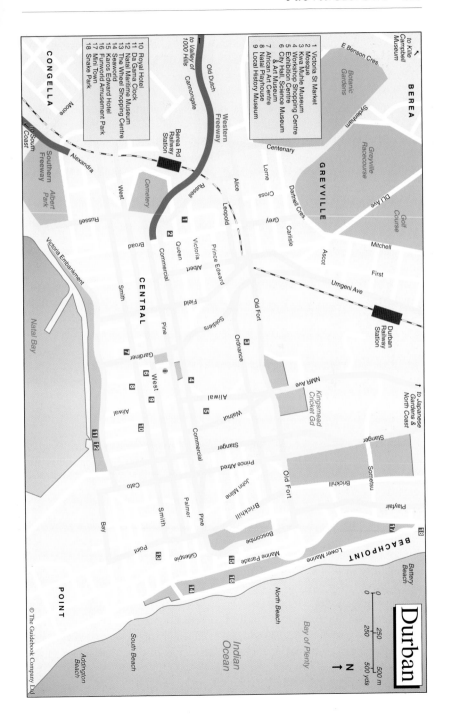

Durban

1 Victoria St Market
2 Mosque
4 Kwa Muhle Museum
5 Workshop Shopping Centre
6 Exhibition Centre
6 City Hall, Science Museum & Art Museum
7 African Art Centre
8 Natal Playhouse
9 Local History Museum

10 Royal Hotel
11 Da Gama Clock
12 Natal Maritime Museum
13 The Wheel Shopping Centre
14 Seaworld
15 Karos Edward Hotel
16 Funworld Amusement Park
17 Mini Town
18 Snake Park

BEREA

CONGELLA

GREYVILLE

CENTRAL

BEACHPOINT

POINT

Natal Bay

Indian Ocean

Bay of Plenty

telephone 376 336/329 776); and **Minitown**, a miniature replica of Durban's best-known buildings (09.30–20.30 Tuesday–Saturday, 09.30–17.30 Sunday, telephone 377 892). On Addington Beach there is a 100 metre-long **Waterslide** (telephone 323 804).

In the city proper there are several places worth visiting. At the west end of the city, at the corner of Victoria and Queen Streets is the largely Indian **Victoria Street Market**, (06.00–18.00 Monday–Saturday, 10.00–16.00 Sunday, telephone 306 4021), an enormous spice, herb and food market, where you can also find African *muti* (medicine) stalls. The original market burned down in 1973; today's is in a modern building, built in 1990. This is the heart of what's known as **Oriental Durban**, with a mass of shops selling silks, oriental baubles and trinkets and much else. Close by, on Grey Street, is the impressively-decorated **Jumah Mosque**, with large golden domes; it's reputedly the largest mosque in the southern hemisphere; tours can be arranged by telephoning the Islamic Propagation Centre on 306 0026.

The other major **shopping** delights are **The Workshop**, a huge, new purpose-built shopping centre just north of the centrally-placed tourist information centre, on Pine Street; **The Wheel**, on Gillespie Street, South Beach (telephone 324 324); **The Pavilion**, at Westville (telephone 265 0558); and the **African Art Centre**, on Gardiner Street, close to the Royal Hotel (telephone 304 7915).

But despite giving every appearance of being devoted entirely to sun-tans and shopping bags, Durban also has a fine array of museums and galleries. A useful telephone number giving detailed information concerning all museums is 300 6911. All museums (unless specified otherwise) are open 08.30–17.00 Monday–Saturday, and 11.00–17.00 Sunday and public holidays.

Of particular interest is the new **Kwa Muhle Museum**, on **Ordnance Road**, a short walk beyond The Workshop shopping centre. The museum is housed in the formerly derelict building which was the headquarters of the municipal authorities responsible for implementing the odious Section 10 of the Group Areas Act, ie vetting black South Africans for passes. It has an excellent half-hour video documenting 20th-century race relations in and around Durban, as well as various photographic and other exhibits. The video clearly explains the way in which the local authorities manipulated alcohol consumption as a means of political and economic control of the lives of black South Africans; there's also a small but very good shop attached.

Other museums feel a little stuffy after that, but some of them are very good. The **Killie Campbell Museum** has an excellent collection of Africana but is open only by appointment—telephone 207 3432. It's out in the suburb of Berea, so do not go there without having made a prior arrangement. The **Local History Museum** on **Aliwal**

Street (at the corner of Smith) has a good collection of colonial art and artefacts concerning Natal. The **Natural Science Museum** in the **City Hall** in the middle of Smith Street, between Aliwal and Gardiner Streets, has some interesting exhibits, including a skeleton of the extinct dodo (telephone 300 6212). In the same building is the **Durban Art Museum** which has some notable European work, including Rodin sculptures, as well as a growing number of exhibitions of contemporary South African and black township art. The **Natal Maritime Museum** (08.30–16.00 Monday–Saturday, 11.00–16.00 Sunday, telephone 300 6320/306 1093) in the harbour, on Victoria Embankment at the corner of Aliwal, has the minesweeper SAS *Durban* and other seafaring stuff. Next door is the **Da Gama clock**, a Victorian work commemorating the discovery of Natal by Vasco da Gama in 1497.

Durban also has some delightful **parks**. The **Botanic Gardens** (off Sydenham Road) were founded in 1849; there's a good tea-garden. The **Japanese Gardens**, north of the city on Tinsley Road, Virginia, are also a tranquil spot. Up in the suburb of Morningside is the **Robert Jameson Park**, which has more than 200 varieties of roses. The **Kenneth Stainbank Nature Reserve** (06.00–18.00, daily) is on Coedmore Road, Yellowwood Park, behind the suburb of Berea. It has a variety of antelope and several walking trails. The 76-hectare **Beachwood Mangroves Nature Reserve** is north of Durban via the Leo Boyd Highway en route to Umhlanga; it's one of the area's last mangrove swamps, mangrove being a general term for any tree able to survive in salt water, and has a variety of typical mangrove bird and fish life.

DURBAN NIGHTLIFE

The **Natal Playhouse** is on Smith Street, almost exactly opposite the City Hall. It has five theatres and for an idea of what's on call 304 3631. The local **Computicket** office (selling tickets for all types of activities and also a good source of information) is on 304 2753. Local newspapers have full listings of local cultural events. Durban is well-endowed with nightclubs but they come and go like the wind, so check when you are there.

SPORTS GROUNDS

Cricket is played at the **Kingsmead** ground on Old Fort Road, slightly north of the downtown centre; it's also the spot where the **Comrade's Marathon** starts/finishes; further north still is the King's Park soccer stadium off the M12; golf is played everywhere; and the Greyville race course is also centrally located. Boat charters for fishing can be easily obtained—ask for details at your hotel or the tourist information office. It's also worthwhile checking out what's on at the Durban Exhibition Centre on Aliwal Street, which besides trade fairs has sporting events.

(Opposite) Zulu woman in traditional costume;

(above, below and right) Zulu dancers prepare for wedding ceremonies

NORTH COAST

The N2 highway follows the coast north and south of Durban, with the north being much less frenetically given over to beach-side resorts.

Eighteen kilometres north along the coast is **Umhlanga**, a beach, hotel and shopping outgrowth of Durban proper. It's also home to the **Natal Sharks Board**, which has daily audio-visual shows as well as a well-stocked aquarium; telephone 561 1001. There is a small lagoon nature reserve; telephone the Wildlife Society for details (213 126). There are other, smaller resorts (**Umdloti, Tongaat Beach, Ballito, Shaka's Rock, Salt Rock** and **Sheffield Beach, Blythedale Beach, Zinkwazi Beach**) all along this strip, with one larger town, Stanger (where Shaka was murdered in his *kraal* in 1828—there is a small monument on Couper Street), for long the centre of the province's sugar industry. Beyond the Tugela River mouth you begin to enter Zululand proper, where Nature re-asserts itself.

On the south bank of the Tugela is the **Harold Johnson Nature Reserve**, 104 hectares of coastal forest with a couple of interesting sights: the **Ultimatum Tree** at Fort Pearson was where on 11 December 1878 the British authorities gave the Zulu king Cetshwayo a choice—either he accept dismemberment of the traditional Zulu military ways, allow missionaries into Zululand, and agree to a British representative to be permanently stationed with him—or there would be war. It was not a proposal he could accept, as the British well understood, and the Anglo-Zulu war started on 12 January 1879, with a three-pronged invasion by the British forces into Zululand. There is also a 2-kilometre **Rituals and Remedies** walking trail, through a glade of trees each with supposed healing properties.

There are two large towns between Tugela Mouth and the far northern resort of St Lucia. **Empangeni**—inland off the N2—and **Richard's Bay**—on the coast—are not terribly attractive, Richard's Bay in particular being a newly-developed industrial port. South of Richard's Bay is the more attractive and rather popular **Ulalazi Nature Reserve**, a 1,000 hectare mangrove reserve with log cabins that can be booked through the Natal Parks Board (see National Parks' appendix, page 307).

Beyond that are several important nature reserves—**St Lucia, False Bay, Sodwana Bay** and **Kosi Bay**—all of which have excellent accommodation (which can be booked through the Natal Parks Board) and are well worth visiting; for details of these and the inland Hluhluwe and Umfolozi parks, see the National Parks' appendix, page 307. There is also a luxurious but expensive, 15,000 hectare private game reserve—the Phinda Private Nature Reserve—modelled on similar such reserves around the Kruger Park, north of St Lucia and inland off the N2 (PO Box 1211, Sunninghill Park 2157, telephone 011 803 8421/8616, fax 011 803 1810 for reservations).

RURAL LIFE

One of the founders of the South African Native National Congress, Solomon Tshekisho Plaatje was an interpreter at Mafeking during the siege in the Second South African War, and later a newspaper editor at Kimberley. His *Native Life In South Africa* was a closely-argued, passionate protest against the 1913 Land Act, which banned white landowners from renting land to black South Africans, on pain of a fine of £100 or six months' jail. Many Africans were brutally evicted from land they had long rented.

A drowning man catches at every straw, and so we were again and again appealed to for advice by those sorely afflicted people. To those who were not yet evicted we counselled patience and submission to the absurd terms, pending an appeal to a higher authority than the South African Parliament and finally to His Majesty the King who, we believed, would certainly disapprove of all that we saw on that day had it been brought to his notice.

It was cold that afternoon as we cycled into the 'Free' State from Transvaal, and towards evening the southern winds rose. A cutting blizzard raged during the night, and native mothers evicted from their homes shivered with their babies by their sides. When we saw on that night the teeth of the little children clattering through the cold, we thought of our own little ones in their Kimberley home of an evening after gambolling in their winter frocks with their schoolmates, and we wondered what these little mites had done that a home should suddenly become to them a thing of the past.

Kgobadi's goats had been to kid when he trekked from his farm; but the kids, which in halcyon times represented the interest of his capital, were now one by one dying as fast as they were born and left by the roadside for the jackals and vultures to feast upon.

This visitation was not confined to Kgobadi's stock, Mrs Kgobadi carried a sick baby when the eviction took place, and she had to transfer her darling from the cottage to the jolting ox-wagon in which they left the farm.

Two days out the little one began to sink as the result of privation and exposure on the road, and the night before we met them its little soul was released from its earthly bonds. The death of the child added a fresh perplexity to the stricken parents. They had no right or title to the farm lands through which they trekked: they must keep to the public roads—the only places in the country open to the outcasts if they are possessed of a travelling permit. The deceased child had to be buried, but where, when, and how?

The young wandering family decided to dig a grave under cover of the darkness of that night, when no one was looking, and in that crude manner the dead child was interred—and interred amid fear and trembling, as well as the throbs of a torturing anguish, in a stolen grave, lest the proprietor of the spot, or any of his servants, should surprise them in the act. Even criminals dropping straight from the gallows have an undisputed claim to six feet of ground on which to rest their criminal remains, but under the cruel operation

Charlestown residents returning to their ancestral land

Nimrod Mthetwa's first afternoon back in Charlestown, their ancestral home

of the Natives' Land Act little children, whose only crime is that God did not make them white, are sometimes denied that right in their ancestral home.

Numerous details narrated by these victims of an Act of Parliament kept us awake all that night, and by next morning we were glad enough to hear no more of the sickening procedure of extermination voluntarily instituted by the South African Parliament. We had spent a hideous night under a bitterly cold sky, conditions to which hundreds of our unfortunate countrymen and countrywomen in various parts of the country are condemned by the provisions of this Parliamentary land plague. At five o'clock in the morning the cold seemed to redouble its energies; and never before did we so fully appreciate the Master's saying: 'But pray ye that your flight be not in the winter.'

Sol Plaatje: Native Life In South Africa, 1916.

SOUTH COAST

The coast south of Durban, down which runs the N2 highway for most of the strip as far as Shelley Beach, leaving the rest of the route to **Port Edward** to the R61, is not an attractive sight. It's one large built-up beach house, but for all that is very popular with South African tourists and pensioners who want to retire to somewhere with year-round warmth. There are a score of towns, mostly indistinguishable, and some excellent swimming areas.

Heading south, you will encounter: **Amanzimtoti**, 30 kilometres south of Durban but feels just like the big city. **Kingsburgh** has a 10-kilometre beachfront. **Scottburgh** is a popular, larger town, inland from which is the 2,190 hectare **Vernon Crookes Nature Reserve**, with nature trails and some accommodation (telephone 0323 422 222). **Hibberdene** has an 80-metre tidal pool. **Umzumbe**, like **Banana Beach** to the south, is a quieter spot. **Port Shepstone**, at the mouth of the Umzimkulu River, is a busy town, 20 kilometres inland from which is the delightful **Oribi Gorge Nature Reserve** (see National Parks' appendix, page 300). Beyond Port Shepstone is **Margate**, with some lovely beaches and hotels; then **Ramsgate** (like Margate, named after a much less attractive couple of British seaside towns) until you reach **Port Edward**—one of the coast's quieter and less brash spots—and the Eastern Cape border.

NATAL MIDLANDS

One of South Africa's most unknown delights is a short drive north of Durban; take the N3 highway out of the city and beyond the Mariannhill Toll Plaza look for signs to the M13 road; take that road and at a T-junction turn left onto the R103, towards **Hillcrest**; from there look out for signposts to **Valley of a Thousand Hills**, a beautiful valley formed by the **Umgeni River**, which has its source at the 2,146-metre Spioenkop, in the Natal Midlands. The Umgeni flows into the **Midmar Dam** before falling over the **Howick** and **Albert Falls**; from Pietermaritzburg to Durban it winds a 64-kilometre course through the Valley of a Thousand Hills. There are no good roads here, and there have been violent political clashes between ANC and IFP supporters in this area in recent years, but it's still a wonderfully beautiful area, though with a dark history. It was, in the 19th century, home to the Debe people, who according to some historians suffered so badly at the hands of warring Zulus.that they were forced to take up cannibalism; some retreated to a 959m flat-topped peak in the valley, known as **Natal Table Mountain**, a good if strenuous hiking spot. Unfortunately there is nowhere to stay in this area.

Eighty kilometres along the N3 highway north of Durban lies one of South Africa's most pleasant towns, **Pietermaritzburg**, the telephone prefix for which is **0331**. Its airport is 6 kilometres from the centre. It feels a very English, ex-colonial

nial town but was actually founded in 1838 by Voortrekkers who called it Pietermauritzburg, in memory of their leader, Pieter Mauritz Retief, who had been murdered by the Zulu chief Dingane on 6 February 1838. Eventually the 'u' was dropped.

It's a very bustling place, with all the usual chain stores and a sprinkling of markets, but it's also a town with many important historical associations, besides those of the Voortrekkers: Louis Napoleon, the prince imperial of France, stayed in the **Imperial Hotel** on Loop Street, and rode from it to his death in 1879 in a Zulu ambush; Alan Paton, the novelist, was born here in 1903; his study has been relocated to the Pietermaritzburg campus of the **University of Natal** (to visit it, telephone the archivist on 955 622).

The 1893 **City Hall**, which must be visited by appointment, is a fine example of red-brick late-Victorian architecture, on one of the main roads in the centre, **Commercial Road**; as you face City Hall, a few metres to the right is the town's publicity association, one of the best in the country, at the corner of **Longmarket Street**.

Across the road from there is the **Tatham Art Gallery**, (09.00–16.30 Monday–Saturday), one of the unsung treasures of South African gallery life. Built 1865–71, it housed the country's supreme court between 1906 and 1983; in 1990 it re-opened as a gallery. It contains some excellent 19th and 20th-century European and South African art, including works by Marc Chagall, Pablo Picasso, Oscar Kokoschka and David Hockney. It also has a splendid cafe upstairs.

Continue along Commercial Road to **Loop Street**; turn right onto Loop, and just after Witness Lane is the rather dull **Natal Museum**, (09.00–16.30, Monday–Saturday), one of five national museums in the country. Cut back onto Longmarket through one of the narrow side streets to find the enormous grey-stone **Post Office** which although—or maybe perhaps—it's distinctively ugly, has been declared a national monument. Turn left in Longmarket and then right into **Theatre**

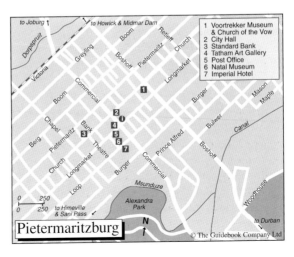

Lane, down which there is an interesting second-hand bookshop called **Bloomsbury Books**, with a wide stock at good prices. Carry on down Theatre Lane until you reach Church Street; immediately across the road on the corner of Church and Bank Streets is the **Standard Bank**, which contains some beautiful new stained glass windows designed by Philip Dudgeon; the windows depict the months of the year. Unfortunately, Dudgeon is a northern hemisphere inhabitant and he has accordingly constructed the months as he knows them—ie a wintry December and sunny August, entirely the reverse from what the seasons are like in (southern hemisphere) South Africa.

The Drakensberg mountains

Walk along Church Street back towards City Hall; at the far end of the street, before you get to Boshoff Street, there is on the right the **Voortrekker Museum** and the original **Church of the Vow**, built by the Voortrekkers in 1841 to commemorate their victory over the Zulus at the Battle of Blood River on 16 December 1838. It contains a good collection of old Voortrekker memorabilia, including what is alleged to be Piet Retief's prayer book.

From Pietermaritzburg publicity association you can get hold of a free brochure detailing something called the Midlands Meander, a combined arts-and-craft, restaurant, hotel and activities route map covering villages and towns along the 50-kilometre stretch of the N3 highway between Pietermaritzburg and Estcourt; it's quite useful. Not all the spots it mentions are worth visiting, the **Midmar Dam** theme park being especially dull. **Howick**, however, is a pleasant village, on the Umgeni River, and it has an impressive 95-metre waterfall in the centre, around which there are several pleasant walks. At Howick publicity association you can see how little impact has been made by the recent democratic reforms; the association has a 'tourist guide' which carefully tells you that (in 1996) the 'population of Whites, Indians, Blacks and Coloureds is approximately 48,000...'. Who said things have changed? There are a couple of nearby nature reserves—**Umgeni Valley** and **Game Valley**, both close to **Karkloof Falls**, also near Howick.

THE DRAKENSBERG

SOUTH

From Pietermaritzburg take the R617 to **Himeville**, where there is a nature reserve that makes a good jumping-off point for the **Sani Pass**, the only route over the Drakensberg connecting South Africa with Lesotho. (Himeville Nature Reserve, PO Himeville, 4585, telephone 033 702 1036; the reserve has 10 campsites and a hotel). The final 8 kilometres of the Sani Pass are restricted to four-wheel drive vehicles; there are several tour operators you can contact for assistance to get to the top: Mokhotlong Mountain Transport, telephone (033) 702 1615; Himeville Hotel, telephone (033) 702 1305; Molumong Tours, telephone (033) 701 1490; and Sani Top Chalet, telephone (033) 702 1069.

Beyond Howick on the N3 turn left to **Nottingham Road**, from where minor roads lead to two more important nature reserves, **Loteni** and **Kamberg** in the Drakensberg foothills; both are good trout fishing spots.

CENTRAL

Further along the N3 turn left just beyond **Mooi River** to reach the 35,000 hectare **Giant's Castle Game Reserve**, run by the Natal Parks Board (to book accommodation, see National Parks' appendix, page 300). Its name derives from the 3,314-metre central peak—said to resemble a slumbering giant—above the reserve. San rock paintings can be found in this reserve, as in many other parts of the central Drakensberg region.

Further up this central part of the Drakensberg are other equally towering peaks, including **Champagne Castle** (3,348 metres), so called because two British army surveyors took a bottle of champagne with them when they attempted to climb it in the 1860s. They were intending to drink it when they reached the top; they gave up and decided to crack the bottle anyway. They found that it was already half empty and, as neither would admit to sneaking a drink, they decided to blame the mountain instead. The nearby **Cathkin Peak** (3,148 metres) is detached from the main wall of the escarpment. Further north up the N3 beyond Estcourt turn left onto the R615 and head for Winterton, from where one of the most famous peaks, **Cathedral** (3,004 metres), one of the easier climbs in the region, can be reached; there is a good resort hotel at its base (see section on Hotels, page 284). It's possible to walk a (rather complicated, 60-kilometres) route between Cathedral and Cathkin. Between Cathedral and Champagne Castle lies the **Ndedema Gorge**; Ndedema is believed to be a corrupt version of the word Ndidima, meaning 'place of reverberation'. The gorge has 17 rock shelters, and an estimated 4,000 rock paintings, many of which are deteriorating badly.

JUST ROUTINE POLICE PROCEDURE

Miss Hazelstone was telephoning [her local police station] to report that she had just shot her Zulu cook. Konstabel Els was perfectly capable of handling the matter. He had in his time as a police officer shot any number of Zulu cooks. Besides there was a regular procedure for dealing with such reports. Konstabel Els went into the routine.

'You wish to report the death of a kaffir,' he began.

'I have just murdered my Zulu cook,' snapped Miss Hazelstone.

Els was placatory. 'That's what I said. You wish to report the death of a coon.'

'I wish to do nothing of the sort. I told you I have just murdered Fivepence.'

Els tried again. 'The loss of a few coins doesn't count as murder.'

'Fivepence was my cook.'

'Killing a cook doesn't count as murder either.'

'What does it count as, then?' Miss Hazelstone's confidence in her own guilt was beginning to wilt under Konstabel Els's favourable diagnosis of the situation.

'Killing a white cook can be murder. It's unlikely but it can be. Killing a black cook can't. Not under any circumstances. Killing a black cook comes under self-defence, justifiable homicide or garbage disposal.' Els permitted himself a giggle. 'Have you tried the Health Department?' he enquired.

It was obvious to the Kommandant that Els has lost what little sense of social deference he had ever possessed. He pushed Else aside and took the call himself.

'Kommandant van Heerden here,' he said. 'I understand that there has been a slight accident with your cook.'

Miss Hazelstone was adamant. 'I have just murdered my Zulu cook.'

Kommandant van Heerden ignored the self-accusation. 'The body is in the house?' he enquired.

'The body is on the lawn,' said Miss Hazelstone. The Kommandant sighed. It was always the same. Why couldn't people shoot blacks inside their houses where they were supposed to shoot them?

'I will be up at Jacaranda House in forty minutes,' he said, 'and when I arrive I will find the body in the house.'

'You won't,' Miss Hazelstone insisted, 'you'll find it on the back lawn.' Kommandant van Heerden tried again.

'When I arrive the body will be in the house.' He said it very slowly this time.

Miss Hazelstone was not impressed. 'Are you suggesting that I move the body?' she asked angrily.

The Kommandant was appalled at the suggestion. 'Certainly not,' he said, 'I have no wish to put you to any inconvenience and besides there might be fingerprints. You can get the servants to move it for you.'

There was a pause while Miss Hazelstone considered the implications of this remark. 'It sounds to me as though you are suggesting that I should tamper with the evidence of a crime,' she said slowly and menacingly. 'It sounds to me as though you are trying to get me to interfere with the course of justice.'

'Madam,' interrupted the Kommandant, 'I am merely trying to help you to obey the law.' He paused, groping for words. 'The law says that it is a crime to shoot kaffirs outside your house. But the law also says it is perfectly permissible and proper to shoot them inside your house if they have entered illegally.'

'Fivepence was my cook and had every legal right to enter the house.'

'I'm afraid you're wrong there,' Kommandant van Heerden went on. 'Your house is a white area and no kaffir is entitled to enter a white area without permission. By shooting your cook you were refusing him permis sion to enter your house. I think is is safe to assume that.'

There was a silence at the other end of the line. Miss Hazelstone was evidently convinced.

'I'll be up in forty minutes,' continued van Heerden, adding hopefully, 'and I trust the body—'

'You'll be up here in five minutes and Fivepence will be on the lawn where I shot him,' snarled Miss Hazelstone and slammed down the phone.

The Kommandant looked at the receiver and sighed. He put it down wearily and turning to Konstabel Els he ordered his car.

As they drove up the hill to Jacaranda Park, Kommandant van Heerden knew he was faced with a difficult case. He studied the back of Konstabel Els's head and found some consolation in its shape and colour.

If the worst came to the worst he could always make use of Els's great gift of incompetence and if in spite of all his efforts to prevent it, Miss Hazelstone insisted on being tried for murder, she would have as the chief prosecution witness against her, befuddled and besotted, Konstabel Els. If nothing else could save her, if she pleaded guilty in open court, if she signed confession after confession, Konstabel Els under cross-examination by no matter how half-witted a defence attorney would convince the most biased jury or the most inflexible judge that she was the innocent victim of police incompetence and unbridled perjury. The State Attorney was known to have referred to Konstabel Els in the witness box as the Instant Alibi.

Tom Sharpe; Riotous Assembly: 1971.

NORTH

Still further north, reached by staying on the R615 after Winterton, passing through Bergville and after 45 kilometres taking a small road left, just before the spectacular Oliviershoek pass, is Mont-aux-Sources, source of the Tugela River. Here you will find the **Royal Natal National Park**, some good hotels (see appendices, page 274) and marvellous scenery.

ZULULAND

From the right of the N3 highway, stretching east, lies some of the most bitterly contested land in the country, where Voortrekker battled Zulu, Zulu fought Brit, and Brit clashed with Boer. It also has some of the most impoverished rural areas you will see, and some very bad roads. Yet it is a beautiful landscape, where you will climb high and see what appear to be endless vistas of empty grassland, dotted with hills and rocky outcrops. For those interested in getting a grip on the many military engagements of this area, the **Dundee** information centre is well set up to

Preparing for the feast at a Zulu wedding

give advice and arrange specialist tours: Private Bag 2024, Dundee 3000, telephone (0341) 22 121, fax (0341) 23 856.

Ladysmith has romantic associations for British military history, as the place where a small British force held out against a Boer siege for 115 days between October 1899 and February 1900. In fact the siege was poorly conducted and the defence incompetently handled, a clash between anarchic fervour and plodding stupidity that was to be repeated throughout the Second South African war. Today, Ladysmith is a dull place, not worth spending time upon. South-west of Ladysmith is **Spioenkop**, now a resort and nature reserve (telephone 0331 471 981, fax 0331 471 980) constructed around a dam. On 24 January 1900 the area witnessed one of the most bloody engagements of that war, when 1,200 British troops died in a futile defence of the small hill called Spioenkop; the Boer farmers lost about 300 men.

There is a small museum close to the battlefield.

Between Estcourt and Ladysmith is **Colenso**, a small town famous for a battle of the Second South African war; it was here that Winston Churchill was captured by Boer commandos. From Colenso take the R74 heading south-east towards **Greytown**; you will pass through Weenen, which means 'weeping', after the massacre of 500 Boer women and children by Dingane's Zulus in 1838; Weenen also has a nature reserve which is due greatly to expand and become one of the country's largest. At Greytown turn north again, up the R33 to **Keate's Drift**, **Tugela Ferry** and **Pomeroy**, all of which are small places where the devastation wrought by apartheid can be clearly seen in the immense poverty and wretched shacks that line much of the road. The road itself, like many in this part of the country, is very poor, particularly in the towns, where gaping potholes will crack your vehicle's suspension if you are not careful. These are lonely spots, not to be driven through at night, not least because of wandering cattle.

At Helpmekaar take a dirt road right to **Rorke's Drift**, where the Anglo-Zulu war of 1879 came to a crisis point. At nearby **Isandhlwana** on 22 January 1879 some 1,200 British troops and local levies were slaughtered by a 20,000-strong Zulu army, some of whom then went on to Rorke's Drift. The Zulus were there kept at bay by a resolute defence of this small mission station by 150 poorly-equipped and non-combatant British troops. There is a small but fascinating **museum** at Rorke's Drift (08.00–17.00, daily), and also an excellent local handicrafts centre called the **Evangelical Lutheran Church** Arts and Crafts Centre (08.00–16.30, Monday–Friday, 10.00–15.00, Saturday, telephone 03425 627). To get to Isandhlwana from Rorke's Drift you will need to return to the R33, and head north 42 kilometres to **Dundee**, a small and not terribly interesting town, though there are a couple of interesting battlefield sites, Talana and Elandslaagte, close to the town. From Dundee take the R33 heading east towards **Vryheid**. After a short distance, turn right onto the R68; Isandhlwana is about 80 kilometres south on that road. On the battlefield itself, hundreds of white cairns mark the positions of buried British troops.

Further along the R33 towards Vryheid, some 48 kilometres east of Dundee, is another important historical battlefield, **Blood River** (*see* HISTORY *chapter, page 84*). Once again, having left the tarred road, it requires a lengthy drive on dirt roads actually to reach the site of the clash, where on 16 December 1838 a small group of Voortrekkers formed an ox-wagon *laager* and defeated a large Zulu army, killing some 3,000 in the process—hence the name Blood River. But the site is worth visiting, if only to gauge just how deeply self-righteous Afrikaners—some, anyway—have felt in the past. For on the site of the battle there has been erected an exact replica of the original *laager*, with 64 life-size bronze ox-wagons. It's a very gloomy place. There is nothing to commemorate the Zulus.

APARTHEID

Black people may find it hard to believe, but the main purpose of apartheid was not racial segregation, nor even racial domination; it was to enrich the ruling class.
Ken Owen, newspaper editor.

We did what God wanted us to do.
Hendrik Verwoerd, former prime minister.

If we'd called it ethnic cleansing we might have got away with it.
Evita Bezuidenhout, ambassador (aka Pieter-Dirk Uys, satirist)

*I*t might seem perverse to consider an ideology which is now officially dead, but those who forget their errors are condemned to repeat them.

An Afrikaans word which may be translated as 'apartness' or 'separateness,' and which is pronounced 'apart-ate' (and not 'apart-ite'), the concept came to the forefront of South African politics after the 1948 general election, won by the National Party under its leader D F Malan. Apartheid was the single most powerful slogan of the 1948 election, in which only whites had the vote. Under Malan and his minister of 'Native Affairs' (and future prime minister) Hendrik Verwoerd, a whole bundle of legislation was passed, aimed at systematizing and reinforcing the racial segregation which had in any case long been practiced, although in a fairly ad hoc fashion.

The distinction between the segregation of pre-1948 and the apartheid of 1948–1990 was one of emphasis; apartheid was systematized segregation run mad, segregation followed to the point of logical insanity.

The roots of apartheid stretch far back into the history of the country. Many of the early British colonialists also favoured racial segregation and considered black indigenous peoples as uncivilized. In 1897 James Bryce, who would later act as British ambassador to Washington, voiced the prevailing view of Victorian England when he wrote in *Impressions of South Africa*: 'Here in South Africa the native races seem to have made no progress for centuries, if, indeed, they have not actually gone backward; and the feebleness of savage man intensifies one's sense of the overmastering strength of nature.' Even relatively enlightened commentators, such as Theophilus Shepstone, born on a Methodist mission station in the Cape Colony, and secretary of native affairs in Natal, could not escape a patronising tone in 1853: 'I do not think them wanting in capacity or intelligence[...] I see no absolute bar to their civilization or to their usefulness, in any position which their intelligence and capacity may hereafter place them.'

But while the predominant view of British colonists was that black people were inferior, they nevertheless generally paid lip-service to the patronizing notion that they had a moral duty to 'educate' black Africans, in order that they might one day take an equal place in society.

On the other hand the early Boers were implacably hostile. In 1852, before the same British colonial government of Natal commission at which Shepstone spoke, one Dewald Johannes Pretorius spoke for many of his compatriots when he averred that 'black and white races in large masses cannot live together in peace and safety in the same land.' A century later, Boer racial attitudes gained the upper hand. The 1948 National Party government took its revenge on the hitherto politically influential English-speaking whites, by systematically eliminating them from positions of state influence.

But the Nationalists' main target was black South Africans, around whose necks they drew a legislative noose. They were to be removed from white society in every possible way;

Prime minister D F Malan who in 1948 became the godfather of apartheid

their role was to be restricted to that of a reservoir of cheap labour. As Verwoerd said in his maiden speech to the Senate on 3 December 1948: 'South Africa is a white man's country and he must remain the master here. In the Reserves [rural areas designated for black occupation] we are prepared to allow the Natives to be the masters [...] but within the European areas we, the white people of South Africa, are and shall remain the masters.'

Verwoerd appealed to the hard-line racism of many whites; and he cleverly appealed to white voters who doubted his proposals by disguising them as being of benefit to both black and white. The word apartheid is now so loaded with repugnant connotations it is difficult to realise that, initially, its euphemistic character— which Verwoerd utilised to the full, by describing his racism as 'separate development'—gained it easy acceptance among many whites. For politically conscious, unfranchised blacks, the 1948 election was almost an irrelevance. Albert Luthuli, who

Hendrik Verwoerd, the architect of apartheid, meets some fans

was to become president of the African National Congress, wrote in his autobiography, *Let My People Go*: 'The Nationalist win did not either surprise nor extremely interest us, though we did realise that there would probably be an intensification of the hardships and indignities which had always come our way. Nevertheless, I think it is true that very few (if any) of us understood how swift the deterioration was to be.'

The deterioration was indeed rapid, as the new Afrikaner government passed a stream of racist legislation in the 1950s, designed to formalise this new, radical separation of white from black, 'coloured' and Indian races. Strikes by African workers were banned; black Africans were subject to forced removals (individually and en masse) from 'white-only' areas; education was segregated—in future, black Africans were to be educated only as 'hewers of wood and drawers of water'; sexual relations between whites and non-whites were criminalized; and the limited voting rights enjoyed by so-called coloureds in the Cape were ended.

The underpinning legislation was the 1950 Population Registration Act, which compelled racial classification on all South Africans. In future, a South African's public and private rights increasingly came to depend on his or her racial classification. This grotesque distortion of the notion of citizenship, bearing an obvious similarity to the racial laws of Nazi Germany, was the core of apartheid.

As the Nazis sought to remove Jews and other peoples from its territories, so too did the Nationalist Party set about removing black South Africans from 'white' areas. One of the most devastating laws of the National Party was the Bantu Self-Government Act (1959), which provided for the establishment of ultimately 10 black African mini-states within South Africa, based on the geographical land carve-ups embodied in the Land Acts of 1913 and 1936, which had put more than 80 per cent of South Africa's land mass into 'white-only' ownership. A further Act, the Black Urban Areas Act of 1952 gave authority to the government to decide which black South Africans could legally stay in 'white' South Africa. Without the right permit, a black South African was allowed a maximum 72 hours in a white area.

The supposedly independent self-governing black states of Bophuthatswana, Ciskei, Transkei, Venda, which came to be known as homelands or Bantustans, gained almost no international diplomatic recognition. Following the release from jail of Nelson Mandela in February 1990, and the elections involving all South Africans, the homeland governments swiftly collapsed; the artificially-created territories returned to being an intrinsic part of the country.

Formally, apartheid is dead. Informally, racism has of course not disappeared; laws cannot stop individuals being prejudiced. Visitors to the country will not see much public evidence of apartheid; but casual conversations with some whites over a drink or two will show that attitudes have changed little.

TOWNSHIP LIFE

On the outskirts of Johannesburg is Soweto (an abbreviation of South Western Township), a sprawling urban area and home to more than two million people—black people, by and large. Segregation and apartheid created urban ghettos all over the country. They still exist, though no law any longer enforces who can and cannot live there.

But white South Africans do not live in townships, the collections of slum dwellings, shacks and hovels seen on the outskirts of almost every town and city. Townships are the most visible and distressing legacy of apartheid. Some, such as large parts of Soweto, are well-established and contain impressive homes. The majority, however, are shameful slums, lacking the most basic amenities of running water, sewage disposal and electricity.

From the 1940s onwards black South Africans sought a better life on the fringes of white-only urban areas. Various pieces of legislation sought to prevent this influx, but still they came, driven by rural poverty and the hope of a job. Throughout the apartheid era many forced removals of these townships were conducted by the white authorities, causing enormous suffering for the families whose flimsy shacks and tenuous existences were bulldozed into the ground.

Disgracefully, even where black families did have freehold title to the land they occupied, they were nevertheless often forced out. Perhaps the most famous example of such a forced removal was that of Sophiatown, a suburb of Johannesburg. The very word Sophiatown was for many anti-apartheid activists a potent symbol of how the country's different races might have happily co-existed, but for the viciousness of the apartheid regime. Sophiatown started life in 1897 when Herman Tobiansky bought 237 acres of land and named it after his wife, Sophia. He hoped to create a classy suburb, but Johannesburg's municipal authorities first built a sewage works nearby, and then soon after a

(top) Black pupils concentrate on their lessons
(bottom) Alexandra township, Johannesburg

(top) *Krugersdorp 1990: a typical migrant worker's hostel*
(bottom) *Rural poverty has long been a way of life for black South Africans*

municipal location for blacks—both of which deterred whites from buying property in Sophiatown. Tobiansky thereupon sold freehold plots to blacks, whites, anyone who would give him the price. The result was that by the 1950s Sophiatown was a genuinely multi-racial, vibrant district—and utterlyloathed by the apartheid regime of Hendrik Verwoerd.

Its inhabitants said that Sophiatown had a gregarious, cosmopolitan feel, where musicians, writers, journalists, and even priests rubbed shoulders with *tsotsis*—small-time criminals who formed themselves into gangs with names such as 'Russians', 'Americans' and 'Berliners'. All would meet up in one of Sophiatown's many shebeens, or illicit drinking dens. Essential reading for its inhabitants—and blacks throughout the country—was *Drum*, a *Picture Post*-style magazine that started life in 1951 and bred a generation of black intellectuals and journalists, who wrote about beauty queens, shebeens, jazz, big-city life, the gang fights, as well as more serious issues, such as the exploitation of black workers.

Most townships were not like Sophiatown, it must be said. They were—and the majority of those that persist today still are—miserable places of deprivation and squalor. But even in such ghettos an underground culture thrived, widely known to township-dwellers as *marabi*, a blend of music, drinking, posing, preening, sexual freedom and sheer exuberance. The heart of *marabi* was its music, a mish-mash of spirituals, rags, jazz, swing, traditional African rhythms and anything novel from America, immediately incorporated into the unique local *marabi* sound. It was as if the sheer awfulness of life under apartheid inspired township-dwellers to find whatever *joie de vivre* they could, be it from a tin whistle or bottle of booze.

Sophiatown's bohemian culture has to some extent been sentimentalised in recent times. It was a rough, tough place, where kidnappings and assaults regularly happened, and casual death, either at the hands of a tsotsi or through too much home-brew, was common. But its inhabitants claimed to feel a greater degree of freedom to live their lives as they pleased than they were permitted elsewhere in apartheid-ridden South Africa. That in itself offended the white authorities, who on 10 February 1955 sent in 2,000 heavily-armed police to begin the forced removal of the first 110 families ear-marked for internal deportation to Meadowlands, part of Soweto. Over the next few years, Sophiatown was broken up, its streets demolished and its people dispersed. With unashamed arrogance, the district was renamed Triomf (Afrikaans for triumph), and reconstructed as a whites-only suburb. The district can still be found today, north-west of the central business district of Johannesburg, though, by now, probably under a more politically-correct name.

In his book *Naught for your Comfort*, Father Trevor Huddleston, an Anglican priest in Sophiatown, wrote at the time: 'Here in Sophiatown we have been engaged in building a Christian Community. It is that community which is now being smashed to pieces in the interests of racial ideology. And as we watch our people's homes being reduced to heaps of rubble, we watch also the destruction of something which cannot be built again so easily or so far. When Sophiatown is finally obliterated and its people scattered, I believe that South Africa will have lost not only a place, but an ideal.'

Township culture in the mid-1990s bears little or no resemblance to the heady days of Sophiatown. Today's townships, such as Crossroads, an enormous squatter camp that runs alongside the motorway leading from Cape Town's International Airport, are an ugly scar, slums which will take many years and much cash to replace with adequate housing and acceptable infrastructure. Moreover, most of them are not organic creations like Sophiatown but artificial constructions, imposed on people by the apartheid regime. The integration of their inhabitants into South African society can take place on one level, by simply building houses for them in areas once reserved for whites. Yet on another, more profound level, the damage that has been done in terms of human relationships cannot so easily be healed. In hindsight, Huddleston's words seem distressingly prophetic.

(above) *One of South Africa's largest townships—Soweto* (below) *Khayalitsha township, near Cape Town*

(above) *KTC squatter camp, part of Crossroads, on the outskirts of Cape Town*
(below) *Kwanobgle Township in the Western Cape*

Provinces Part Two

Mpumalanga

Formerly known as Eastern Transvaal, Mpumalanga is bordered by Swaziland and Mozambique to the east, and Gauteng to the west. The provincial capital, **Nelspruit**, is one of South Africa's fastest-growing cities, 375 kilometres east of Johannesburg on the N4 highway. The telephone prefix for Nelspruit is **01311**. The eastern *lowveld* is an astonishingly fertile part of the country, with everything from tobacco to pineapples thriving in the rich, red soil. The province is one of the more interesting places for the traveller, with lots of nature reserves, spectacular scenery, and a sprinkling of superb country house hotels.

The greatest part of the eastern border with Mozambique is occupied by the **Kruger Park**, a wilderness as large as a small country and one of the world's most important conservation areas. While most flock to the Kruger Park, on the park's western border are some of the world's most glorious natural sights. Little wonder that this part of the country is a very popular tourist destination.

From the Witwatersrand highveld heading east along the N4 highway there is little to detain you. **Witbank**, 100 kilometres from Joburg, is coal city; there are 22 open-cast mines in this area, which has an estimated 75 million tons of coal, South Africa's biggest reserve. At **Middelburg** you can turn left onto the R35; about 40 kilometres along this road you will see the **Botshabelo Mission Station**, a restored Ndebele village which makes and sells various handicrafts; telephone (0132) 23 897. Ten kilometres further is the 15,000 hectare **Loskop Dam and Nature Reserve**, popular with anglers and with several species of large game and some 250 species of birds. Be careful of crocodiles and bilharzia; there is a swimming pool, restaurant and accommodation on the north-eastern side of the dam.

To continue to Kruger Park you must return to the N4, passing through **Machadodorp** and, if you have time, deviating north onto the R539, which takes you through **Schoemanskloof**, a pretty valley village; the R359 will rejoin the N4.

If you don't take that detour but stay on the N4, 70 kilometres before Nelspruit are two villages, **Waterval Boven** and **Waterval Onder**, where the high escarpment comes to an abrupt end at the 228-metre **Elands River Falls**. At Waterval Boven a major railway yard was built in 1894, part of Paul Kruger's plan to build his own 700km railway route to the Indian Ocean, in order to avoid being dependent on the

British control of the Cape and Natal railway systems. The railway line here moves down a very steep 1:20 gradient.

Beyond Waterval Boven you can deviate left to the **Sudwala Caves**, a major tourist attraction. The caves were used in the early 19th century as a bolt-hole by Swazi people fleeing attacks by other marauding tribes; they stretch for many kilometres and have not been completely explored. Visitors may only go 600 metres into them, on a supervised tour, but even that small section covers 14,000 square metres of weirdly-shaped rock formations. Guided tours are conducted seven days a week between 08.30–16.30. On the final Saturday of each month is the six-hour **Crystal Cave Tour**; telephone (01311 64 152). Nearby is a pleasant small resort.

You can continue on the N4 to Nelspruit and then, just before that city, either turn south to **Barberton**, head north to **White River**, or carry on the N4 to either the **Malelane** or **Crocodile Bridge** entrance gates to the **Kruger Park**; the N4 continues another 150 kilometres to **Komatipoort**, the border-town with **Mozambique**.

As you travel along the N4 you will notice how the landscape gradually alters, from the flat highveld—about 1,000 metres above the lowveld—to the dramatic ridge, running for about 300 kilometres north of **Nelspruit** north to **Tzaneen** (part of Northern Province) and beyond, overlooking the savanna lowveld beyond; this ridge is part of South Africa's **Great Escarpment**, here known as the **Transvaal Drakensberg**. All along this 300-kilometre ridge, criss-crossed with ancient paths linking highveld and lowveld, are awe-inspiring gorges and individual buttresses, sometimes covered in cloud, more often bursting through into sunshine.

NELSPRUIT, WHITE RIVER AND POINTS NORTH

Nelspruit is a lively, friendly, bustling place with good air connections to Gauteng and Durban, and an excellent centrally-located tourist information office, very well set-up to give lots of local information. The town has a number of good curio shops as well as all the major stores. **White River** has several excellent hotels and lodges, making it the perfect spot to stay over before entering the 350 by 70-kilometre Kruger Park, the major tourist magnet of this province. Details of the park and its accommodation are in the National Parks' appendix.

But there is much beautiful countryside and many historically important places outside the Kruger Park. From White River take the R537 to **Sabie**, a small town with some interesting bric-a-brac and second-hand bookshops, and a good pancake house (Petena Pancakes on Main Street, telephone 01315 41 541). Eleven kilometres north of Sabie on the R532 are the **Mac Mac Pools**, a small set of natural rock pools in a forest setting, falling from the twin Mac Mac Falls a kilometre further on; it's a popular place to swim, and there are small changing huts.

Ten kilometres west of Sabie on the R37 is the **Lone Creek Falls Trail**, an easy

(top) *A typical South African 'cafe'*; (bottom) *The beer flows freely in Soweto's shebeens*

walking trail leading to a 70-metre waterfall set amid mountains forests. Further along is a spectacular drive up to the 57-kilometre-long **Long Tom Pass**, at the top of which (2,149 metres) is a 1984 replica of one of the four French-made Long Tom heavy artillery pieces used by the Boers to bombard the British during the 1899–1902 war. The Boers paid the then huge sum of R125,700 for the four 155mm cannons plus 8,800 shells; rather than let them fall into the hands of the British towards the end of the war the Boer generals decided to melt them down. It's only when you see this replica (the original was last used in action at this site on 8–11 September 1900) do you realize what an enormous effort it must have been to drag these beasts all around the country, fleeing British regiments in hot pursuit.

Beyond Long Tom Pass, just before you reach **Lydenburg**, is the 2,200 hectare **Gustav Klingbiel Nature Reserve**, on the slopes of Mount Anderson. The reserve also has a collection of later Stone Age ruins. A short distance on you reach the 19th- century town of Lydenburg, the Afrikaans name of which means 'place of suffering', a reflection of the hardships endured by its Voortrekker founders. It has an original 1851 Voortrekker School, an 1852 church, and an old powder magazine. From Lydenburg take the R36 heading north towards Krugerspos; beyond that, turn right onto the R533, heading towards Pilgrim's Rest. A short distance along the R533 is the **Mount Sheba Nature Reserve**, a beautiful woodbush area with many ancient indigenous trees.

Twenty kilometres further along the R533 is **Pilgrim's Rest**; the whole town— originally a gold-rush site—has been declared a conservation area, and it is well worth pausing at, both for refreshments and its various museums. The Victorian single-storey tin-roofed buildings have been carefully restored and the setting of the whole village is delightful. A handful of (highly optimistic) prospectors still work away in the area.

Heading west beyond Pilgrim's Rest you reach **Graskop**, a tiny forestry village with lots of camping and caravan sites, and the southern point at which to start perhaps the most beautiful drive in the whole country. North along the R532 you travel by the side of the 35 kilometre-long **Blyde River Canyon**, a massive, winding sandstone gorge with a cliff-face plunging a kilometre, a sheer drop to the small Blyde river below, which can hardly be seen at many points. The canyon, which is within the overall Blyde River Nature Reserve, is home to a wide variety of birds, primates and antelope.

One and a half kilometres north of Graskop on a slight detour from the R532 and before the canyon proper, at its southern end, is **Pinnacle Rock**, a tall, jutting isolated rock standing amid steep forest slopes, and **God's Window**, another stunning viewpoint. Further along the same detour are the **Lisbon Falls**, which may easily be reached on foot from a nearby carpark. A very short drive beyond are the

Berlin Falls, an 80-metre waterfall plunging into a rocky pool.

Beyond that detour you rejoin the R532 proper and travel through 30 kilometres of dense forest before getting to the run-off for **Vaalhoek**, where you can turn onto a smaller road that will lead back to Pilgrim's Rest. But much better carry on up alongside the Blyde River canyon; along the road there are many excellent places to stop and view various parts of the canyon, including (at the northern end) the **Three Rondavels** and the flat-topped **Mariepskop** peak (1,944 metres). At the middle of the canyon is a very useful information centre and hiking trail starting-point, at **Bourke's Luck Potholes**, a series of strange, circular potholes eroded over centuries by the powerful force of the river. The 69-kilometre **Prospector's Trail** from the potholes to the Mac Mac forest station, near the falls, takes five days; telephone (01315) 41 058. The information centre also has a leaflet mapping out several short walks of a couple of hours.

The northern end of the canyon, off the R532, now has the **Blydepoort Resort** (telephone 01323 80 158) with restaurant, garage, supermarket and some accommodation.

There is the **Blyderivierspoort Hiking Trail**, which in its entirety is 56 kilometres, from God's Window through the canyon to the smaller, older resort of **Swadini**, which is off the R531, on the north-eastern part of the Blyde River Nature Reserve.

Following the R532 to its junction with the larger R36, you will find almost opposite the R532 the **Echo Caves** (08.00–17.00, daily), a large cave system once occupied by Stone Age man, as the many rock paintings indicate. One section, called Cannibal Cave, is a bat sanctuary and is closed to the public. Inside the caves it becomes clear how they gained their name; if tapped with a metal object the stalagmites and stalagtites will 'echo' the sound.

BARBERTON

Forty kilometres south of Nelspruit is **Barberton**, a pretty town set in the De Kaap valley. It has some interesting historical associations, little evidence of which remain today. In 1883 gold was discovered at Barberton and three years later it was the stock exchange centre of the country; but in 1886 the Barberton boom collapsed, and the Rand gold finds rapidly overshadowed Barberton's. A short walk from the town on the Sheba ridge overlooking Barberton are the heavily-overgrown ruins of **Eureka City**, built in 1885 to house miners working on the so-called Golden Quarry, which produced 519,565 ounces of gold before it was exhausted within 10 years. **Golden Quarry** yielded 50,000 ounces of gold from the first 13,000 tons of crushed ore, one of the highest yields in gold-mining history.

In the bar of the original **Phoenix Hotel**, built 1886, on Barberton's **Pilgrim Street**, one of the resident tarts was known as 'Cockney Liz'; legend has it that each night she would auction herself to the highest bidder. She later joined the Salvation Army. The gold ran out, the bubble burst, and the prospectors and hangers-on left as quickly as they had arrived. Today's Phoenix Hotel was raised in 1942 on the same site as the original.

Another of Barberton's other famous characters, the huge fig tree in **Coronation Park**, where it was alleged that Paul Kruger spoke to the local miners, has also gone. Of the old **Stock Exchange** on Pilgrim Street, only the facade remains.

A cableway runs between the town and neighbouring Swaziland, transporting not humans but asbestos and coal.

In front of the town hall there is a statue of the dog Jock, from the classic novel *Jock of the Bushveld* by Percy Fitzpatrick, a hunter, explorer and writer who trekked across much of this region at the turn of the century. By the time you leave this part of South Africa you will be thoroughly sick and tired of this wretched dog, who pops up everywhere and on everything.

On the corner of Lee and Judge Streets is a fine example of a **blockhouse**, a tiny fortified box of the type erected in thousands across South Africa during the 1899–1902 Second South African war. The blockhouses were intended to be strongpoints from which a small unit could hold off raiding Boer commandos.

South of Barberton on the R40 is the 56,000-hectare **Songimvelo Nature Reserve**, via the Saddleback Pass; the reserve has a wide range of large game and an expensive though luxurious lodge; telephone (0134) 830 800.

Northern Province

This province shares borders with Botswana, Zimbabwe and Mozambique, right at the top right-hand corner of the country. Formerly the **Northern Transvaal**, its major towns are (heading north) **Potgietersrus**, **Pietersburg** (the capital), **Louis Trichardt** and **Messina**, all on the N1 highway. Pietersburg is 300 kilometres from Johannesburg; its telephone prefix is **0152**. Its eastern border is formed by the Kruger Park.

The major towns are not that interesting; but there are some splendid nature reserves and some fascinating indigenous cultural aspects to this rather remote, little-visited region.

If travelling up from Mpumalanga, either through Kruger Park or further inland, from Blyde River canyon, you should try to visit **Phalaborwa**, just outside the Kruger Park. The town itself was created in the 1950s and is uninteresting, but outside it is Africa's greatest open-cast copper mine, which can be viewed from above. The whole area around Phalaborwa is rich in various mineral and phosphate deposits.

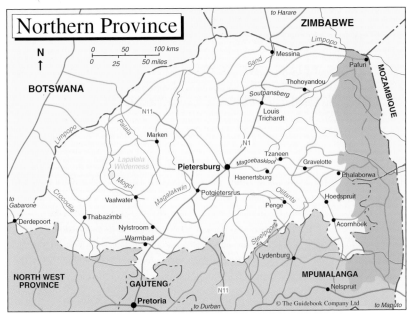

From Phalaborwa head west on the R71 to **Gravelotte**, and then take a small road to **Leydsdorp**, a ghostly remnant of a former gold-rush town in the centre of the Murchison Range of mountains. A hundred metres off the road linking the two is a strange, huge, **baobab** tree, whose trunk is hollowed-out; it once was used as a bar where drinks were served (room for up to a dozen customers at a time) to gold miners. Leydsdorp itself is in the process of being restored. Return to Gravelotte and continue north along the R71 until you reach the junction with the R529; turn right onto the R529 and head 40 kilometres (beyond the town of **La Cotte**) to the **Hans Merensky Dam Nature Reserve** (telephone 015 386 8633), set within the former 'homeland' of Gazankulu, a very deprived area. The Hans Merensky has a great variety of game including sable, giraffe and blue wildebeest, and three walking trails, including a three-day Giraffe Trail on almost no gradients.

An alternative to heading north from Leydsdorp is to continue on the dirt roads to **Ofcolaco**, and from there to a small settlement called **The Downs**, through the foothills of this part of the Transvaal Drakensberg, the site of the relatively new forest and grassland **Lekgalameetse Nature Reserve**, which has accommodation and hiking trails; telephone (0152302) and ask for 1514. If you go through the reserve you will eventually join the R37, where you should turn right and head for Pietersburg.

From the Hans Merensky return along the R529 and at the junction, turn right onto the R71, which will take you to Tzaneen, a thriving town and the jumping-off point for many outdoor activities in the area. Immediately north of Tzaneen (on the R36) is the **Fanie Botha Dam Nature Reserve**, which now officially seems to be called the **Tzaneen Dam Nature Reserve**—presumably because 'Fanie' (Stephanus) Botha, minister of forestry and water from 1968 to1976, is regarded as no longer politically kosher. North of Tzaneen on the R36 you will reach Duiwelskloof, which has a small holiday resort and four walking trails; telephone (0152) 309 9651. Twenty eight kilometres beyond **Duiwelskloof** on the R36 watch for signposts for the Modjadji Cycad Forest, wherein resides the Modjadji Rain Queen, a reclusive Queen who inherits the title and is supposedly able to conjure up rainfall. The forest is covered with a rare cycad (see **Flora and Fauna**, page 108); it's well worth a visit.

Return south to Tzaneen and from there take the R71 west through the winding mountains of the **Magoebaskloof**, to the village of **Haenertsburg**, where the Letaba River enters the **Ebenezer Dam Nature Reserve**. This is a beautiful area, popular for boating and angling (you will need a fishing licence if over 16—available from the magistrate's office on Morgan Street, Tzaneen, telephone 0152 307 3770). South of Haenertsburg is the **Wolkberg Wilderness** area, 19,000 hectares of hiking trails and camping sites; no accommodation facilities; telephone the directorate of nature and environmental conservation for details, on (0152) 276 1303.

For a more strenuous hike, try the the Woodbush and De Hoek Forest areas, with two trails starting and ending at the De Hoek Forest Station north of the Ebenezer Dam; telephone (01315) 41 058.

From Haenertsburg it's about 60 kilometres west to Pietersburg, which has little to detain you. The **Civic Plaza and Square** has some pleasant landscaped gardens to rest in. Nearby the city is **Zion City Moria**, the national headquarters of the Zion Christian Church, the largest of some 2,000 evangelical Christian churches, whose adherents are almost entirely from the black population. At Zion City more than 1m pilgrims gather every Easter.

Forty three kilometres south on the N1 from Pietersburg is **Potgietersrus**, which today is an uneasy town, following some nasty racist trouble in 1996; several local white racists attempted to prevent black children from attending a previously whites-only secondary school. Further south down the N1 towards Joburg are the even duller towns of **Nylstroom** and **Warmbad** (which has some mineral springs).

So from Potgietersrus drive north-west for about 150 kilometres to find the 20,000 hectare **Lapalala Wilderness Game Reserve**, in the **Waterberg** range of mountains, through which runs the **Palala River**, heavy with hungry crocodiles. It has rhino, wildebeest, zebra and other game but is particularly good for walking and camping; there are some self-catering camps. Next door is a large private game reserve, **Touchstone Game Ranch**; telephone (01536) 50 230, with horse riding, hiking and guided tours.

From there it's possible to drive on dirt roads south-west to join the R517 at **Vaalwater**; turn right and head along the R517 to where the road splits after 90km, whereupon take the R510 south-west again to **Thabazimbi**, an iron-ore rich area, and where there is an annual **Game Festival and Auction**; telephone the Thabazimbi tourist office to find out the date of the next one (*see* PUBLICITY ASSOCIATION APPENDIX, *page 317*). Around Thabazimbi are a couple of smaller game reserves, the **Ben Alberts Nature Reserve** and the relatively new **Marakele National Park**, 20 kilometres north-east of Thabazimbi. East of Thabazimbi on the R571/R516 roads there is also the **Mabula Private Game Reserve** (telephone 011 883 7140 for details and accommodation; it's part of the Protea chain, *see* HOTELS *page 278*). If you carry on driving down the R510 in a southerly direction you will eventually end up close to **Sun City** and the **Pilansberg National Park**, in North-West Province.

In the far north of this province is the **Soutpansberg** ('salt pan mountains') range, with Louis Trichardt at their centre on the N1 highway. The Soutpansberg— which stretch about 130 kilometres from west to east—get their name from the brine spring which surfaces at their western end. Famous for the baobab trees that dot the northern, hotter and drier area, the region normally has good rainfall and is heavily forested. South of Louis Trichardt is the **Ben Lavin Nature Reserve**, which has driving and walking trails, bird-watching and a number of different antelope species; telephone (01551) 3834. Around Soutpansberg mountain itself are circular hiking trails, from the **Hangklip Forest Station** and the **Entabeni Forest**; call Louis Trichardt publicity association for further details.

The Soutpansberg are held sacred by the **Venda** people, who have long populated this area. (For more on the Venda see the special topic on the country's different peoples, page 65). The Venda still practice much of their traditional ways, including divination, magic, ritual murder—to obtain body parts for the preparation of *muti* (magical medicine)—and witchburning, the latter two of which of course are illegal under South African law. They also revere **Lake Fundudzi**, surrounded by the **Thathe Vondo** sacred forest, as being the home of their most important deity, the Python God. It's prohibited—and certainly inadvisable—to visit the lake without permission, which may be obtainable, if you call the Venda tourist office (see relevant appendix for the telephone number, *page 316*), which is located in **Thohoyandou**, east of Louis Trichardt on the R524. You can however walk through the Thathe Vondo forest.

Thohoyandou is not an attractive town, having been artificially created to be the capital of the 'independent homeland' of Venda, now reintegrated into South Africa. For exploring any of this area it is best to employ a trained local guide, who will be relatively inexpensive; the Venda tourist office will be happy to help supply one.

There are a couple of hot mineral spring resorts close to Thohoyandou, **Sagole Spa** and **Mphephu Hot Springs**, both with accommodation that can be booked through the Venda tourist office.

Further north, **Messina** is the last South African town before the Zimbabwe border, 16 kilometres away. The landscape is wild, almost untouched, and antelope are to be found everywhere. It's also a large copper-mining centre, and the true home of the baobab tree. In the **Messina Nature Reserve**—telephone (01553) 3235—6 kilometres south of the town, are some particularly fine specimens, some thought to be several thousand years old; one giant is 25 metres tall, with a circumference of 16 metres.

WHERE LAW THREATENS JUSTICE

It's time to talk law. Where other regimes have no difficulty tyrannizing their citizens under the cloak of constitutions guaranteeing universal human rights, South Africa's white rulers have been unusually conscientious about securing statutory authority for their abuses. When a right, even a birthright, such as citizenship, is to be annulled, it is always done with a law. Most whites are uncomprehending of the argument that law is brought into disrepute when it is used to destroy habeas corpus, the presumption of innocence, equality before the law, and various other basic freedoms. Law is law. It's the principle of order and therefore of civilization, the antithesis advanced by the white man to what he knows as a matter of tribal lore, his own, to be Africa's fundamental thesis: anarchy. Excessive liberty, in his view, is what threatens civilization; law is what preserves it. The opposing view that law might preserve liberty is thus held to be a contradiction; in Africa, a promise of surrender. On this basis it has been possible to build apartheid not simply as the sum of various kinds of segregation, or the disenfranchisement of the major-

In the 1980s, police dealt brutally with demonstrators

During apartheid, squatter camps witnessed almost daily clashes

ity, but as a comprehensive system of racial dominance. A decade after the South African authorities announced their intention to move away from 'hurtful and unnecessary discrimination,' I thought I would get the feel of the basic statutes by holding them in my hands as you might if you were apprizing an eggplant or a melon. Some laws, especially those reserving the best industrial jobs for whites, had been repealed. Others, such as the Prohibition of Mixed Marriages Act, seemed destined for repeal as part of a calculated effort to lower the level of ignominy attaching to the system. I wanted to feel, literally to weigh, what remained.

What remained weighed slightly more than 10 pounds when I stepped on a scale with an up-to-date volume of all the laws in South Africa that relate specifically to blacks—laws, that is, that can normally be broken only by blacks (or by persons of other racial groups only when they interfere with the state's master plan for blacks). The figure of 10 pounds had to be halved immediately because the volume of 4,500 pages contained both the Afrikaans and English versions of 64 basic statutes that regulate the lives of blacks.

These then amounted to about 2,250 closely printed pages, weighing about 5 pounds. But the small print that followed the statutes indicated that they had given rise to some 2,000 regulations, adding 3 pounds at least. These, in turn, would have given rise to hundreds or maybe thousands of official circulars that were not in the public domain but were treated as law by the officials who regulate blacks. And that was only the racial law for blacks. There were also laws, regulations and circulars for coloreds and Indians, running to hundreds of additional pages and another couple of pounds. And there were the laws, regulations and circulars relating to the administration of the Group Areas Act, the basic statute guaranteeing absolute residential segregation. Gathering all the materials for a precise weighing was more than I could manage; but the basic corpus of South African racial law still ran to more than 3,000 pages, and when all the regulations and circulars were added in, its dead weight was bound to be well over 10 pounds. Apartheid was not wasting away. For argument's sake, there was enough of it left to give someone a concussion. [...]

If this structure were suddenly dismantled, if whites stopped regulating black lives, there would still be migrant workers by the hundreds of thousands in South Africa and millions of impoverished blacks. There would still be wealthy suburbs, huge ranches, black townships, and squalid rural areas. But it would then be possible to think of the society as a whole and talk rationally about its needs. Apartheid ensures that the language for such a discussion hardly exists. It does so for its own cunning reasons. Once you think of the society as a whole, it is impossible not to think of the distribution of land— 50,000 white farmers have 12 times as much land for cultivation and grazing as 14 million rural blacks—or of the need to relieve the pressure in those portions of the countryside that have been systematically turned into catchment areas for surplus black population.

Joseph Lelyveld, Move Your Shadow: 1986

Provinces Part Three

North-West

Apart from one or two spots, this is a desperately dull corner of South Africa. North-West province borders Botswana to the north; Northern Cape province to the west; the Free State to the south; and on its eastern side is Gauteng and the Northern province. The problem is that there isn't a single town in which it's worth spending more than a couple of hours.

The countryside—apart from the area around the **Pilansberg National Park**—is generally flat, the *platteland* where arable farmers eke out a living producing *mealies* (maize corn) and sunflower oil, and herds of cattle nibble at miserably scrubby pasture. Spend a few days here amid the numbing emptiness, and you begin to understand why **Zeerust**, a one-horse farming town close to the provincial capital of **Mmabatho**, stages an annual *mampoer* festival, *mampoer* being a wickedly potent home-brewed peach, apricot and other fruit liquor. The only surprise is that it isn't a weekly event.

RUSTENBURG

About 120 kilometres west of Pretoria on the R27 is **Rustenburg**, centre of the largest platinum producing area in the world. An indication of the sort of town Rustenburg is can perhaps be obtained from a leaflet obtainable from the local tourist information office. Among the highlights of the town it identifies a statue of a Voortrekker girl, on Plein Street, which 'symbolizes the light of Christian civilization brought to this area by the Voortrekkers.' A civilization which included shooting people if they didn't want to give up their land.

Rustenburg is also the spot where **Paul Kruger** farmed, until he went into exile in 1902. The statue of Kruger in front of the town hall was sculpted by the Frenchman Jean Jacques Archard. It was originally intended for Pretoria but for some reason Jan Smuts—no mean ego himself—had it placed in Rustenburg in 1921, perhaps because he thought Pretoria already had more than its fair share of Kruger memorabilia. You can visit **Boekenhoutfontein**, Kruger's farm (10.00–17.00, Tuesday–Sunday, telephone 0142 733 199), which is north-west of Rustenburg.

Fortunately Rustenburg also possesses a very good **Nature Reserve**, a marsh and woodland area with a two-day 21 kilometres hiking trail, with overnight accommodation in basic huts (telephone 0142 31050). The reserve, which is at the

Sun City

western end of the Magaliesberg range, has a variety of antelope, including sable, as well as eagles, vultures and other bird life. It's south of the town and is well sign-posted.

South-west of Rustenburg (via the N4 and then the R52) is **Lichtenburg**, another dusty farming town but one which has some attraction for those interested in the Anglo-Boer war, in the shape of the **Town Museum** (10.00–12.00 13.00–17.00 Tuesday–Friday, 10.00–13.00 Saturday), with memorabilia and gear that once belonged to perhaps the best General the Boers possessed, the *bittereinder* Koos de la Rey. North-east of Lichtenburg is a 6,000 hectare **Nature Reserve**, telephone (01441) 22 818, with a few rare species such as pygmy hippo and sable; there's a camp site. About 80 kilometres along the R47 south-west of Lichtenburg is an interesting and unusual inland wetland reserve, the **Barberspan Nature Reserve**, telephone (0144322) 1202, which also has a camp site. Barberspan has a myriad of waterbirds, including flamingos, ibis, geese, ducks and storks.

PILANSBERG

Fifty kilometres north of Rustenburg is **Sun City**, the creation of one of South Africa's larger-than-life entrepreneurs, **Sol Kerzner**. Sun City acquired a notoriety in the days of apartheid. It was deliberately placed in the supposedly independent 'homeland' of Boputhatswana, which meant that Kerzner's large hotel complex could get away with all kinds of things—such as gambling, porn movies, and interracial mingling—not permitted in South Africa proper. A convenient short drive from Joburg and Pretoria, it neatly allowed white South Africans to zip up for a weekend's illicit flirtation with softcore naughtiness. **Sun City** is the spiritual core of what was formerly Boputhatswana, one of the supposedly independent black 'homelands'. It's astonishing how many tourists are sucked into staying at this slot-machine soft-porn mockery of human happiness, plonked in the middle of a dumping-ground of tens of thousands black South Africans, people who were deemed 'surplus' to the requirements of white society.

The Lost City complex at Sun City

Now that 'Bop' has disappeared, and South Africans can get hard-core by the bucketload, hand-crafted and with doorstep delivery, the raison d'etre for Sun City (and the other Sun casino-hotels dotted around the former homelands) has disappeared. Financially, these are beginning to look like expensive follies; even at the height of summer Sun City's casinos are like ghost towns. You don't have to be a puritan to despise Sun City. It's not what it does, so much as how it started doing it, that makes one's flesh creep.

Miss World competition at Sun City

But surrounding Sun City is one of the country's best National Parks, the 50,000 hectare **Pilansberg**, set within a large range of extinct volcanoes. The park has excellent accommodation (see National Parks' appendix, page 305) and a good road system of some 100 kilometres, enabling the visitor a good chance of seeing a large amount of game, including not only the 'big five' but also giraffe, zebra, antelope of all kinds, hippos and 300 different species of birds.

THE SPECTACULAR GROWTH OF A CITY

At first, few international observers took the slow-moving Transvaal mining industry particularly seriously—and why should they have? In 1886, the year that the Rand was discovered, the new industry produced only 0.16 per cent of the world's gold output and was still clearly dwarfed by its more formidable Australian and American rivals. By 1898, however, the new giant was already firmly on its feet, without serious challengers, and producing no less than 27 per cent of the world's gold. By 1913 the Witwatersrand mining colossus bestrode the economic world, producing no less than 40 per cent of the world's gold output. Highly visible from even the most far-flung of financial outposts, this imposing new profile of profit captured the attention and imagination of a whole generation of European capitalists[...]

This dramatic shift, as the Transvaal abruptly transferred its economic weight from its agricultural to its industrial leg over a brief period of 30 years, transformed the Witwatersrand and, in time, the whole of southern Africa. For a length of some 40 miles along the line of reef, from Springs in the east to Krugersdorp in the west, the accommodating ridges and depressions of the Witwatersrand became pock-marked with all the signs of an industrial revolution—mining headgear, ore dumps, battery stamps, reduction works, slimes dams and the frayed ends of railway lines. Besides, and in between these starker thickets of technology, the same revolution also spawned a series of urban sponges—the mine compounds and towns—that were called upon to absorb the ever-increasing numbers of black and white miners who made their way to the new goldfields at the turn of the century. And, in the midst of all of these developments, almost exactly half-way along the new line of the reef outcrop, lay the social, political and economic nerve centre of the new order—Johannesburg.

Fathered by gold and mothered by money, Johannesburg's impatient and demanding parents scarcely allowed their charge time to pause in infancy or linger in adolescence before pushing it out onto the streets of the economic world. The tented diggers' camps of the '80s soon gave way to the corrugated iron structures of the mining town of the mid-'90s, and then to the more substantial brick buildings of an industrial city with suburban homes during the first decade of the 20th century. By 1896 the 3,000 diggers of the original mining camp were lost in a town of 100,000 residents and, by 1914, these 100,000 were in turn becoming harder to find in a city with over a quarter of a million inhabitants. The inexorable pressure exerted by people, houses, shops, offices and factories pushed back the municipal boundaries from 5 square miles in 1898, to 9 square miles in 1901, and then—more ambitiously still—to an enormous 82 square miles in 1903.

Given the company that the parents kept, it is scarcely surprising that the child lost its innocence at an early age. With white workers ranged against black, skilled miners against the mine owners and the Randlords against the state, Johannesburg was racked by class conflict during much of this period. By the outbreak of the First World War the city had been chosen as the centre of an unsuccessful attempted uprising against the government of the day, been occupied by the army of an invading Imperial power, and subjected to at least three bouts of such serious industrial unrest that troops had to be called in to help maintain order. It was these turbulent events, the city's cosmopolitan immigrant population and the all-consuming worship of wealth which, in 1910, prompted the visiting Australian journalist, Ambrose Pratt, to comment: 'Ancient Nineveh and Babylon have been revived. Johannesburg is their 20th century prototype. It is a city of unbridled squander and unfathomable squalor.'

Charles van Onselen: New Babylon: 1982

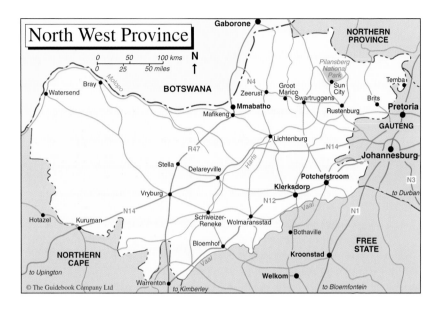

Doubling back from Sun City to Rustenburg, if you take the N4 heading west to Zeerust, and then from Zeerust north towards Gaborone, you will find a new, even larger reserve, the 75,000 hectare **Madikwe Game Reserve**, which is 300 kilometres from Johannesburg and 28 kilometres from the South African-Botswana border. Under the auspices of the North-West Parks authority, Madikwe now has some (rather expensive) private lodges and is currently being stocked with animals taken from other reserves around the country. Since 1990 some 10,000 animals, from 27 different species, have been introduced into the reserve; by the time the relocation programme is completed, there will be about 31,000 animals. It's a major, laudable project; but for the next few years it's not going to be a good place to go to if you want to see animals. In 1996 even game such as zebra and impala, which happily let vehicles approach in other such parks, scampered away at Madikwe; the animals were very skittish and will need a few years to get used to visitors. In fact, even the rangers seem bored; when I visited in early 1996 the most laid-back game to be spotted was a group of three rangers enjoying an after-dark puff of *dagga*.

MMABATHO AND MAFIKENG

Three hundred kilometres west of Joburg—drive from Rustenburg along the R27, passing through Groot Marico and Zeerust, which are of interest only because the writer Herman Bosman set so many of his short stories there—are the twin towns of **Mmabatho** and **Mafikeng**, which are three kilometres apart. Not even its admirers—there may be as many as a dozen—could describe Mmabatho as anything but ugly. Mafikeng is slightly less of a waste of time, but only because of its historical associations (Mmabatho has none). Better known as Mafeking, it was one of the three places besieged by the Boers in the 1899–1902 war with Britain. If you really must visit Mmabatho and Mafikeng, there are only two places to see, one in each: **Mega City** is a massive shopping arcade at Mmabatho where you can find some interesting local craftwork; at Mafikeng, there is a tired museum in the town centre; it has some dusty remains of the October 1899–May 1890 siege, and a few snaps of **Colonel Baden-Powell**, who led the defence. Boy scout fanatics will no doubt wish to pay homage. Thirty one kilometres from Mafikeng is the **Wondergat** (Wonderhole), a 100-metre deep and 70-metre-wide sinkhole, filled with clear water. Legend has it that it was used as a place of execution by the Ndebele in the 19th century.

Then there is **Potchefstroom**, whose strongest point is that it's only about 80 kilometres south-west of Joburg. For Potchefstroom was invented the ancient joke: 'What's the difference between X (in this case, Potchefstroom) and yoghurt? Yoghurt has an active culture.' Actually, 'Potch' (as locals call it) has a sort of shuffling culture, all of it thoroughly Afrikaans. On the N12, half-way between Joburg and Potch is a strange 24-metre high concrete, stone and steel structure, on the top of which is a 'flame of freedom' in burnished copper. This is the **Danie Theron memorial**, placed on the spot where he was killed in October 1900 while fighting off a British unit, single-handed, so the story goes. Theron gained a certain notoriety in 1899 by thrashing W F Monypenny, editor of the *Johannesburg Star* newspaper, for writing a supposedly insulting article about the Boers. When the war started Theron formed a unit of armed young cyclists, called the Wielrijders Rapportgangers; he deserves immortality for that alone.

In Potch itself, the **Potchefstroom Museum** is yet another dedicated to the Voortrekkers; it has an original waggon from the battle of Blood River (08.30–16.30 Mon-Fri). The Old Fort (08.30–16.30, Monday–Friday) is the site of a siege of British forces in the first South African War, when after a very short campaign the British caved in. **President Pretorius Museum** (10.00–13.00 and 14.00–17.00 Monday–Friday, 09.00–12.45 Saturday, 14.30–17.00 Sunday), was built in 1868 by the first president of the South African Republic. The Totius House Museum (10.00–13.00 and 14.00–1.00 Monday–Friday, 09.00–12.45 Saturday, 14.30–17.00 Sunday), was the former home of the Afrikaans poet J D du Toit, who translated the Bible into Afrikaans.

Stay on the N12 going south and head for Kimberley, a town that has a completely unjustifiable reputation for being boring. It has hidden depths.

STARING INTO THE ABYSS

As the [Kimberley] mine is one of the most remarkable spots on the face of the earth I will endeavour to explain it with some minuteness.[...]

The Colesberg hill is in fact hardly a hill at all—what little summit may once have entitled it to the name having been cut off. On reaching the spot by one of the streets from the square you see no hill but are called upon to rise over a mound, which is circular and looks to be no more than the debris of the mine though it is in fact the remainder of the slight natural ascent. It is but a few feet high and on getting to the top you look down into a huge hole. This is the Kimberley mine. You immediately feel that it is the largest and most complete hole ever made by human agency.

At Du Toit's Pan and Bultfontein [other excavations] the works are scattered. Here everything is so gathered together and collected that it is not at first easy to understand that the hole should contain the operations of a large number of separate speculators. It is so completely one that you are driven at first to think that it must be the property of one firm—or at any rate be entrusted to the management of one director. It is very far from being so. In the pit beneath your feet, hard as it is at first to your imagination to separate it into various enterprises, the persons making or marring their fortunes have as little connection with each other as have the different banking firms in Lombard Street.[...]

You are told that the pit has a surface area of 9 acres; but for your purposes as you will care little for diamondiferous or non-diamondiferous soil, the aperture really covers 12 acres. The slope of the reef around the diamond soil has forced itself back over an increased surface as the mine has become deeper.[...]

You stand upon the marge and there, suddenly, beneath your feet lies the entirety of the Kimberley mine, so open, so manifest, and so uncovered that if your eyes were good enough you might examine the separate operations of each of the three or four thousand human beings who are at work there. It looks to be so steep down there that there can be no way to the bottom other than the aerial contrivances which I will presently endeavour to explain. It is as though you were looking into a vast bowl, the sides of which are smooth as should be the sides of a bowl, while round the bottom are various marvellous incrustations among which ants are working with all the usual energy of the ant-tribe. And these incrustations are not simply at the bottom, but come up the curves and slopes of the bowl irregularly—half-way up in perhaps one place, while on another side they are confined quite to the lower deep[...]

But though there are but 408 claims there are subdivisions in regard to property very much more minute. There are shares held by individuals as small as one-sixteenth of a claim. The total property is in fact divided into 514 portions, the amount of which of course varies extremely. Every master miner pays 10 shillings a month to the Government for the privilege of working whether he own a claim or only a portion of a claim. In working this the number of men employed differs very much from time to time. When I was there the mine was very full, and there were probably almost 4,000 men in it and as many more employed above on the stuff. When the 'blue' [diamondiferous soil] has come up and been deposited in the great wooden boxes at the top it is then lowered by its own weight into cart, and carried of to the 'ground' of the proprietor. Every diamond digger is obliged to have a space of ground somewhere round the town—as near his whim as he can get it—to which his stuff is carted and then laid out to crumble and decompose. This may occupy weeks, but the time depends on what may be the fall of rain. If there be no rain, it must be watered—at a very considerable expense. It is then brought to the washing, and is first put into a round puddling trough where it is broken up and converted into mud by stationary rakes which work upon the stuff as the trough goes round. The stones of course fall to the bottom, and as diamonds are the heaviest of stones they fall with the others. [...]

I must add also that a visitor to Kimberley should if possible take an opportunity of looking down upon the mine by moonlight. It is a weird and wonderful sight, and may also be called sublime in its peculiar strangeness.

Anthony Trollope: South Africa: 1877

Northern Cape

The Northern Cape is by far the biggest province; it's also the most sparsely populated, with just 1.9 per cent of South Africa's total population. It has a remarkable beauty all its own; a combination of massive, empty space, and an enduring silence, broken only by the gusting wind and the occasional bird. Few tourists bother to come here, which makes it even more of a delight.

KIMBERLEY

Four hundred and nintey-six kilometres along the N12, south-west of Johannesburg, brings you to Kimberley, capital of this province; its telephone prefix is **0531**. Kimberley's airport is 8 kilometres from the centre, and its railway station, on Florence Street, is a 10-minute walk from the centre.

On his deathbed Cecil Rhodes is supposed to have said: 'So little done, so much left to do.' It's a fitting epitaph for Kimberley, perhaps the most overlooked city in the whole of South Africa. There's always something else to be discovered in Kimberley; ignore the modern, ugly centre and search the tucked-away corners, which have some unique glories.

You really ought to try to see inside the **Kimberley Club**, on Du Toitspan Road. Although it's a members' only establishment, it now also takes non-members on a B&B basis (see **Hotels**, page 285). The club was founded in August 1881 by senior diggers and diamond dealers who wanted a refuge from the rowdy, dusty bars and pubs that sprang up near the 'Big Hole', as the Colesberg diamond workings quickly became known. Initial membership was limited to 250; today it's more than 500. Rhodes, still then only 28 years old, was a key figure in forming the club; among the founder members was Rhodes' friend and political stooge, Leander Starr Jameson, and another diamond magnate, Barney Barnato. In its early days it was said of the club that it held more millionaires per square foot than any other place in the world. Sadly, the original building burned down in 1886. It was rebuilt in 1887, only to be gutted by fire yet again, in 1895. The kitchen escaped on that occasion—and meals were being served three days after the fire. The third club was finished in 1896. Among the many historically interesting pieces inside the club are a weighing chair, donated by Lord Randolph Churchill (father of Winston Churchill) in 1892, which is in the lounge on the ground floor; a portrait of Rhodes painted by Hubert Herkomer in 1898; much late 19th-century furniture imported from London; and a well-preserved Spandau machine-gun from the World War I, which stands, almost on guard it seems, in the entrance foyer. Telephone 24 224 or 28 567 to arrange a visit.

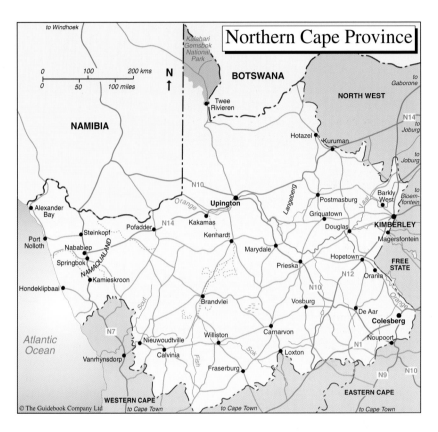

The **Big Hole**, situated in the well-designed 'living history' **Kimberley Mine Museum** (on Tucker Street, 08.00–18.00, daily, telephone 31 557), a short distance from the city centre, should not be missed. Until you see its vastness—the opencast workings went down 400 metres, though underground workings continued for another 900 metres; it covers 17 hectares—you cannot really comprehend what passions must have driven the early white and black miners who flocked there. Before it ceased being worked, on 14 August 1914, 22.5 million tonnes of earth and rocks were shovelled from its bowels, yielding 2,722kg, or 14.5 million carats, of diamonds. Next to the Big Hole are three cocopans containing broken glass weighing the same as the excavated diamonds; it's a very graphic method of drawing the contrast between effort and gain.

The large museum site has lots of good exhibits, including Barney Barnato's original boxing academy, a 1901 ballroom, a diamond exhibition (including the

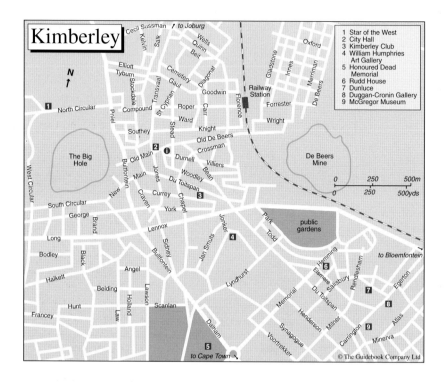

'Eureka', the diamond which started the ball rolling, and the '616', the world's largest uncut diamond, so called because its carat weight is 616, and 616 is coincidentally also the De Beers PO Box number in Kimberley), plus a restaurant and cafe. There is also an oddly moving letter from Erasmus Stephanus Jacobs, who found the 'Eureka' (first known as the 'O'Reilly'). The letter is dated 9 August 1932, when Jacobs was in his 82nd year. He writes that he is living in destitution; and that his discovery has not benefitted him at all, except for a charitable donation of £30 in 1920.

It's very easy to get to the Big Hole: a tram operates daily between the Hole and City Hall (09.00–16.15, daily, tickets sold on the tram). The tram passes by a number of historical sites, including a stop at the **Star of the West**, Kimberley's oldest pub.

Elsewhere in Kimberley you should make an effort to visit the excellent **McGregor Museum** (2 Egerton Road, 09.00–17.00 Monday–Saturday, 14.00–17.00 Sunday, telephone 32 645/6). This was built by Rhodes in 1897 as a sanatorium; he lived in two quite spartan rooms on the ground floor during the Kimberley siege in the Second South African war. It has some interesting natural history displays but the most interesting are those relating to the siege. It's also a magnificent building, both internally and externally, with a fine central staircase.

The **Duggan-Cronin Gallery**, also on Egerton Road (09.00–17.00 Monday–Friday, 09.00–13.00, 14.00–17.00 Saturday, and 14.00–17.00 Sunday), is a superb collection of more than 8,000 photographs of the culture and lifestyles of indigenous South African people, the core of which were taken by Alfred Martin Duggan-Cronin between 1919 and 1939.

Another excellent, little-known spot is the **William Humphries Art Gallery**, which has some very fine South African and European works; it's in the Civic Centre on Cullinan Crescent (10.00–13.00 and 14.00–17.00, Monday–Saturday, 14.00–17.00 Sunday, telephone 811 724/5).

There are also some fine late 19th-century buildings, embedded in the rock of modern eye-taxing architecture. The **City Hall** (corner of Old Main Street and Transvaal Road) was completed in 1899; in the 1899–90 siege it was used as a ration distribution-centre. **Rudd House**, 5–7 Loch Road (viewing by appointment only, telephone 32 645/6), is now under the auspices of the McGregor Museum; it was owned by one of the original diamond magnates and is now being restored to its former state. **Dunluce**, an elegant building, was built in 1897; on Lodge Road, it can be visited by appointment during weekdays, through the offices of the McGregor Museum. Kimberley was also long the centre for flying training in South Africa. There is a **Memorial to the Pioneers of Aviation** 3.5 kilometres from the airport, on General van der Spuy Drive (09.00–13.00, 14.00–17.00, Monday–Saturday, and 14.00–17.00 Sunday, telephone 32 645/6); it's on the site of the continent's first flying school, established in 1912. There is also a **Museum** dedicated to one of the country's most famous flying units, **Group 22**, on Scanlan Street; viewing by appointment only, telephone 811 303 or 612 452.

One oddity is the **Halfway House Inn**, which claims to be the only drive-in pub in the world; on 229 Du Toitspan Road.

You can tour a working diamond mine, the **Bultfontein Mine**, on Molyneux Road; surface tours are at 09.00 and 11.00, Monday–Friday; underground tours (by appointment only) at 08.00, Monday–Friday (except Tuesday); telephone 29 651 or 32 855 after office hours. There is a minimum age of eight for surface tours, and of 16 for underground tours.

You might care to pay your respects to **Sol Plaatje**, one of the founders of the ANC, who for many years lived in Kimberley; his house, which in 1996 was being restored, is in the grounds of a nursery school on **Angel Street**; a Tswana-language library is likely to be one of its features. Plaatje is buried nearby.

There is a fairly monstrous sandstone monument, called the **Honoured Dead**

Impala at a watering hole

Memorial, (intersections of Memorial, Dalham and Oliver Roads), dedicated to those who died during the 124-day siege at the start of the 1899–1902 war; beneath it is 'Long Cecil', a heavy artillery piece commissioned by Rhodes during the siege in order to reply to the Boers' 'Long Tom'. A more interesting monument (because it commemorates soldiers largely forgotten) is the **Square Hill Memorial** (corner of Lennox and Du Toitspan Roads), which stands in honour of the members of the Kimberley Cape Coloured Corps who died in the World War I.

AROUND KIMBERLEY

South Africa is littered with battlefields, but perhaps the most fascinating is **Magersfontein**, 31.5 kilometres south-west of Kimberley, off the N12 highway. At midnight on 10 December 1899 the flower of the British army, the Highland Brigade, marched north towards the 60-metre-high hill called Magersfontein. Through a violent storm 4,000 men struggled across the flat plain, the thorny, thickly-bunched mimosa bushes tugging at their every step, heading to what they believed was a lightly-defended position, en route to relieve the besieged Kimberley. By early morning they had come within point-blank range of Magersfontein's base. One of the most able Boer generals, De La Rey, had dug an extended line of trenches at the base of the hill, well-hidden and following its winding course. This was a novel approach for the Boers, who normally used hit-and-run guerilla tactics.

When the Highlanders came within 100 metres of the trenches, the Boers opened fire. In the course of the next 24 hours, until the British troops could effect a withdrawal, the Boers inflicted a tremendous defeat. British losses were more than 1,000 men killed and wounded; the Boers lost a quarter of that figure.

If you drive to the top of Magersfontein and look south, there is a most remarkable sight; at the base of the hill can clearly be seen the original trench line, almost untouched after nearly 100 years. The area has a sombre atmosphere. Nearby the battlefield is an ugly monument to the Boer dead; there is a memorial to the British fallen on a nearby hill. In the Boer memorial site there is a single stone on which is engraved the simple sentence: 'A young Scottish bugler who died of wounds and was buried here by the burghers.'

Thirty-two kilometres north-west of Kimberley on the R31 towards **Barkly West** (where working alluvial diamond diggings can be visited) is **Nooitgedacht**, an important geological site where you can see Ice Age lava, dating some 2.5 million years, formed into large 'pavements', on some of which are San rock carvings. At **Dreikopseiland** there are other lava pavements in the Riet River, with more than 3,000 Stone Age abstract engravings, which are submerged when the river is in flood; appointments to visit this site must be made through the McGregor Museum in Kimberley (telephone 32 645).

Fifty kilometres north-west of Kimberley, also on the R31, is the **Vaalbos National Park** (see **National Parks appendix** on page 306 for details). If you continue heading west you will arrive at **Postmasburg**, a centre of a district for asbestos mining. 20 kilometres south-west of Postmasburg (on the R383) you might be lucky enough to hear a very unusual sound at an area known as Witsand, a region of high, white sandy dunes in the Langeberg range, some 12 kilometres long and three kilometres wide; in dry weather, when the wind blows, there is sometimes an uncanny moaning or even roaring sound which seems to emanate directly from the dunes.

South of Postmasburg on the R386 is **Griquatown**, once the capital of an independent state, Griqualand, led by the Griqua leader, Nicolaas Waterboer, until (following the diamond rush) it came under British control. Today it's a small trading town; there are San rock paintings at Pannetjie five kilometres outside the town. **Kuruman**, some 100 kilometres north of Postmasburg, is a remarkable spot. In the midst of one of the country's driest areas, Kuruman has a permanent supply of water from a natural underground spring called Gasegonyane (meaning 'little water calabash'). More popularly known as **The Eye**, this spring produces 20–30 million litres of pure spring water every day. The Scottish missionary Robert Moffat, the first person to translate the Bible into Tswana, lived in Kuruman between 1820 and 1870; his church (built 1838) still stands and services are regularly held there.

The Eye, which is the source of the Kuruman River, is on Main Street and may be visited between 06.00–20.00 (telephone 05373 30 343). It's still believed to be the largest natural fountain in the southern hemisphere, and a nearby pool is home to an enormous amount of fish, including an endangered species, the *Pseudocrenilabrus philander*.

There are several interesting nature reserves near to Kuruman, including the small **Billy Duvenhage Nature Reserve** (telephone 05373 21 095) which is open to day visitors; the **Kalahari Raptor Rehabilitation Centre** (telephone 05373 30 464), also open to visitors; and also an 11 kilometres **walking trail** which starts at The Eye (telephone 05373 21 095/6).

About 130 kilometres south of Kimberley on the N12 is **Hopetown**, the spot where the fist diamond that sparked the rush was discovered by Erasmus Jacobs in 1866. If you want a taste of real weirdness, turn left at Hopetown onto the R369 and head for **Orania**, which in 1991 decided that it would declare itself an Afrikaner volkstaat and stand against the changes happening in the country. It's not a friendly place for anyone not white and who doesn't speak Afrikaans.

Continue south along the R369 from Orania for about 150 kilometres and you will arrive at the 19th century town of **Colesberg**, which has (beside sheep-farming—the whole of the Karoo is famous for its mutton and lamb) a formerly important landmark, the **Tooverberg** or Towering mountain, a 1,707-metre-high flat-

topped mountain that was used by early travellers as an important signpost. From Colesberg you have several directional choices; either north along the N1 highway to **Bloemfontein**, or south to **Beaufort West** (in Western Cape Province); or south along the N9 to **Graaff-Reinet** (in Eastern Cape province).

Alternatively, you can double-back from Orania along the R369 heading northwest; about 200 kilometres later you will arrive at **Prieska**, (the name derives from the Khoikhoi expression meaning 'the place where the goat was lost'), another typical Karoo town, famous for its semi-precious stones, particularly 'tiger's eye'; on the crest overlooking the two is a small British fort, made largely from 'tiger's eye' rock, built during the 1899–1902 war. From Prieska it's a drive of about 260 kilometres north along the N10 to **Upington**.

Some 200 kilometres west of Kuruman on the N14 is Upington, which is not a particularly interesting spot, more a staging-post for travellers heading deeper into the Kalahari. The small **Spitskop Nature Reserve** is nine kilometres north of the town on the R360. If you want to visit the largest inhabited inland island in South Africa, **Kanoneiland** is close to Upington on the Orange River; telephone (054) 491 1147 for a guided tour, including spit-roasted sheep, home-baked bread and locally-produced wines.

One hundred and forty kilometres south of Upington is the small, oasis-like town of **Kenhardt**, just south of which is a forest of several thousand giant aloes or quiver trees.

KALAHARI GEMSBOK NATIONAL PARK

This two million-hectare national park is one of the glories of southern Africa. Owned jointly by South Africa and Botswana, it's one of the most inaccessible spots in the country, yet one of the most beautiful. Approached either via the R31 from Kuruman (passing through a town called **Hotazel**, so christened in 1917 by two surveyors, Dirk Roos and J W Waldeck, who obviously experienced the worst of the area's baking heat), or the R369 from Upington, the journey takes you along generally very poor, badly-rutted dirt roads that should not be tackled unless your vehicle is in sound health and you have adequate water, food and clothing for the cold nights. You should not drive these roads after dark; they are too dangerous, due to their poor surfaces. It's almost 400 kilometres from Upington to the entrance into the park at **Twee Rivieren**, where there is a rest camp. You should allow yourself a day simply for that journey. There are two more restcamps, **Mata Mata** and **Nossob**. Through the park run the Nossob and Auob rivers, which rarely have water but there are some drinking holes which are good for game spotting. The temperature normally reaches 40°C during the day in the summer, and often below freezing at night.

The Kalahari desert occupies almost the whole of Botswana, the eastern third of Namibia, where in the south-west it merges with the Namib, the coastal desert of Namibia. It's largely a featureless, sand-covered plain, of about 900 metres above sea level, characterized by large, red-coloured undulating dunes.

There is only one way out of the park—back the way you came. From Upington take the N8 west, towards **Kakamas**. 110 kilometres west of Upington is another fine national park, the **Augrabies** (for details on both this and the Kalahari Gemsbok's accommodation, see the **National Parks' appendix**, page 302). En route to the Augrabies you will pass through Kakamas, 80 kilometres west of Upington; **Kakamas** is a pleasant small town, with 14 operational water-wheels, powered by the Orange River, which passes through the centre of the town. From Kakamas it's about 300 kilometres to along the N8 to **Springbok**, the main town of the north-west, and the heart of **Namaqualand**, which for most tourists is the place to visit to see carpets of flowers in August and September. Following the winter rainfall, flowers arising as if from nowhere, out of what is for most of the year a semi-desert arid landscape. You will pass through the inventively-named though quintessentially boring **Pofadder**, named after a certain Klaas Pofadder who led a gang of cattle-rustlers until they were killed at this spot in a shoot-out in 1875. Eight kilometres to the east of Springbok is the **Goegap Nature Reserve**, a 15,000 hectare park of flat plain and granite hillocks, which has some interesting antelope and—when the season is right—some splendid flowers. There's no accommodation but the reserve is open daily between 08.00–16.00, telephone (0251) 21 880.

Springbok is 1,274 kilometres west of Johannesburg, 550 kilometres north of Cape Town, and 115 kilometres south of the Namibian border. Originally a copper-mining centre, today it's a commercial, farming and industrial centre. In the centre of town is a hillock called **Koppie**, the site of a British fort from the 1899–1902 war; the fort was destroyed in a raid by the Boer commander (and later prime minister) Jan Smuts. If you feel inclined you can visit the country's Atomic Energy Corporation's waste disposal site at **Vaalputs**, 100 kilometres south-east of Springbok on the R355 beyond Gamoep, but telephone first (0251) 22 882; there is a nature reserve on the same site. To the west of Springbok much of the coastline is intensively-mined for diamonds and is closed to the public.

North of Springbok on the N7 you pass through granite hills and into Namaqualand's copper-belt, beginning at the town of **Okiep**, which was once the world's richest copper mine; it was also under a short siege during the 1899–1902 war. Forty nine kilometres north of Springbok, off the N7 on the R382, is the town of **Steinkopf**, originally constructed in 1818 as a Rhenish Mission Station; 93 kilometres further west along this road is **Port Nolloth**, on the coast. Port Nolloth is both a fishing and alluvial diamond centre. It's a remote place and the only spot on

Young cheetah attacking a young wildebeest

Lion bringing down a buffalo

A leopard rests in a tree, its prey safely out of the reach of scavangers

Indiscriminate poaching has put the rhino's future in jeopardy

Always on the alert, this cheetah mother watches over her young cubs

this part of the coast which is set up for tourists; nearby **McDougall's Bay** is a sea-side resort with chalets and a caravan park (telephone 0255 8657/8345), and is a very good spot to get away from it all. There is a very interesting coastal road lead-ing still further north, to **Alexander Bay**, at the mouth of the Orange River. As the area around Alexander Bay is the world's richest alluvial diamond area (diamonds were first discovered there in 1836 by Sir James Edward Alexander) the road is restricted access. You can use it but only with an official permit, which you can obtain either from Alexander Bay tourist office (Private Bag X5, Alexander Bay 8290, telephone 0256 330, fax 0256 364) or other tourist offices in this region (see **appendix on publicity associations** on page 317). From Alexander Bay, on the Namibian border, you can continue along this road to the **Richtersveld National Park**, via the town of **Sendelingsdrift**. The Richtersveld was declared a National Park in 1991; there are no facilities—though you can camp at various spots—and you need to stock up with food, water and petrol at Alexander Bay. This is one of South Africa's driest regions, with average rainfall of less than 50mm a year; it's very rich in endemic succulent plants and trees. There are also leopard, various antelope, zebra, and a variety of lizards and snakes.

SOUTH OF SPRINGBOK

The N7 highway heads south from Springbok to Cape Town; there are several diver-sions worth making, both inland and to the coast, which is unspoilt and not at all developed for tourism.

About 15 kilometres south of Springbok the dirt road to the utterly remote sea-side village of **Hondeklipbaai**, following a steep gradient over the **Messelpad Pass**; there is a caravan park at Hondeklipbaai, telephone (025222) 53. If you follow the N7 south instead of heading to the coast you will after 68 kilometres arrive at Kamieskroon, perhaps the centre for walking trails into the surrounding country-side during the peak of the flower season (roughly August-September). **Kamieskroon** is surrounded by a range of granite mountains, the Kamiesberg, the peak of which is called the Crown; for guides along the unmapped walks, telephone (0257) 762, fax (0257) 675. Nearby is the ghost town of **Bowesdorp**, from which all the inhabitants were removed to Kamieskroon in 1924, when it was decided that the valley in which Bowesdorp stands was too narrow for the village to grow.

Continuing south in the direction of Cape Town you pass through the villages of Garies and Bitterfontein—the scene in 1931 of a major diamond robbery—to **Vanrhynsdorp**, where you should divert left, heading east along the R27 to **Nieuwoudtville**, via a spectacular pass called **Vanrhyns Pass**. Nieuwoudtville has a 120 hectare flower reserve, and there is good nature reserve at **Oorlogskloof** to the south.

From Nieuwoudtville follow the R27 east to **Calvinia**, a dull town but historically notable for the gruesome story of the role played by one of its citizens, **Abraham Esau**, in the 1899–1902 war. Esau was a blacksmith who became the leader of the Coloured community in the town. After being refused the right to bear arms on behalf of the British against the Boers, he formed a network of intelligence-gatherers covering the northern Cape, who took it upon themselves to keep the British informed of the whereabouts of marauding bands of Boer commandos. On 10 January 1901 a Boer commando rode into town, shot a number of Coloured people and threw others, including Esau, into jail. Over the course of two weeks he was beaten, smeared with dung, flogged numerous times, stoned and then finally chained to horses and dragged out of town, where he was shot. Neither Calvinia nor Esau's story get mentioned in many of the locally-produced glossy brochures and guidebooks.

Western Cape

Western Cape is beyond question the province most densely-packed with tourist attractions. Wonderful beaches, beautiful wine-producing areas, excellent mountain ranges, some exquisite nature reserves, and one of the world's most attractive cities—Cape Town. It's the perfect place for business or pleasure.

The province can be divided into several parts: Cape Town and the Cape peninsula; the winelands; the Garden Route; north of Cape Town, into the Cedarberg mountains and along the coast; and inland from the southern coast. Each of these can easily take a week to explore, though a week is probably enough time to see the best of both Cape Town and the Cape Peninsula.

CAPE TOWN

Cape Town is about 1,500 kilometres south-west of Johannesburg, well-connected to the rest of the country by air and coach, and is also a major destination for the more important trains. It's the provincial capital and also the seat of the national parliament. Sometimes known as 'The Mother City', its airport is 25 kilometres east of the city centre; the telephone prefix is **021**.

The city centre's streets are laid out on a grid-like pattern. Two hours are ample to stroll its length and breadth, though it can easily take a couple of days to see the major sights. As in all South African cities, local tourist offices, Yellow Pages and newspapers have a huge number of local multi-lingual tour operators offering to ferry you around, which is perhaps a good idea if you are pressed for time. But if you are in a hurry, you've come to the wrong place. Cape Town has a languid, laid-back atmosphere unlike anywhere else in the country, which is perhaps why South Africans resident in Johannesburg sometimes mock Capetonians for their supposed easy-come, easy-go attitudes. But Cape Town is a sophisticated city, with little of the neurotic fear-and-guilt syndrome hanging over Joburg like a miasma.

Long Street runs through the middle of the centre. The street is these days looking a bit dingy and run-down, but it's a useful thoroughfare from which to plot your walk round town—and walk it should be as parking can be a problem. If you walk from the far end (starting where Orange Street leads into Buitensingel) heading towards the dock, you will find on either side streets down which you can meander and discover some of the city's finest attractions. Long Street has many junk, antique and book shops, **Clarke's** bookshop (211 Long Street, telephone 235 739) being possibly the best in South Africa for old and new Africana, though it's not cheap. Further down Long Street turn right into **Church Street**, which has open-air antique and bric-a-brac stalls. On the corner of Church and Burg Streets is the **Cape Heritage House**, (telephone 249 590), selling a wide range of excellent locally-produced ceramics, toys, jewellery, fabrics and other handicrafts.

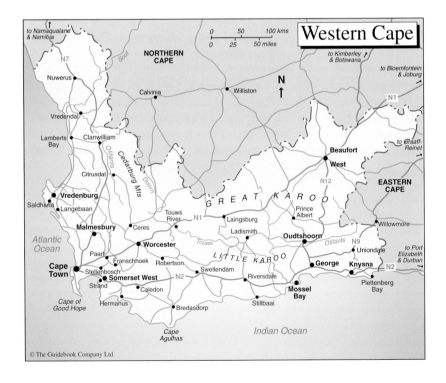

The Royal Yacht Britannia sails into Cape Town, 1995

From there turn left along Burg Street; it crosses **Longmarket** and **Shortmarket**, where you come into Greenmarket Square, where there is daily (except Sunday) a flourishing flea market. **Greenmarket Square** is the city's geographical centre and was originally the place were public proclamations were read, including an 1834 declaration freeing slaves. Created in 1710 as a market, it's the site of Cape Town's first civic building, the Burgher Wachthuis, built 1751–61 with the original purpose of housing the town guard. It's now known as the **Old Town House** (10.00–17.00, Monday-Sunday, telephone 24 6367), and houses a collection of Dutch and Flemish oil paintings, as well as exhibitions of contemporary art and sculpture. Its exterior—reckoned to be one of the finest examples of Cape Baroque—is little altered from when it was first built, though the interior was remodelled in 1916 to resemble a 17th-century Dutch guildhall. It's an excellent spot for an afternoon cup of tea.

Also on Greenmarket Square is the **Metropolitan Methodist Church**, the second oldest building in the square, constructed in 1876. It's the only example of a late Victorian town church in the city. Across the square is the **Holiday Inn on the Square**, built in 1929; it was the first South African headquarters of the Shell Oil Company, as its exterior shell motifs reveal.

From Greenmarket Square turn into **St George's Mall**, a semi-pedestrianized precinct and the heart of the shopping district. If however you continue down

Longmarket you cross **Adderley Street**; almost exactly opposite is the **Groote Kerk**. The building currently standing dates from 1841 and is on the site of the first Dutch Reformed Church built in the country, in 1704. Of the original church only the clock tower remains, constructed in 1701. Its chiming bell was made in Amsterdam in 1726; several early Cape governors are buried here.

Further along at 49 Adderley Street is the **Cultural History Museum** (09.30–16.30 Monday–Saturday, closed Sunday, telephone 461 8280), first built as a slave lodge (to house 600 slaves) for the Dutch East India Company in 1679, then later turned into the Cape's Supreme Court under the British. The museum houses an oddly diverse collection ranging from the history of currency and postage in South Africa to several rooms of antiquities from Greece, Rome and elsewhere.

At this end of Adderley Street the road does a sharp right turn and becomes **Wale Street**; on the corner is the Victorian-built **St George's Cathedral**, the parish church of former Archbishop Desmond Tutu and the focus in the past for many anti-apartheid protests. Almost opposite Adderley and heading in the same direction is **Government Avenue**, a delightful pedestrian walk which should be avoided at night—it's become a favourite spot for muggers. During the day however it's perfectly safe and brings you into the **Company's Botanical Gardens**, the area where the Dutch East India Company's first settlers started growing their own produce in 1652. It's now a wonderfully attractive park, a favourite spot for office-workers having their lunchtime snacks. The garden has more than 8,000 species of exotic plants, flowers and trees, and a large conservatory, as well as an aviary and a tea-garden.

The gardens are bracketed by some of the finest architecture in the city; the **Houses of Parliament** (on **Parliament Street**) were built in 1884 and then enlarged in 1910. During parliamentary sessions visitors can take gallery seats; tickets are available from room V12, Old Assembly Wing, with overseas visitors being required to show their passports. Out of session, guided tours are available between 11.00–14.00 Monday–Thursday and at 11.00 on Friday, telephone 403 2460/1. Adjacent to parliament is **De Tuynhuys**, the office of the state president, which is not open to the public but the exterior of which is very much on view, replete with a grandiose statue (in **Stal Plein**, on **Plein Street**) of General Louis Botha, one of the Boer's 1899–1902 war heroes, and, later, the first prime minister after union in 1910.

Beyond De Tuynhuys the gardens broaden out into a delightful rectangular area, at one end of which is the **South African National Gallery** (10.00–17.00 Tuesday-Sunday, 13.00–17.00 Monday, telephone 451 628), which holds more than 6,500 works of art and is deservedly considered to be one of the city's foremost attractions. There is some astonishingly good contemporary South African art here, as well as an interesting shop and good cafe. Next door to this gallery is the **Jewish Museum** (on Hatfield Street, a dizzyingly complex variety of opening hours, telephone 434 6605), which beside being the country's oldest synagogue has some interesting exhibits. At the other end of the rectangle (on Queen Victoria Street) is the **South African Museum**, founded in 1825 and claiming to be the biggest museum in the country. (10.00–17.00, daily, telephone 243 330). It's full of local discoveries, including the famous 'Lydenburg Heads', reconstructed pottery heads dating from the early Iron Age. Next door is the **Planetarium** (same telephone number).

Once you leave the gardens and reach the end of Government Avenue you arrive at an annexe of the University of Cape Town, a small collection of buildings among which is **Bertram House** (corner of Orange and Government, 09.30–16.30, Tue-Sat, telephone 249 381), which has a collection of furniture, ceramics and silver.

From here you need to turn left and walk along Annandale , which turns into Mill Street. After a short distance turn left into **Buitenkant Street**. At number 78 is **Rust-en Vreugd** (09.00–16.00, Monday-Friday, telephone 453 628), which has an excellent collection of early watercolours and lithographs, some of the William Fehr Collection (other parts of which are on show at the Castle).

Continue along Buitenkant until you get to 25a, the Buitenkant Methodist Church, which now houses the **District Six Museum** (10.00–16.30 Monday–Saturday, Sunday by appointment, telephone 461 8745), one of the city's most important sites. The building itself is nothing special but inside is some fascinating historical research in the making. District Six was the name given to the sixth municipal district of Cape Town in 1867. Originally a vibrant centre where freed slaves, immigrants and merchants all rubbed shoulders, in 1966 it was declared a 'white' area; a total of something like 60,000 people were forcibly removed to a barren area known as the Cape Flats, far from Cape Town. Cape Town had its own Sophiatown; District Six was bulldozed to the ground. The Museum is now busily gathering all manner of materials from the people who were chucked out of their homes; it's well worth a visit. Scattered around the museum are original street name-plates, which had supposedly been thrown into Table Bay, but were returned by one of the (white) municipal authorities responsible for the forced removals' programme—he had kept them in his back garden. The volunteers running the museum will be only too pleased to provide you with a historical map enabling you to walk round the district, which is very close to the museum. With considerable irony, the museum is directly opposite the city's grim-looking police station.

If you continue along Buitenkant and turn left into **Darling Street** you will pass the imposing **City Hall**, completed in 1905. Opposite is a large car-park, beyond which is the bus terminus. At the bottom of Buitenkant to the right is the city's

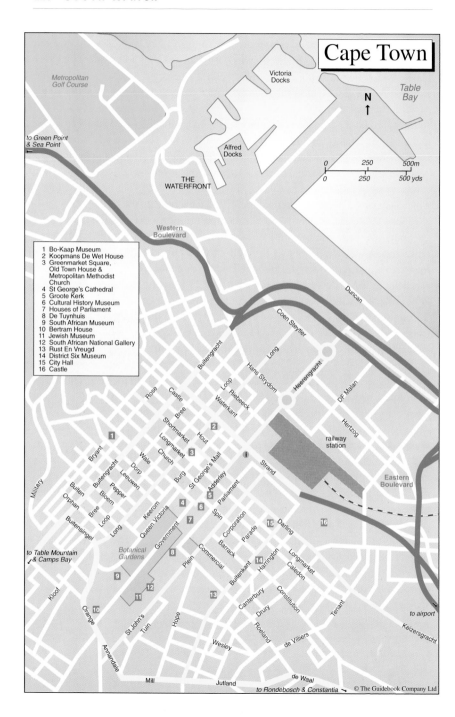

Cape Town

Victoria Docks

Table Bay

N

Metropolitan Golf Course

to Green Point & Sea Point

Alfred Docks

THE WATERFRONT

0   250   500m
0   250   500 yds

Western Boulevard

Duncan

1   Bo-Kaap Museum
2   Koopmans De Wet House
3   Greenmarket Square,
    Old Town House &
    Metropolitan Methodist
    Church
4   St George's Cathedral
5   Groote Kerk
6   Cultural History Museum
7   Houses of Parliament
8   De Tuynhuis
9   South African Museum
10 Bertram House
11 Jewish Museum
12 South African National Gallery
13 Rust En Vreugd
14 District Six Museum
15 City Hall
16 Castle

Coen Steytler

Long

Hans Strydom

Heerengracht

DF Malan

Buitengracht

Hertzog

railway station

Rose

Castle

Bree

Shortmarket

Longmarket

Hout

Loop
Riebeeck
Waterkant

Eastern Boulevard

Bryant

Wale

Dorp

Church

Burg

St George's Mall

Adderley

Strand

Military

Buiten

Buitengracht

Leeuwen

Bloem

Pepper

Keerom

Parliament

Orphan

Bree

Loop

Long

Queen Victoria

Government

Spin

Corporation

Parade

Barrack

Darling

Longmarket

Caledon

to Table Mountain
& Camps Bay

Botanical Gardens

Plein

Commercial

Buitenkant

Harrington

Constitution

Kloof

Buitensingel

St John's

Tuin

Hope

Canterbury

Drury

Roeland

Tenant

to airport

Orange

Mill

Jutland

Wesley

de Villiers

de Waal

Keizersgracht

to Rondebosch & Constantia   © The Guidebook Company Ltd

Castle. In fact it's more the size of a medium-scale fort, its walls being so low that they are dwarfed by the city's skyscrapers. The pentagonally-shaped Castle of Good Hope (to give its full title) is the site of South Africa's oldest (white-constructed) building, having been built between 1666 and 1679. As it is also the HQ of Western Province army command, you

A windswept Cape Point set in Cape Peninsula National Park

cannot go round independently but must take a guided tour, which happens every hour between 10.00–15.00, Monday-Sunday, and on the half-hour in December and January; telephone 469 1249/50. The parts of the interior which you are permitted to see are not terribly interesting, and the William Fehr collection of various art-works is badly laid-out, with no informational inscriptions about dates, artists or suchlike. The various other military history galleries are very dull. You might be fortunate to have a guide who is able to bring it to life; bad luck otherwise.

From the Castle walk along **Strand Street** back into the city centre, up to where it intersects with Adderley. You cannot miss here the **Golden Acre**, an enormous multi-storey shopping and cinema complex, owned by Sanlam, one of South Africa's leading conglomerates, an Afrikaner-inspired company which started life in the 1930s as an assurance company aimed at helping Afrikaners. If you carry up Strand to where it crosses Long Street you will find **Koopmans De Wet House**, built in 1701, now a museum dedicated to 18th-century artefacts (09.30–16.30 Tuesday–Saturday, telephone 242 473).

From there, continue up Strand until you reach Loop Street; turn left onto Loop until it crosses Wale Street, then turn right; at number 71 Wale Street is the **Bo-Kaap Museum**, an 18th-century house which contains an exhibition of Cape Malay life in the 19th century (09.00–16.30 Monday–Saturday, closed Sunday, telephone 243 846). This is on the edge of Muslim Cape Town, the quarter known as Bo-Kaap ('above Cape') and traditional home to Cape Malays.

After all this walking you may be in need of a steam bath to ease your legs. So head for Long Street, at the junction of Orange (the opposite end from the docks); at the start of Long is a **Turkish Steam Baths**; women's days are Monday, Thursday and Saturday, men's are Tuesday, Wednesday, Friday and Sunday, all at various hours; telephone 400 3302. There's also an indoor heated swimming pool.

THE WATERFRONT

One of the major tourist developments Cape Town has seen in recent years is the massive shopping and entertainment complex known as **The Waterfront** (general details telephone 418 2369), a five-minute drive from the city centre, on the Victoria and Alfred docks. The docks are still used by fishing vessels, but the whole area has been re-developed, retaining the old buildings, as a place for shopping, eating, strolling, and enjoyment. It's not to everyone's taste but it is a lively centre, with excellent family facilities and a good sense of security. It has had a deleterious effect on the city centre's nightlife; most people now head to the Waterfront, not least because it feels much safer to stroll there than in the city centre. It has everything from South Africa's only IMAX cinema, an aquarium, boat charters, helicopter rides and guided tours. It is a fantastically good place to take children who can have hours of amusement. There are shuttle buses running very frequently between it and the city centre.

TABLE MOUNTAIN

One of few landmarks that is immediately, internationally recognisable, **Table Mountain** gives Cape Town its special feel; in 1996 it was declared a National Park. In good weather it can sometimes be seen out at sea from as far away as 200 kilometres. This 1,086-metre high sandstone block dominating the skyline has a northern face of a sheer precipice more than three kilometres long; but enterprising climbers have ascertained at least 350 different ways of getting to the top. The easiest by far is to take the cable-car from Kloofnek Road; **buses** go from Adderley Street outside the OK Bazaar supermarket. The cable-car takes about six minutes, and at the top there's a tea-room in case the journey tires you out. The queues for the cable-car can be horrendously long in the summer peak season (though you can and should book in advance); in the winter the mountain can often be closed due to awful weather. The mountain is frequently garbed in cloud, making it occasionally dangerous; many climbers have died on its slopes. The weather around the mountain's higher reaches is notoriously changeable, swiftly altering from bright sunshine to cold mists; be careful if walking up without an experienced guide.

The danger is largely the fault of Cape Town's notorious south-easterly winds, which can sweep across the city with speeds of up to 120 kilometres per hour during the months of November–March. As well as being a nuisance for locals—though some claim it creates a healthy atmosphere—the wind can cover the mountain very rapidly. It's always a good idea to telephone the mountain's administrators before setting off, in case it's closed; telephone 245 148 or 248 409. If you want to climb it, contact **Captour** (the main tourist office, on Adderley Street), which has good maps giving clear walking routes up the mountain; Captour can also put you in touch with experienced local guides.

Table Mountain is one of the more spectacular peaks of the Cape Peninsula range, which includes **Devil's Peak** (which towers above the plush southern suburbs, such as **Rondebosch**); behind Table Mountain are the **Twelve Apostles** (seen from the road linking **Camps Bay** and **Llandudno**), and overlooking **Green Point** (a short drive from the centre of the city) is the lower (335 metres high) but no less interesting peak called **Lion's Head** and its rump, **Signal Hill**, the top of which is accessible by car. At the top is a ceremonial gun, fired electronically at midday every day except Sunday. A good few years ago the gunner left the ramrod in the barrel; it shot across the roofs of the city and landed in Greenmarket Square, killing a horse.

Beyond the city centre the northern and eastern suburbs are quite industrialized; out along the N2 highway towards the airport the route passes through some notorious township and squatter-camp names familiar from the worst days of apartheid—**Langa**, **Guguletu** and **Crossroads** being perhaps the most well-known. These places are still areas of massive social deprivation and severe unemployment, and should not be entered; crime levels here are high. North of the airport the other main highway heading east, the N1, passes through some ugly industrial areas such as **Bellville**, which is also home to the University of the Western Cape, a hotbed even today of student activism. None of these places need detain you.

CAPE TOWN: SOUTHERN SUBURBS

East and south of the city centre are several suburbs linked by means of a network of highways—confusingly marked and at peak times feeling like a Formula 1 racetrack—following the shape of Devil's Peak. Both the N1 and N2 highways run right into town. Most of these suburbs are not very interesting, but some are worth a visit.

APARTHEID FALLING

They tell me,
my educated brothers do,
that the colour bar in South Africa
is coming down
I'm not impressed.

They show me signs
that are no longer there
on park benches and on lift doors
those signs, they used to say
whites only—blankes alleen.

They point out to me
black men and black women
khaki-clad office boys and
overall-wearing street diggers
and they say
don't you see
all those people
sitting on those benches
where only whites were allowed
to sit all these years?
we tell you, man,
apartheid is dying
I'm not impressed.

They tell me
my educated brothers do
about other educated brothers
who eat and sleep
in hotels

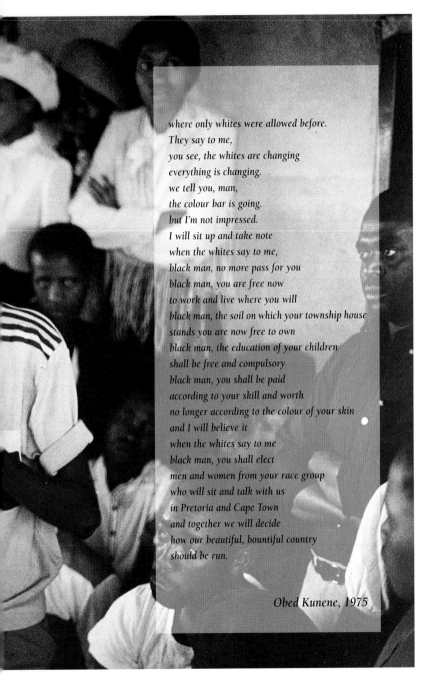

where only whites were allowed before.
They say to me,
you see, the whites are changing
everything is changing.
we tell you, man,
the colour bar is going.
but I'm not impressed.
I will sit up and take note
when the whites say to me,
black man, no more pass for you
black man, you are free now
to work and live where you will
black man, the soil on which your township house
stands you are now free to own
black man, the education of your children
shall be free and compulsory
black man, you shall be paid
according to your skill and worth
no longer according to the colour of your skin
and I will believe it
when the whites say to me
black man, you shall elect
men and women from your race group
who will sit and talk with us
in Pretoria and Cape Town
and together we will decide
how our beautiful, bountiful country
should be run.

Obed Kunene, 1975

Young poet recites militant verse during funeral of student activist, Bethal 1985

The M4 heading first east then south out of town (which starts as **Sir Lowry**, then **Victoria** and then **Main** roads) takes you past **District Six**, through **Woodstock**, on the edge of **Salt River** and then into **Observatory**, suburbs which are home to students and the poorer sections of the city. It then moves through wealthier suburbs; **Mowbray**, **Rosebank**, **Rondebosch**, **Newlands**, **Claremont**, **Kenilworth**, **Wynberg**, **Plumstead**, before passing into much poorer suburbs such as **Dieprivier** and **Retreat**, suburbs which once were for 'non-whites', until finally arriving at **Muizenberg**, on the Indian Ocean coast.

Observatory has the **Groote Schuur Transplant Museum** (off De Waal Drive, 10.00–16.00, telephone 404 5232/404 9111), the site of the world's first heart transplant in 1967. The prestigious **University of Cape Town**, 10 kilometres from the city centre, is in Rondebosch, at the foot of Devil's Peak. Off Main Road close to the UCT campus is **Groote Schuur** (which means 'great barn') estate, on which is which was Cecil Rhodes' old house. The estate contains the Cape Town state residences of the president, prime and deputy prime ministers. Weekly guided tours are staged when the state president is in Pretoria (to arrange one contact The Household Manager, Westbrooke, Rondebosch 7700); among the opulent oddities of Rhodes' quarters is a large marble bath, which apparently immediately chills the hottest of water. Behind the university campus is the **Rhodes Memorial**, a picturesque spot giving wonderful views across the city. Eight lions stand guard over a bronze head of Rhodes. Underneath are words written by Kipling (who stayed here with Rhodes) on hearing of Rhodes' death:

> *The immense and brooding spirit still shall quicken and control*
> *Living he was the land and dead his soul shall be her soul.*

A generous epitaph for one who was so immoral.

One of the delights of these southern suburbs is **Constantia**; to get there take the M41 exit (in Wynberg) from Main Road, or, if coming south from the UCT campus, turn right onto Klipper Road, following it round as it becomes Newlands and then Rhodes Avenue (the M63). Constantia is the suburb where the immensely wealthy choose to buy property, but don't let that put you off. If driving along Rhodes Avenue, in the suburb of Bishopscourt (just before Constantia) you will see an exit for the **Kirstenbosch National Botanical Gardens**, one of the loveliest spots in the city. Kirstenbosch has yet another Rhodes' connection, as this area was bought by him in 1895 and donated to the nation. The gardens cover some 560 hectares and contain some 9,000 of South Africa's 21,000 indigenous flowering plants. (April–August 08.00–18.00, September–March 08.00–19.00, open daily, telephone 762 1166). It also has a restaurant.

In Constantia itself are three of the finest vineyards of South Africa—**Groot Constantia**, **Klein Constantia** and **Buitenverwachting**, the first being also the oldest and perhaps the grandest homestead in the Cape, originally granted to governor Simon van der Stel in the 17th century. All three are open for tasting and sales during weekdays and weekends; Buitenverwachting also has a particularly fine restaurant. All are well-signposted off Constantia Road from Wynberg. (Telephone: Groot Constantia— 794 5128; Klein Constantia—794 5188; Buitenverwachting— 794 5190/1).

CAPE PENINSULA

If you continue down Main Road from Constantia you will eventually reach **Muizenberg**, 28 kilometres from Cape Town and one of the most famous beach areas of the Peninsula. If you turn left and head east along the coast road you will travel parallel to one of the world's finest stretches of white-sand beaches, eventually reaching the Cape Flats, where there are two huge townships, **Mitchell's Plain** and **Khayelitsha**, dumping grounds in a dusty, remote spot far away from the wealthy southern suburbs. It was once possible to drive round these townships in relative safety, but not today, unless you have an experienced local guide who knows what they are doing. There are several local tour firms who will take you round; contact Captour for their telephone numbers.

The **False Bay** or eastern side of the Peninsula at this section is largely given over to beach resorts; the warmer Indian Ocean makes it rather more pleasant to bathe here than on the western, Atlantic Ocean side of the Peninsula. **Strandfontein** is a short drive east of Muizenberg along the coast road; it has a tidal pool safe for swimming. Muizenberg itself has a grass embankment and a long beach popular with surfers and families, along with the Carousel, where there are swimming pools, restaurants and a water slide. Although sharks can sometimes be spotted, the relatively shallow shoreline usually prevents problems. Muizenberg also has several buildings of minor interest, including the **Natale Labia Museum** (10.00–17.00, Tuesday–Sunday, telephone 788 4106, on Main Road), once the home of an eccentric Italian diplomat; it has a good restaurant serving hearty breakfasts, good lunches and delicious teas. A complete oddity is the nearby **South African Police Museum** (08.00–15.30, Monday–Friday, 09.00–13.00 Saturday, 14.00–17.00 Sunday), which was opened in June 1990 in what must have been a belated attempt by the police force to do some public relations' work. For those not yet exhausted by **Rhodes**, his **seaside cottage**, where he died in 1902, is also on Main Road, a short walk from the Natale Labia museum. (10.00–13.00 and 14.00–17.00, Tuesday–Sunday, telephone 788 1816).

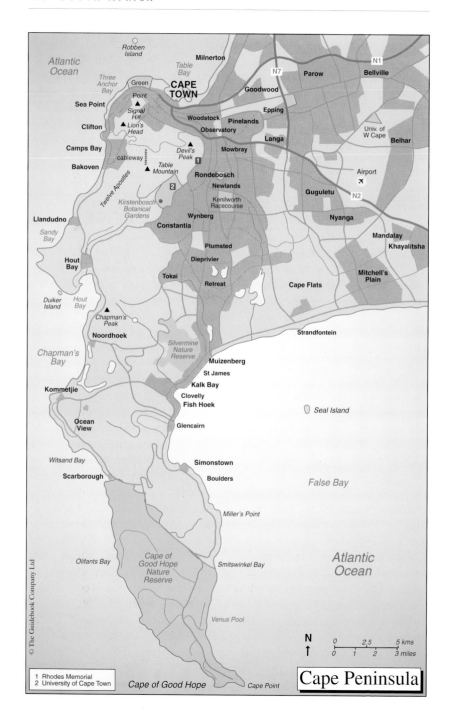

Atlantic Ocean

Robben Island

Three Anchor Bay

Green Point

Sea Point

Signal Hill ▲

Clifton

Lion's Head ▲

Camps Bay

Bakoven

cableway

Twelve Apostles

Table Mountain ▲

Devil's Peak ▲

Milnerton

Table Bay

CAPE TOWN

Goodwood

Woodstock

Observatory

Pinelands

Mowbray

Rondebosch

Newlands

Kenilworth Racecourse

Wynberg

Constantia

Plumsted

Dieprivier

Tokai

Retreat

Llandudno

Sandy Bay

Hout Bay

Duiker Island

Hout Bay

Chapman's Peak ▲

Noordhoek

Chapman's Bay

Kommetjie

Ocean View

Witsand Bay

Scarborough

Silvermine Nature Reserve

Muizenberg

St James

Kalk Bay

Clovelly

Fish Hoek

Glencairn

Simonstown

Boulders

Miller's Point

Kirstenbosch Botanical Gardens

Milnerton

N7

Parow

N1

Bellville

Goodwood

Epping

Langa

Univ. of W Cape

Belhar

Airport ✈

Guguletu

N2

Nyanga

Mandalay

Khayalitsha

Mitchell's Plain

Cape Flats

Strandfontein

Seal Island

False Bay

Atlantic Ocean

Olifants Bay

Cape of Good Hope Nature Reserve

Smitswinkel Bay

Venus Pool

N
↑

0   2,5   5 kms
0   1   2   3 miles

Rhodes Memorial
University of Cape Town

Cape of Good Hope

Cape Point

Cape Peninsula

Further south round the coast is **St James**, which has a safe tidal pool, ideal for children, and is very sheltered. Nearby are a couple of other beaches, **Danger** and **Dalebrook**, the latter being more of a tidal pool than a beach, again very good for families. Beyond is **Kalk Bay**, a busy fishing harbour and home to one of the area's better fish restaurants, the **Brass Bell**. There's also an interesting bric-a-brac store called **Quagga Trading**, on Main Road—but don't expect to find any real bargains.

Next beach along is the sand dune resort of **Clovelly**, which is next to the railway station; there may still be signs on the station saying 'no fishing from the platform'. Clovelly runs into **Fish Hoek**, a small town which until quite recently was the only 'dry' place in the country—no alcohol was sold here, though apparently it's now possible to get a drink in some restaurants. It's a dull place but it has a long, safe beach and play park, making it popular with families.

President Nelson Mandela and Queen Elizabeth II in Cape Town 1995

Further on you reach **Glencairn**, with a tidal pool offering safe swimming; it's now also a wetlands reserve where, if you are fortunate, you might see the Cape clawless otter. Beyond Glencairn you reach **Simonstown**, the home to South Africa's navy. It's an attractive town, though it's few museums are not enticing. Perhaps its greatest interest lies in the British Hotel, a splendid place to stay, great value and very much off the regular tourist beat, even though it's only 38 kilometres from Cape Town. (See **Hotels** appendix, page 287). Beyond Simonstown is another secluded beach, **Boulders**, though when the tide is in the beach is almost covered. It's also a favourite spot for Jackass penguins. Further south, **Miller's Point** has a small pool. About eight kilometres south of Simonstown is **Smitswinkel Bay**, above which you can park and follow a footpath down to a very secluded cove and sheltered swimming area.

Here the M4 route parts; if you head further south you will eventually reach **Cape Point**, within the **Cape Peninsula National Park**. Cape Point is not the southernmost tip of Africa—that distinction goes to Agulhas (also in Western Cape province, near Bredasdorp)—but it is nevertheless a wild, windswept spot. The park covers some 7,750 hectares of unspoiled *fynbos* vegetation, and is open from dawn to dusk. Walking maps for the area are available from the entrance gate. The area is home to many different species of birds, and hordes of baboons, who can prove nasty, so give them a wide berth. There are also various antelope and zebra. At the very tip is a lighthouse, from which some have claimed to have seen the mythical *Flying Dutchman*, a sailing ship which is supposedly forever condemned to try to round the Cape. The story has it that anyone seeing the ship will soon die; one recorded sighting on 11 July 1881, by a young British junior naval officer, sailing on the Bacchante, might seem to confirm that. The lookout man on the Bacchante reported seeing a brig less than 200 metres distant, from which a strange red glow emanated. The lookout man soon died, falling from a mast; the recorder of his sighting was later to become King George V of the United Kingdom. Within the park there is a road to the western side, to **Olifants Bay**, which is good for walking and picnicking but not safe for swimming.

From Cape Point you must return to the main road; turn left onto the M65/Plateau road towards **Scarborough**, you will head towards some more beach areas, along the western side of the Peninsula. Scarborough, **Witsands**, **Kommetjie** and **Long Beach** are all popular surfing spots; further along there is also **Noordhoek**, a 10-kilometre stretch of unsheltered beach with cold waters; good for walking but not swimming. From there is a spectacular drive via Chapman's Peak (592 metre) along what has become the M6 road, to Hout Bay, a rather busy tourist spot which has been spoilt by development. It has a bustling harbour, restaurants and in a collection of giant aviaries (called **World of Birds**, 09.00–17.00, daily) a major local tourist attraction.

From Hout Bay the M6 road continues north but if you wish to visit the Peninsula's only official nudist beach, then you must park along the road and take an easy footpath (two kilometres, no gradients to speak of) from **Llandudno**—a beautiful beach, but not safe for swimming—to the north. This path will lead you to **Sandy Bay**, a remote spot; it's not mandatory to be a nudist to sunbathe there.

From Llandudno north to Cape Town along the M6 the beaches get more crowded. **Camps Bay** has a wonderful backdrop, the Twelve Apostles, a range of peaks so named by Sir Rufane Donkin, an early Cape governor who believed he could detect the various apostles in the shape of the peaks. Like all of the beaches along this coast, the water is cold and the surf can be very strong; unless you are a very strong swimmer it's best not to go out of your depth anywhere along here.

Like Camps Bay, the next beach along, **Clifton**, is these days largely given over to body obsessives who like to parade their muscles and skimpy costumes. The roads behind these beaches are lined with trendy bars and restaurants, and generally there's an overcrowded feel and a narcissistic atmosphere; not much frequented by families who just want a day out building sandcastles.

Approaching still closer to Cape Town centre, the next suburb along is **Sea Point**, which is not great for swimming or simply sitting on the beach; it's quite

ROBBEN ISLAND

This island represents more completely than any other patch of South African earth that which has been unspeakable...in the last three centuries and more of the country's history.

Stephen Watson, poet and academic at the University of Cape Town.

A small oval outcrop, 10 kilometres north of Mouille Point (itself no more than a couple of kilometres from the centre of Cape Town), Robben Island—South Africa's Alcatraz—has an ugly reputation, as the place where many ANC and other political prisoners were harshly jailed. The island has also been the last resting place of sailors, drowned in nearby shipwrecks. There have been many since the first recorded, the *Schapenjacht*, foundered in August 1660.

Jan van Riebeeck started the practice of banishing troublesome individuals on Robben Island, and his successor, Zacharias Wagenaar, turned it into a major prison. When the British occupied the Cape in 1806, Robben Island (which gets its name from 'robbe', the Dutch word for seals) also became a whaling station, under the control of the Englishman John Murray; the island's bay and harbour are named after him. In 1819 a self-proclaimed Xhosa prophet, Makanna, was jailed there for leading an uprising against the white inhabitants of Grahamstown, in the eastern Cape. Murray's whaling business was closed by the authorities in 1820, after a series of prisoners had escaped, using ships and boats attracted there by his whaling business. Among those who managed to escape was Makanna—though he drowned when his boat capsized in the rough seas.

But by the middle of the 19th century Robben Island was more a leper colony and lunatic asylum than a prison. This change of emphasis was largely the work of John Montagu, Secretary to the Government of Cape Colony. Montagu had a mission to build passes and roads throughout the new British colony. He determined to use Robben

Island's convicts—all but the most dangerous—as cheap, expendable labour. In exchange, Montagu suggested consolidating various Cape Colony establishments for lepers, paupers, lunatics and the chronically sick, lumping together on the island the 250 or so men and women who lived in them. This was done in November 1845.

The misery suffered by those unfortunates thus cast away—out of sight and out of mind, existing in conditions of appalling squalor and ignorance—was extreme. By 1861 there were 361 inmates of all categories, those classified as lunatic nevertheless being required to work—hard labour for the men, (collecting rocks to build a new jetty) and sewing for the government for the women. Their lives were supervised by about 40 poorly-qualified staff, though some missionaries were seemingly well-motivated. The lepers lived in equally squalid conditions as the lunatics, but were at least not forced to work.

By 1890 the island's total population was more than 700. It had become quite a thriving community, with its own newspaper—the *Robben Island Times*, published by the postmaster—a couple of schoolteachers, priests, medical staff and storekeepers. In 1889 a Select Committee report resulted in greater public awareness of conditions on the island, and for its enforced inhabitants, life slowly began to improve. In 1890 female paupers were removed and housed in Grahamstown. In 1913 all lunatic patients began to be removed.

By 1920 the island's 2,000-strong community had a bakery, fire station, library, mule-drawn train and dairy. In January 1931 the leper colony was transferred to Pretoria and their wards burnt down. In the 1950s, the South African navy took control of the island, and started up a bus service for the hundreds of families who lived there. In June 1965 the Prisons Department took it over, and turned it once more into a notorious detention centre and dumping ground for those regarded by the authorities as dangerous and nasty—including the first black president of the country, Nelson Mandela.

It is now possible to visit Robben Island, though not without considerable preparation. Visits for up to 50 people at a time, at R80 each, are arranged by the Department of Correctional Affairs—as the prison service is now euphemistically called-but there is always a lengthy waiting list, of several months. To make the booking you must call the Department of Correctional Affairs on (021) 411 1006.

It's also quite possible that, having waited patiently for your pre-arranged visit, you will find it cancelled on the day, due to bad weather making impossible the short sea journey, which takes about an hour, from Cape Town. And be warned that all local tour operators selling 'trips to Robben Island' are being economical with the truth; all they do is organise a boat trip out to and around the island, they cannot actually land there. But the trip on a sunny day is very pleasant. And perhaps a distant observation of the island, from the security of a comfortable boat, is as close to the ghosts of the former leper colony and grisly prison as we may wish to get.

May 1994: Former inmate of Robben Island, Nelson Mandela becomes South Africa's first black President

PRISON LIFE FOR THE FUTURE PRESIDENT

We were awakened at 5.30 each morning by the night warder, who clanged a brass bell at the head of the corridor and yelled 'Word wakker! Staan op!' (Wake up! Get up!) I have always been an early riser and this hour was not a burden to me. Although we were roused at 5.30, we were not let out of our cells until 6.45, by which time we were meant to have cleaned our cells and rolled up our mats and blankets. We had no running water in our cells and instead of toilets had iron sanitary buckets known as 'ballies'. The ballies had a diameter of 10 inches with a concave porcelain lid on the top that could contain water. The water in this lid was meant to be used for shaving and to clean our hands and faces.

At 6.45, when we were let out of our cells, the first thing we did was to empty our ballies. The ballies had to be thoroughly cleansed in the sinks at the end of the corridor or they created a stench. The only pleasant thing about cleaning one's ballie was that this was the one moment in those early days when we could have a whispered word with our colleagues. The warders did not like to linger when we cleaned them, so it was a chance to talk softly.

During those first few months, breakfast was delivered to us in our cells by prisoners from the general section. Breakfast consisted of mealie pap porridge, cereal made from maize or corn, which the general prisoners would slop in a bowl and then spin through the bars of our cells. It was a clever trick and required a deft hand so as not to spill any of the porridge.

After a few months, breakfast was delivered to us in the courtyard in old metal drums. We would help ourselves to pap using simple metal bowls. We each received a mug of what was described as coffee, but which was in fact ground-up maize, baked until it was black, and then brewed with hot water. Later, when we were able to go into the courtyard to serve ourselves, I would go out there and jog around the perimeter until breakfast arrived.

Like everything else in prison, diet is discriminatory. In general, Coloured and Indians received a slightly better diet than Africans, but it was *not much of a distinction. The authorities liked to say that we received a balanced diet; it was indeed balanced—between the unpalatable and the inedible. Food was a source of many of our protests, but in those early days, the warders would say, 'Ag, you kaffirs are eating better in prison than you ever ate at home!' [...]*

After inspection we would work in the courtyard hammering stones until noon. There were no breaks; if we slowed down, the warders would yell at us to speed up. At noon, the bell would clang for lunch and another metal drum of food would be wheeled into the courtyard. For Africans, lunch consisted of boiled mealies, that is, coarse kernels of corn. The Indians and Coloured prisoners received samp, or mealie rice, which consisted of ground mealies in a soup-like mixture. The samp was sometimes served with vegetables, whereas our mealies were served straight.

For lunch we often received phuzamandla, which means 'drink of strength,' a powder made from mealies and a bit of yeast. It is meant to be stirred into water or milk, and when it is thick it can be tasty, but the prison authorities gave us so little of the powder that it barely coloured the water. I would usually try to save my powder for several days until I had enough to make a proper drink, but if the authorities discovered that you were hoarding food, the powder was confiscated and you were punished.

After lunch we worked until 4, when the guards blew shrill whistles and we once again lined up to be counted and inspected. We were then permitted half an hour to clean up. The bathroom at the end of our corridor had two seawater showers, a saltwater tap and three large galvanized metal buckets, which were used as bathtubs. There was no hot water. We would stand or squat in these buckets, soaping ourselves with the brackish water, rinsing off the dust from the day. To wash yourself with cold water when it is cold outside is not too pleasant, but we made the best of it. We would sometimes sing while washing, which made the water seem less icy. In those early days, this was one of the only times when we could converse.

Precisely at 4.30 there would be a loud knock on the wooden door at the end of our corridor, which meant that supper had been delivered. Common-law prisoners used to dish out the food to us and we would return to our cells to eat it. We again received mealie pap porridge, sometimes with the odd carrot or piece of cabbage or beetroot thrown in—but one usually had to search for it. If we did get a vegetable, we would usually have the same one for weeks on end, until the carrots or cabbages were old and mouldy and we were thoroughly sick of them. Every other day we received a small piece of meat with our porridge. The meat was usually mostly gristle...

A 8pm the night warder would lock himself in the corridor with us, passing the key through a small hole in the door to another warder outside. The warder would then walk up and down the corridor, ordering us to go to sleep. No cry of 'lights out' was ever given on Robben Island because the single mesh-covered bulb in our cell burned day and night. Later, those studying for higher degrees were permitted to read until 10 or 11pm.

Nelson Mandela:
Long Walk To Freedom: 1994

Ellis Park, Johannesburg, May 1990: Musicians came together to celebrate Mandela's freedom

rocky. There is a strange little alcove on the beach called **Graaff's Pool**, an all-male venue where nude bathing is practised. Sea Point was until quite recently a very trendy spot, its main road being lined with bars and restaurants; but these days it has a rather seedy, run-down atmosphere—many of those once attracted by its night-life seem to have deserted it for the Victoria and Alfred complex. Beyond Sea Point are **Green Point** and **Mouille Point**, neither of them of much interest either for beaches or anything else, being little more than a stone's throw from the city centre. Mouille Point however does have the oldest lighthouse on the Peninsula, which, when the fog is up in the winter months, emits an eerie, regular blast.

TABLE BAY

This brings you back to Cape Town centre, and you should consider driving north, around Table Bay, to get some of the best views of Table Mountain. Take the R27 road up through Milnerton (an uninteresting spot) and head for **Bloubergstrand**, 19 kilometres north of Cape Town, which is a reasonable spot for lunch. This is the spot which produces the best photographs of Table Mountain, and you can also see Robben Island.

CAPE TOWN: NIGHTLIFE

The whole Cape Peninsula sometimes seems to throb at night, as people head off for restaurants, theatres, cinemas and clubs. As everywhere, local newspapers are the best places to see what's currently on and what's fashionable. The following are established, professionally-run theatres: The **Baxter Theatre Complex** is part of UCT in Rosebank (telephone 685 7880); the **Nico Theatre Complex** is in the centre of town on D F Malan Street (telephone 215 470); and there is an open-air theatre, the **Maynardville**, in Wynberg, which puts on performances of Shakespeare, but only during the summer season.

CAPE TOWN: SPORTS GROUNDS

Western Province rugby union has its ground on Boundary Road, Newlands, telephone 689 4921; the **Kenilworth Racecourse**, on Lansdowne Road in Kenilworth, is home to the South African Turf Club, telephone 762 7777; **Western Province cricket** is also in Newlands, telephone 644 146. There are dozens of golf and tennis clubs, Captour will be able to supply current information on a wide range of activities.

WINELANDS

One of the more delightful things to do in this part of the country is to drive to **Franschhoek**, **Paarl** and **Stellenbosch**—all within one easy hour's drive east of Cape Town—and sample wines at the vineyards where they are produced. This area, the

Boland, is a combination of rugged mountain ranges and sheltered valleys, with hundreds of neatly laid-out vineyards. It is perhaps the most charming area in the country, and although a favourite tourist spot, rarely has the feeling of being at all crowded. Some of the finest Cape Dutch architecture, with its distinctive roof-gables, is to be found on the wine estates, all of which feel as though they have been there since time immemorial. Many of the wine estates run a wine-tasting and sales' service; most will charge a token sum for the tastings. Do not feel compelled to purchase wine just because you have tasted it; estate prices are frequently higher than those of bottle stores.

If you plan to tackle seriously the wine routes it's best to arm yourself with a specialist guidebook such as John Platter's *Wine Guide*, which has detailed maps and telephone numbers. Alternatively the Stellenbosch tourist bureau is well equipped to give you more general guidance and maps. Don't get the wrong idea from tourist offices which tout the 'wine routes'—there are no logically laid-out routes, just collections of estates, all over the place. You really need to plan your own routes.

One of the most scenic routes to take in this area is that known as the 'Four Passes'; from Cape Town take the N2 and beyond Somerset West you enter Sir Lowry's Pass, a 402-metre high point from which are panoramic views of Cape Town and False Bay, cut through the Hottentots-Holland mountain range. Continue as far as Grabouw on the N2, then take the R321 left, through Viljoen's Pass, which has a 525-metre summit. After a few kilometres the R45 (again left) towards Franschhoek, via Franschhoek Pass (a winding 1:12 gradient), which has a 701m summit giving breath-taking views across the upper part of the Berg River valley. After Franschhoek continue along the R45 until you reach the junction with the R310; turn left here towards Pniel, beyond which is the 366-metre Helshoogte Pass, through which lies Stellenbosch. The 'Four Passes' encircle the 22,570 hectare Hottentots-Holland Nature Reserve, which has peaks of 1,600+ metres; the closest one can get to it by car is through the Jonkershoek Forest, five kilometres east of Stellenbosch. There are various hiking trails through the Reserve, details of which can be obtained from local tourist information offices. Enquiries about general hikes in the area can be answered by calling (021) 886 5858, and for Jonkershoek in particular telephone (021) 886 5715.

FRANSCHHOEK

Franschhoek has a particularly beautiful setting, in the Berg River valley. It is a small, simple village—though it has some very sophisticated restaurants and vineyards—where the exiled French Huguenots made their home in the country in 1688.

Most of the wine estates here are within a short drive from Main Street (the R45) which runs through its centre. The **Vignerons de Franschhoek** office on Main Street (telephone 02212 3062) has an excellent map covering all the estates, giving precise visiting times, telephone numbers and locations. Particularly worth visiting are the **Bellingham, Boschendal, Môreson** and **Rickety Bridge** estates. The **L'Ormarins** estate produces some first-class wines, particularly chardonnay, but I dislike the estate for a very simple reason. As you drive into the estate's entrance, a hapless gatekeeper trots out, noting on a clipboard the number-plate of your vehicle. He then asks you to pay R5. Now, many estates make a similar small charge for tasting a selection of their wines. This is a fairly recent innovation—tastings were once free—and is apparently designed to prevent Stellenbosch University students from driving round all the estates and getting plastered for free. But most estates at least normally permit you to see what's on offer *before* you have to pay. L'Ormarins outrageously expects cash up-front, even before you know what you will be sampling, or indeed *if* you will be sampling. R5 is a trifling sum; but the principle of charging for something you haven't even seen is a disgrace.

There is a curiously-designed **monument** commemorating the Huguenots at the end of town, as well as a (uninteresting) museum, on the road towards Franschhoek Pass. Franschhoek is a charming place to spend a summer's day, out in the open, drifting from one estate to another—and taking a lengthy lunch during the interval.

STELLENBOSCH

Stellenbosch is an elegant, pretty, tree-lined town, home to one of the country's most famous (and predominantly Afrikaans-speaking) universities. The early Dutch settlers moved here from Cape Town to develop it as an agricultural centre but today it has the feel of being the epicentre of Afrikaner yuppiedom, as well as being a focus for wine-making. It is such a short drive from Cape Town that you might be tempted not to stay over, but that would be a mistake, even though its historic sites can seem a little repetitious after a while—how many examples of old Cape Dutch houses do you really want to see? You'll have your fill in Stellenbosch. Watch out for the numerous cyclists.

The lengthy **Dorp Street** is worth strolling down, as it has many of the local historical monuments, as well as a droll general store called **Oom Samie Se Winkel** ('Uncle Sammy's Store'). On **Ryneveld Street** is the **Village Museum**, 5,000 square metres of restored old houses. Much of the historical attraction of Stellenbosch is summed up in three words—Cape Dutch architecture. But it's also a lively town to spend an evening in, with plenty of good accommodation and restaurants, as you would expect from a small university town. It's rather like the Cambridge of the Cape. A short distance outside the centre on the R310 heading south is the impres-

WINE

Wine has been produced in the Cape for more than 300 years. The Dutch East India Company planted vineyards there in 1655, in order to help prevent scurvy among its sailors. By 1995, wine had become South Africa's fastest-growing export; in 1989, the year before the end of apartheid, export sales of wine were worth R80m; by 1995 that figure had grown to R480m.

Which is entirely as it should be. The long spell of international isolation meant that South African wine labels were rarely seen outside its borders. Not that people outside the country didn't drink South African wine; only it was not called South African but instead carried an east European label. There was plenty of sanctions-busting going on, with South African wine shipped in bulk to east Europe, where it was bottled

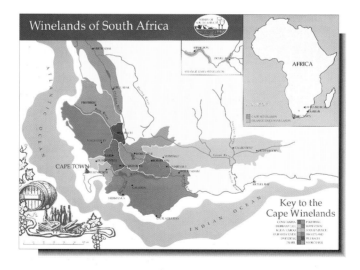

Winelands of South Africa

and re-exported as 'Ruritanian Red' or whatever.

Although the south western Cape, the main wine-producing region, is 35 degrees south of the equator, the confluence of the Atlantic and Indian oceans, plus cold currents flowing up the west coast of Africa from Antarctica, mean that the climate is cooler than might be imagined, giving the region more of a Mediterranean feel. Average annual rainfall is between 450 and 1,000 millimetres, largely between May and August. Summers are warm rather than bakingly hot; winters are mild, with frost only rarely. It's an ideal climate for producing wine.

Not just reds and whites, but ports, brandy, and some delectable late harvest (dessert, Sauternes-type) sweet wines, are produced. Unless you are teetotal, one of the greatest pleasures in visiting South Africa is sampling the wines, particularly its reds, some of which are as fine as any Australian or Californian. While few of the white wines possess the profundities sought from top class wines, some of South Africa's red wines—particularly pinotage, the hybrid unique to the

(above) *The beauties of the Cape*

Cape—can be really superb, and relatively inexpensive. You should expect to pay no more than R40 in a restaurant for an excellent red; restaurant mark-ups can be absurd, as much as 300 per cent on bottle store prices.

There are a dozen distinct wine producing regions, all in the Cape. If you are limited for time, arguably the three most important wine routes—Constantia, Paarl and Stellenbosch—are all within less than one hour's drive from Cape Town.

Constantia is a southern suburb of Cape Town, and is the site of Groot Constantia, Klein Constantia and Buitenverwachting, three farms which in 1685 were granted to Simon van der Stel, the first Dutch governor of the Cape. Groot Constantia is reckoned to be the country's most important example of Cape Dutch architecture and is a popular tourist spot. Stellenbosch is a delightful town with a famous Afrikaans university, and accounts for 15 per cent of the total vineyard area of the country. Paarl is home to an umbrella organisation for 4,300 wine farmers, the Cooperative Wine Growers' Association, KWV (Kooperatiewe Wynbouers Vereniging van Zuid-Afrika), formed in 1918. KWV is the largest wine producer in South Africa; its label is ubiquitous. Covering 19 hectares, the KWV complex is open to the public—as are many individual vineyards—during the week.

A total of almost 5,000 grape farmers cultivate approximately 100,000 hectares in the Cape. There are more than 80 individual estate wineries, making wine only from grapes grown on their own land; several cooperatives apart from KWV; and as many as 73 independent cellars which both buy in grapes and wine from other producers, and make wine from their own farms for bottling under their own labels.

But there is a problem concerning the quality-price relationship, one which has been exacerbated by the way South Africa's wine industry has been bureaucratically managed. The dominating force in wine production has long been KWV. Until 1992 wine could not be grown except on farms with a KWV-granted quota, a system which mitigated against producing wine purely on the basis of quality. Quantity was the overwhelming consideration; there was little incentive to bother too much about quality. Bulk delivery of low quality, low-priced wine was the acid test. Wine growers who stood out against that attitude were rare.

Things are changing fast; the fetters that enabled KWV to bind the industry are being rapidly dismantled, and there has recently been a splash of new wine-producers. But the wine industry is in a state of flux, anxious about the future and struggling to find a place in the highly competitive export business against exceptionally good products from Australia, Chile, New Zealand and the US.

When it comes to experimenting while in the country, the higher the price, the better the quality is not a universal truth, with either reds or whites. A further complication is that bottle stores and restaurant wine lists are crowded, swamped with produce. Most wine experts agree that South Africa's white wines—such as chardonnay, sauvignon blanc, chenin blanc or the various rieslings—are best drunk within a couple of years of production. Some of the best reds—cabernet sauvignon, merlot, pinot noir, pinotage and shiraz—can claim to be world-class, and will last and improve in the bottle.

How to navigate through this ocean? South African wines once carried a confusing series of stickers on their neck capsule, with green, red and blue stripes, indicating respectively variety, vintage and region of origin of the wine. Some wines carried a gold seal, a mark of supposedly superior quality. The gold seal's value was eroded by over-use, until finally it was abolished in 1989. The multi-coloured seal ended in 1993, though it's still possible to find perfectly acceptable older wines embellished with both types of seal—all it means is that they were produced before the change in regulations.

Now all South African wines must sport a Wine of Origin label, a small rectangular seal carrying a set of numbers, issued by the Wine and Spirit Board of South Africa. This should not be interpreted as a quality mark; it is simply a guarantee of the contents meeting the required standards, for example that if it claims to be made from the semillon grape, then it is.

The Boschendal wine estate

Supposedly superior wines are now allowed to place on their labels a Veritas emblem—either a gold or double gold medal, as awarded by 50 judges at the annual SA National Show, or SANS. This quality mark is believed to be more reliable than the old gold seal system, as the SANS panel includes several independent wine critics and a presiding foreign judge. A double gold medal wine must score at least 17 points (out of a total 20) in the estimate of five out of seven judges in its category; a gold medal wine needs to achieve at least 16 points. Double gold awards are rare—less than 10 per cent—while single golds are won by about 15 per cent of the entries, which amount to almost 1,000 wines annually. So if you want to know you are drinking only the best that South Africa can offer, look out for the gold medals.

On the other hand, why play safe when there's so much to choose from?

sive **Oude Libertas Amphitheatre** (telephone 021 808 7474) which has a wide repertoire during November–March.

There are more than 60 wine estates in the Stellenbosch area, nearly all of which are happy to have visitors for tastings, cellar tours and in some cases lunches. Some of the estates are quite far-flung from the centre of town and the trek is not necessarily worth the trouble. For example, when I visited the Thelema estate—which has become intensely fashionable and sells good but relatively expensive wines (by local standards)—in early 1996, there was only one wine available for sampling; the other seven were sold out; a wasted journey. Similarly, some estates give a very cold welcome; the staff at **Kanonkop** for example were more interested in discussing their personal problems among themselves than serving visitors who had come to sample wine. **Louisvale**, a short distance from the town centre, has some truly superb chardonnay and is in a beautiful setting, but requires you to drive past what looks—and smells—like the town dump. **Rustenberg** is well worth the relatively lengthy drive through countryside that looks more English than England; world-class wines and extremely friendly service, on an estate more than 300 years old, inside a delightful Cape Dutch manor.

In short, it can be a hit-and-miss experience, rather more so than in Franschhoek, which has the advantage of its estates being situated rather more closely together, so if you don't like one, there's another just a short drive away.

PAARL AND BEYOND

Another heavily Afrikaans-influenced town, **Paarl** has a couple of interesting sights and several extremely good wine estates.

The **Gideon Malherbe House** on **Pastorie Avenue** is generally recognized to be the place where the cause of promoting Afrikaans as an official language began in the late 19th century. It has the printing press on which the first Afrikaans language newspaper, *Die Afrikaanse Patriot*, was produced on 15 January 1876.

Just outside the town, high above on the southern slope of **Paarl Mountain**, so-called because it looks like a huge white pearl, is the **Taalmonument** or Afrikaans Language Monument, an ugly abstract erection raised in 1975. It's worth driving up there (via Jan Philips Drive from the town centre) simply for the spectacular view. The summit of Paarl Mountain is actually three dome-shaped rocks, the largest granite outcrops in South Africa—Paarl Rock, Bretagne Rock, and Gordon's Rock. The **Paarl Mountain Nature Reserve** surrounds this area, with trout-fishing permitted in the dams and plenty of bird-life.

Paarl has its fair share of good wine estates. **Nederburg** is perhaps the most famous, about five kilometres north-east of the town centre; it produces a wide range of highly-esteemed whites and reds. It's a very large estate so can have a slightly impersonal feel. For something completely different, very personal and small-scale, try the **Welgemeend** estate, about 15 kilometres south-west of Paarl towards Cape Town, just off the N1 highway. It's only open for sales and sampling on Saturdays, but if you just drop in you are certain of a warm welcome and a chat (telephone 02211 5210). A personal favourite is **Landskroon**, where the service is very efficient and friendly and the wines are superb, not least the port and muscat; it also has a pleasant outdoor restaurant. Nor can we forget the **KWV** co-operative, no matter how much we might try. It's the best-known wine label outside South Africa, even though it generally produces only indifferent wine by comparison with some of the private estates. But it is one of the world's largest wine complexes, is right in the town centre on Main Street, and puts on very good multi-lingual cellar tours (telephone 02211 73 007/8).

There are a variety of small towns north and east of Paarl also known for wine and fruit production, many of them pretty and easily accessible. To the north: **Wellington** (named after the Duke of Wellington) was established in 1840. Today it's rather a quiet place; north of the town, next to the railway line, stands the most southerly of a chain of 8,000 blockhouses built by the British during the 1899–1902 war. North of Wellington on the R45 is **Malmesbury**, largest town in the area known as the **Swartland** (or 'black land', probably named thus because of the dark fertile soil in the region). To the north-east of Malmesbury (along the R315) is **Riebeek Kasteel**, where the **Swartland Wine Growers Co-operative** has its head-quarters (open for tastings and sales 08.00–17.00 weekdays, 09.00–12.00 Saturdays; telephone 0224 21 134/5/6). From there is a short drive to **Tulbagh**, which is nestled between the Witsenberg, Winterhoekberg and Saronsberg mountain ranges. In 1969 the town suffered severe damage from an earthquake, and nine people died. It's been carefully restored however. In the town centre is the **Paddagang** cellar, which sells good wines and has a fine restaurant attached (telephone 0236 300 242). Another estate worth visiting here is the **Twee Jongegezellen**, slightly out of town but producing very popular wines (telephone 0236 300 680).

To the east: from Paarl on the N1 via Du Toit's Kloof you reach **Worcester**, in the area known as **Breede River Valley**. The town (founded in 1819) has what is claimed to be the world's largest **brandy distillery**, owned by KWV, on Church Street; tours run daily and you should make a reservation; telephone (0231) 20 255. There are also a large number of wine estates—contact Worcester tourist bureau for details. Off the N1 slightly north of the town is the **Karoo Botanical Garden**, where many of the local plants thrive; it's open to the public. South-east of Worcester (along the R60) is **Robertson**, with more than 20 wine estates sprinkled around this small town. Worth a detour from Robertson is **McGregor**, 21 kilometres south; it's a small, barely-touched village. Beyond Robertson on the R60 is **Montagu**, on the edge of the Little Karoo, a drier, more rugged region stretching for about 250 kilometres east, beyond **Oudtshoorn**. There are two hot springs where you can bath in water at a constant 43°C.

WESTERN COAST AND THE CEDARBERGS

Beyond Malmesbury, heading north, are a variety of coastal spots and inland areas which are infrequently visited by travellers.

If you divert left from Malmesbury (taking the R315 passing through **Darling**, heading west) and then take the coast road (the R27) heading north, after 37 kilometres you will arrive near the **West Coast National Park**, reached via **Langebaan**, which faces onto a lagoon 16 kilometres long by 4.5 kilometres wide, only 6m deep at its maximum. The Park itself (see **National Parks' appendix**, page 306) surrounds this lagoon on both sides, and makes a perfect spot for observing a host of bird life, such as penguins, waders, gannets and so forth. This salt-marsh and mudflat area has a wide range of observation hides, and is an ornithologists' paradise. The lagoon was once home to vast quantities of oysters, but water temperature changes killed them off; it's estimated that there are 30m tons of oyster shells covering the bed of the lagoon.

Beyond Langebaan is **Saldhana**, the southernmost town on the St Helena Peninsula. Saldhana itself is almost entirely given over to the fishing industry, but Saldhana Bay is one of the world's great natural harbours, deep enough for large vessels. In the bay is **Malgas Island**—which may be visited under supervision—where a quarter of the world's Cape Gannet population breeds. North of Saldhana on the peninsula are **St Helena Bay**, **Stompneusbaai** and **Paternoster**, small fishing villages which have scarcely been touched by modern life. Saldhana has a very active publicity association, which has lots of detailed maps and brochures concerning a vast range of hiking, horse-riding, diving and fishing activities (see **Tourist Bureau appendix**, page 318). Following the R27 north you will arrive at **Lambert's Bay**, another fishing industry town which has as its star attraction a crayfish canning centre.

Alternatively head north from Malmesbury up the N7—probably passing straight through **Moorreesburg**, which has little to detain you apart from enthusiasm (it promotes itself as 'the country town with the friendly people'), and also **Citrusdal** (a packing centre for the vast citrus fruit plantations of the Olifants River Valley), and you will arrive at **Clanwilliam**, a good spot to enter the Cedarberg mountain range, and the centre of the country's *rooibos* ('red bush') tea production. The **Cedarberg** range is one of the country's most beautiful set of mountains; it stretches for about 100 kilometres, a sandstone formation with deep red iron oxides, eroded into strange, fantastic shapes, tall peaks and jutting crags. The highest peak is Sneeuberg (2,027m) in this 80,000 hectare reserve, which has some very rare plant species, including the snow protea (which flowers only above the snow line). The cedars which give the range its name are the *Widdringtonia*

Flamingoes on St Lucia Lake

cedarbergensis, the gnarled, small, wind-twisted trees which grow at altitudes of 1,000-1,500m. There are several strange rock formations here, including: the Maltese Cross, a 10m high rock shaped like a cross; the Stadsaal ('town hall'), a mass of rock with chambers, caves and crevices and some San rock paintings; and the Wolfberg Arch. A full exploration of this range would take a week or more; there is a campsite at Algeria Forest Station and horse-riding trails can be arranged.

THE OVERBERG, CENTRAL KAROO AND GARDEN ROUTE

The Overberg extends east from the Hottentots-Holland mountain range, beyond the town of Grabouw on the N2 and slightly beyond Swellendam; it takes in the coastline from Gordon's Bay, down to Cape Agulhas, Africa's southernmost tip, up to Witsand, at the mouth of the Breede River. Much of the coastline is famous for whale-spotting.

The Overberg inland is dominated by the attractions of the relatively bustling town of **Swellendam**, 6 kilometres east of which is the country's smallest National Park, the **Bontebok**, established to protect this large antelope (see **National Parks' appendix**, page 302). Swellendam's main claim to fame is that for a brief period in 1795 it was an independent Republic. The British soon put paid to that by occupying the Cape that same year. Swellendam is 240 kilometres east of Cape Town on the N2, more or less in the middle of nowhere, but its publicity association works overdrive, listing 80 sites of historic interest in and around the town. One is certainly worth a visit; **Suurbraak** (25 kilometres east along the N2) is an old mission station established in 1812; hand-made wooden chairs are produced and sold there (telephone 02921 776).

But if you decide to take the coastal route, then as you leave Cape Town on the N2, and just before Sir Lowry's Pass, you should take the R44 to **Gordon's Bay**; north of there on the coast is the relatively neglected beach resort of **Strand**, which, because it's not terribly fashionable, has some very competitively priced accommodation much of the year. 55 kilometres following this coastal road takes you to **Betty's Bay**, which has some good beaches, safe for swimming, and, nearby, a nature reserve: **Harold Porter Botanic Reserve** (08.00–18.00, daily, telephone 02823 29 311), with a good walking trail and a profusion of flowers during spring-summer. Beyond Betty's Bay the same road runs through **Kleinmond**, which has a small lagoon, excellent for swimming. From there take the R43 to **Hawston** and then onto **Onrus** and **Sandbaai**, another couple of small, safe beach areas. The next point is **Hermanus**, the biggest town on this part of the coast and the best spot from which to look for whales between autumn and spring. There is a **whale-watching hotline** you can telephone for the latest information on sightings; call (0283) 22 629. Above the bay is a 12-kilometre walk, the best position to look for whales. Hermanus has so identified itself with whale-watching that the town even has a 'whale crier,' whose job it is to walk around town, blowing a horn and carrying a sandwich board on which are marked their positions. Also worth a visit near Hermanus are two wine estates, both in Walker Bay: **Hamilton Russel**, telephone (0283) 23 595 and **Bouchard Finlayson**, telephone (0283) 23 515.

From Hermanus the R43 takes a large inland detour via **Stanford**, a small Victorian village which has attracted various arts-and-crafts residents. 22 kilometres further on is **Gansbaai**, a true fishing village, and a good spot to buy fresh-caught fish. The road, now the R406, follows the coastline before turning into the R317, swinging north again to **Bredasdorp**, which has an interesting Shipwreck Museum, open 09.00–16.45 Monday–Thursday, 09.00–15.45 Friday, 09.00–13.00 Saturday, and 11.00–12.30 Sunday (telephone 02841 41 240). The stretch of coast near Bredasdorp is known as the graveyard of ships; more than 120 wrecks have been recorded here, the oldest dating back to 1673.

If being able to say you have been at Africa's southernmost tip is important to you, then you have little option but to drive the 40 kilometres south along the R319 from Bredasdorp to **Agulhas**; there is little of any interest there, however. Much better perhaps to go from Bredasdorp on the R316 south to Arniston, a genuinely delightful spot with long tracts of white beaches; it's a relatively unspoilt place, much-frequented by romantically-inclined couples hoping to get—and generally finding—some privacy. 68 kilometres from Bredasdorp (you will find this back-tracking rather irritating but there is no alternative) is the **De Hoop Nature Reserve**, which has some cottage and camping accommodation (telephone 02922 782); it's a 60,000 hectare reserve, with masses of unspoilt, remote beach, and a very good place to watch for whales, otters, bird-life and some antelope. The reserve stretches as far as **Infanta-on-River**, beyond which commences the **Garden Route**.

The Garden Route is one of the more well-trodden areas of South Africa. It has some excellent coastline, but its towns are frequently over-stuffed with tourists, and compared to the more remote spots to its west it often feels very crowded. Along the coast it starts (roughly speaking) at **Stillbaai**, takes in **Albertinia**, **Mossel Bay**, **George**, **Wilderness**, **Sedgefield**, **Knysna**, **Plettenberg Bay**, the **Tsitsikamma National Park**, and round as far as **Port Elizabeth**, with a host of smaller beach resorts sprinkled in between these larger spots. To the north of this coastal region—through which usefully runs the N2 highway linking Cape Town with Durban—are the **Outeniqua Mountains**.

Inland, across the Outeniqua range, is the region known as the **Klein** (or Little) **Karoo**, which essentially is ostrich country. To the north of the Klein Karoo is the tall, jagged Swartberg range of mountains, dividing the Klein from the more arid **Great Karoo**.

From **Suurbraak** (see above) you enter the Klein Karoo by taking the R324 via the **Tradouw Pass** (403 metres) to **Barrydale**, a village on the outskirts of which is the **Anna Roux Wild Flower Garden**, a charming little detour. From there, head towards Ladismith on the R62. Alternatively you could enter the Klein Karoo from the north, having taken the N1 highway heading north-east from Cape Town and stopping off at **Matjiesfontein**, a highly eccentric small village with a good hotel, called the **Lord Milner**; it's worth spending an overnight here. Matjiesfontein, which is in the central Karoo region, largely owes its existence to one man, **James Logan**, an official on the Cape Government Railways in the 1890s. Logan bought land around Matjiesfontein, which had a natural spring, and turned it into a useful watering-hole for thirsty locomotives. Logan quickly made a fortune and built a large hotel (today called Lord Milner), introduced cricket games and generally turned it into a prosperous place. In the 1899–1902 war it became a major hospital and garrison, a hub of military activity. The novelist Edgar Wallace, then a newspaper correspondent, used to send his despatches from here.

With the end of the war and the decline of steam trains, Matjiesfontein slowly returned to its natural state, a small village in the middle of nowhere. The whole village was declared a national monument in 1975, and it's gradually being renovated. The locals assiduously cultivate their main asset—eccentricity—by doing such things as offering short tours in a London double-decker bus. It's also a favourite spot for Capetonians enjoying romantic weekends away from the city. You really must visit the museum on the railway station—it's a huge and wonderful collection of odds and ends stashed away in the basement.

From Matjiesfontein head for **Laingsburg** (almost completely destroyed by flooding in 1981) on the N1, then turn right onto the R323 and head for **Ladismith**; from Barrydale it's reached via the R62. Ladismith, a small Victorian village overshadowed by the Swartberg's Toorkop (2,203m), is really the start of ostrich country. Ladismith is the second town in South Africa named for Lady Juana Smith, wife of governor Sir Harry Smith; the other is spelt **Ladysmith**, to distinguish it. From Ladismith head east towards **Calitzdorp**, taking a detour left to the **Seweweekspoort** ('Seven Weeks Port') **Pass**, which at 2,326 metres, is one of the world's greatest, if least-known, scenic passes. On the Pass is the old toll-house, which is said to be haunted by the ghost of a former toll-keeper, swinging his lantern after darkness. Double-back to Calitzdorp, 20 kilometres east of which there is a hot mineral spa resort.

Fifty-two kilometres further east along the R62 brings you to **Oudtshoorn**, heart of the ostrich-farming industry. Oudtshoorn itself is—unless you are crazy about ostriches—rather a flat, dull place; it has a couple of moderately interesting museums, including the **C P Nel Museum** (corner of **High** and **Baron Van Reede Streets**) which—would you believe it?—is devoted to the history of the ostrich. The **Arbeidsgenot Museum** (Jan Van Riebeeck Street) was formerly the home of the Afrikaans poet Cornelius Jacob Langenhoven, who today is remembered (if at all) as the author of the Republic's national anthem *Die Stem van Suid-Afrika*, an appropriately dreary, sombre tune. As for the ostriches, there are three show farms where you watch them at close quarters: **Highgate**, telephone (0443) 227 115; **Safari**, (0443) 227 311; and **Cango**, (0443) 224 623. On the road heading north to the Cango Caves is the **Cango Crocodile Ranch and Cheetahland**, open daily from 08.00, telephone (0443) 225 593.

But Oudtshoorn is not all feathers; on the R328 heading north, 27 kilometres from the town are the **Cango Caves**, perhaps the area's greatest tourist attraction.

(top) *Fruit picking in the Cape*; (bottom left) *Farm workers heading for church in the Great Karoo*; (bottom right) *The Klein Karoo*

Black farm labourers go looking for seasonal work

These caves are indeed one of the world's wonders, a one-kilometre, 90-minute walk through strangely-shaped, wonderfully-coloured massive dripstone rock formations. The caves are warm, so wear light clothing. Access is via guided tours only, which happen every hour between 08.00– 17.00 December-January and March-April, and between 08.00–16.00 in other months, 364 days a year—it's closed only on Christmas Day. Telephone (0443) 227 410. The final stages of the walk (which need not be taken) are not for the claustrophobic.

From the Caves you can travel further north up the R328 via the hairpin-bend **Swartberg Pass**, built by convict labour in 1881–1888; there is a nearby mountain reserve with good hiking trails. Beyond the Pass a signposted dirt road takes you to **Gamkaskloof**, once better-known as Die Hel, or The Hell, on **Gamkaspoort Dam**.

The hellish name derives from the intense heat that can develop there in the summer. All round this very isolated spot are walking trails and an abundance of wildlife. From here, double-back and head through Prince Albert up the R353 to rejoin the N1; 85 kilometres north along the N1 is **Beaufort West**, which is not an absorbing town, but nearby is the **Karoo National Park** (see **National Parks' appendix**, page 303).

The **Garden Route** is a fairly compact area criss-crossed by spectacular passes, linking the low-lying coastal towns with inland. It stretches for about 500 kilometres, from (in the west) Stillbaai to (in the east) Port Elizabeth. There are many points of insertion into the route from the north; from the east and west the N2 highway proves a useful through-way. Stillbaai, which is divided in two by an estuary, is a straightforward holiday home resort, deserted apart from school holiday times. At the mouth of the Gourits river, some 25 kilometres east of Stillbaai along a dirt road is **Gouristmond**, a small fishing village.

Further along the coast is **Mossel Bay**, which has a good beach but which scenically has been utterly ruined by the huge industrial refinery, Mossgas. However, Mossel Bay has a fascinating collection of four museums called the **Bartolomeu Dias Museum Complex**; there are Maritime, Shell, Granary and Local History museums (all 09.00–13.00, 14.00–17.00 Monday–Friday, 10.00–13.00 Saturday, 14.00–17.00 Sunday, telephone 0444 911 067). In 1488 the Portuguese explorer Bartolomeu Dias arrived on board two tiny vessels in Mossel Bay. The Maritime Museum is particularly interesting, having a life-size replica of Dias' ship; it's so small that his journey becomes even more miraculous to contemplate.

Further along is another ugly town, **George**, named for George III of England. From here you can take the Outeniqua Choo-Tjoe steam train to Knysna (see **Railways** in A–Z chapter, page 42). George must have changed greatly since 1877, when Anthony Trollope described it as 'the prettiest village on the face of the earth.' The George Museum claims to have South Africa's largest collection of working gramophones, as well as an exhibition of gifts given to former president P W Botha, who was born here. Sort of sums up George, really.

Beyond George is Wilderness, a great beach area and site of the **Wilderness National Park** (see **National Parks appendix**, page 306). Beyond there, past the holiday resort of Sedgefield—which has the largest natural inland salt-water lake in the country—is the delightful **Goukamma Nature Reserve**. On the eastern side of this Reserve is Buffelsbaai, a favourite swimming, surfing and angling spot. Further along is **Knysna**, a very popular tourist destination, set on a lagoon which is almost completely cut off from the sea; a very narrow channel connects it to the ocean. If you like water-sports, oysters, sea-fishing and scuba-diving, Knysna is the place for you.

Knysna has long been a place which seems to attract eccentricity and mystery.

Its surrounding high forest areas were, in the 19th century, home to a hermit-like community of Afrikaner woodsmen, who retreated further into their own thoroughly in-bred world. They shared the forests with wild animals, including herds of elephants, which were ruthlessly hunted for their ivory. There still are elephants in the Knysna forests today, though they are seldom spotted amid the tangled trees and ferns covering the mountains. Other reclusive inhabitants included **George Bernard Shaw**, who stayed here in 1932.

But perhaps the biggest eccentric of all was **George Rex**, who came from England to the Cape in 1797. When he took up residence in Knysna in 1804 he did it in grand style, transporting his wife and four children in a magnificent coach. Stories quickly spread suggesting that he was in fact the illegitimate son of George III of England. George Rex rapidly built up a minor business empire from his homestead, Melkhoutkraal, exploiting the vast local hardwood resources. He died in Knysna on 3 April 1839. There are several interesting museums in Knysna, the best perhaps being **Millwood House** (10.00–12.00 Monday–Friday), on Queen Street. In the 1880s there was a brief gold rush near Knysna and the mining town Millwood was established, dying away almost as fast as it appeared. This building has been relocated to Knysna, and it houses a collection of some of the possessions of George Rex.

From Knysna you can continue along the N2 towards **Plettenberg Bay**, but it's worthwhile taking a lengthy, sometimes hair-raising but always spectacular detour north, along the R339 to **Avontuur** and, beyond, **Uniondale**. This drive is less than 100 kilometres, but it will take you a full afternoon, simply because the gradients are very steep, the roads are not in the best of condition, and the hairpins are some of the tightest you will ever encounter, particularly through **Prince Alfred's Pass**, (named after Queen Victoria's second son, who hunted elephants here in 1867), over the Outeniqua Mountains. This is the heart of dense Knysna forest country which, even in summer, has the sweet smell of slowly rotting pine. At Uniondale, an otherwise dull little town, there is a well-preserved small fort dating from the 1899–1902 war, perched high above the town. It gives a wonderful panoramic view across a beautiful, rugged landscape.

If you continue along the N2, 40 kilometres later you will arrive at Plettenberg Bay, known to most South Africans simply as 'Plett'. This is one of the Garden Route's most heavily-frequented tourist spots, largely because it has some classy hotels and very good beaches. But the town itself is modern and dull. Far better to continue onwards to **Nature's Valley**, a small resort with excellent, little-known beaches, set in the **De Vasselot Nature Reserve**, which borders the **Tsitsikamma National Park** (see **National Parks' appendix**, page 305). Where, after all this dashing about, you should spend at least a week—just to unwind.

OSTRICHES

*I*n the second half of the 19th century the vagaries of fashion in London, Paris and New York had strange repercussions thousands of miles away, in the small South African town of Oudtshoorn, in the Little Karoo, near the Olifants River. The ostrich-feather boom was born, thanks to the Victorian taste for adorning fancy dresses with feathers taken from this large, ungainly, flightless, but immensely strong bird, which has its ideal environment in and around Oudtshoorn.

The ostrich was only domesticated in 1865, when 8,000 kilos of feathers were exported from South Africa, for a total income of £65,736. By 1882 that export figure had reached 115,193 kilos, sold for the (then huge) sum of £1,093,989. With the outbreak of World War I in August 1914, the craze for frivolity and frothy dress rapidly ebbed away—and South Africa's ostrich-feather industry shrivelled almost to nothing.

By 1939, when the following was written in that year's *The South and East African Yearbook and Guide for the Union-Castle Mail Steamship Company*, the heyday of the ostrich-feather industry was over:

'An exceptionally good bird should yield from 20 to 26 ozs of feathers and should give from 60 to 62 long whites and byocks and 60 to 70 long blacks [feathers], in addition to the body feathers. Birds can sometimes be plucked three times in two years, but once a year is a fair average. The cock should yield about one-third more than the hen.'

The birds were and are most numerous around Robertson, Montagu and Oudtshoorn. Climate has a very marked effect on the quality of the feathers; proximity to the sea-coast would seem to be essential.

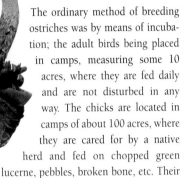

The ordinary method of breeding ostriches was by means of incubation; the adult birds being placed in camps, measuring some 10 acres, where they are fed daily and are not disturbed in any way. The chicks are located in camps of about 100 acres, where they are cared for by a native herd and fed on chopped green lucerne, pebbles, broken bone, etc. Their great enemy is the jackal. The cock-bird is often pugnacious, but can be easily warded off by means of a long thorn bush branch. A man was recently killed by one kick in the abdomen by a male ostrich.

A pair of birds breeds as often as three times in a year and can hatch some 16 or 17 eggs at a sitting.

The birds produce their first crop of feathers at six months old. Six months after this the next crop is ready to clip. The best feathers are grown in the spring and autumn months. They may live to over 100 years.

Around 1880, the great boom in ostriches commenced. People of all sorts left their employment to take part in an undertaking which was thought to show a certainty of a large fortune within a few years. £200 for a pair of birds was a common price. When particularly fine, they sometimes sold for £1,000. In 1886, owing to the fall in prices, many farmers were ruined, but the output was reduced and quotations rapidly recovered.

The following authentic record may prove interesting. In 1912, a breeder bought two adult pedigree birds. On 6 June, the hen laid her first egg. Between that date and November 1913, the pair hatched out 6 clutches (89 eggs) and produced 85 chicks. Of these, 82 were sold for £395 10s, an average of £4 16s 6d each. In addition to this, two clippings of feathers were sold, the first for £22, the second, when prices were lower, for £12. Total proceeds in 18 months, £429 10s.

The average valuation price for export at Port Elizabeth in 1910 was 61s 3d per lb., the record quotation since 1888. In 1914, feathers, nominally 30s just before the war, were almost unsaleable before the end of the year.

The change of fashion and the unsuitability of feathers for motoring has since reduced the number of birds in the Union [of South Africa] to about a fortieth of their former number.

In 1937, ostrich feathers in Paris (the Exhibition year) were said to be 'back in the limelight,' and in June 1938, they were reported as popular in Paris. 'The Duchess of Kent's liking for the feathers has been of service to S. Africa. May 1938 prices are reported to have increased from 10 to 15 per cent. There is a fine of £100 for exporting ostriches and of £5 for exporting eggs for incubating from South Africa.

'Experiments in tanning the skins of ostriches have met with much success, so much so as to threaten the disappearance of the ostrich from many districts. With skins worth about 5s and ostrich biltong 1s per lb. the birds have been worth more dead than alive.'

Today, although the feather boa is no longer a fashion item, there is another ostrich boom. Tourists flock to see South African ostrich farms; the skin is used in a variety of objects; and the low-fat, low-cholesterol meat (though expensive) is becoming increasingly popular, particularly in the context of world-wide scares over diseased beef. The ostrich is making a comeback.

ON BAKING AN ELEPHANT

The trunk and the feet are considered a delicacy, and a detachment [of men] are deployed on these. The four feet are amputated at the fetlock joint, and the trunk, which at the base is about two feet in thickness, is cut into convenient lengths. Trunk and feet are then baked, preparatory to their removal to headquarters. The manner in which this is done is as follows:- A party, provided with sharp-pointed sticks, dig a hole in the ground for each foot and a portion of the trunk. These holes are about two feet deep, and a yard in width; the excavated earth is embanked around the margin of the hole. This work being completed, they next collect an immense quantity of dry branches and trunks of trees, of which there is always a profusion scattered around, having been broken by the elephants in former years. These they pile above the holes to the height of eight or nine feet, and then set fire to the heap. When these strong fires have burnt down, and the whole of the wood is reduced to ashes, the holes and the surrounding earth are heated in a high degree. Ten or twelve men then stand round the pit, and rake out the ashes with a pole about sixteen feet in length, having a hook at the end. They relieve one another in quick succession, each man running in and raking the ashes for a few seconds, and then pitching the pole to his comrade and retreating, since the heat is so intense that it is scarcely to be endured. When all the ashes are thus raked out beyond the surrounding bank of earth, each elephant's foot and portion of the trunk is lifted by two athletic men, standing side by side, who place it on their shoulders, and approaching the pit together, they heave it into it. The long pole is now again resumed, and with it they shove in the heated bank of earth upon the foot, shoving and raking until it is completely buried in the earth. The hot embers, of which there is always a great supply, are then raked into a heap above the foot, and another bonfire is kindled over each, which is allowed to burn down and die a natural death; by which time the enormous foot or trunk will be found to be equally baked throughout its inmost parts. When the foot is supposed to be ready, it is taken out of the ground with pointed sticks, and is first well beaten, and then scraped with an assegai, whereby adhering particles of sand are got rid of. The outside is then pared off, and it is transfixed with a sharp stake for facility of carriage. The feet thus cooked are excellent, as is also the trunk, which very much resembles buffalo's tongue.

Roualeyn Gordon Cumming;
A Hunter's Life In South Africa: *1851*

Gordon Cumming was an officer in the Cape Mounted Rifles,
and frequent explorer of the country's interior.

Food & Restaurants

I tasted elephant's heart, roasted on a forked stick over the ashes, which I thought then, and still consider, to be one of the greatest delicacies that an African hunter is likely to enjoy.
Frederick Courteney Selous.

First, the good news. South Africans are big restaurant-goers, and there are thousands of restaurants. You can eat African, American, Chinese, French, German, Greek, Indian, Indonesian, Italian, Japanese, Middle Eastern, Mexican, Portugese, Thai, Spanish, South African...there's probably even a Venusian diner somewhere. In Johannesburg alone you could dine at a different place a night for a year. Some of the local specialities can be excellent. You can find *bredies* (stews), *bobotie* (a curried mince dish with onions and eggs), various dishes incorporating *waterblommetjie* (water lily buds), *potjiekos* (a meat and vegetable stew), *koeksisters* (plaited or twisted syrupy dough rolls) and *melktert* (milk tart).

The bad news is that it's a very crowded market, and—as with the country's wine—quantity has to some extent driven out quality. To get a first-class meal at a sensible price and without stifling pretentiousness is not easy. To make themselves heard, many restaurants resort to hyperbole, inflating their food and service way beyond its actual quality. Others focus more on packaging than food—you can dine at a place in Cape Town which claims to be the first 'Afro-Euro-Trash-Eatery,' not a boast many would imagine worth making. Most restaurants serve ok food at more or less palatable prices. But a large number believe themselves top-notch when they are merely second-rate. Restaurants can also be economical with the truth; in Cape Town you should try asking where the crayfish you are tucking into was caught—local crayfish are now quite scarce and many restaurants use frozen US imports. In Johannesburg—some considerable distance from the coast—many restaurants offer 'fresh' fish; it might be fresh, but most will have been frozen.

With the current tourist explosion, tour guides (who get a commission—the more visitors, the bigger it is) often take travellers to the same restaurant as every *other* tourist; for example, in the Cape Peninsula the Black Marlin restaurant, which specialises in excellent seafood, has become so popular that at weekend lunchtimes it's rather like eating in a factory canteen—nice food, horrible atmosphere. Far better try slightly further down the road, off the beaten track, the Camel Rock (Main Road, Scarborough, telephone [021] 780 11122—unlicensed, so bring your own wine or beer), where the food is every bit as good and somewhat cheaper, with scarcely a tourist in sight. Wherever you see a couple of coaches, you can reckon on a less-than-special eating experience.

There are no truly independent, objective restaurant guides available, although there are plenty of editorial puffs (as well as brief listings) of particular restaurants in most newspapers and magazines. South Africa's *Living* magazine annually publishes a fairly comprehensive guide, which (rather arbitrarily) identifies a 'top ten'; its greatest value lies in its listing of the addresses, telephone numbers and price ranges of some 250 of the generally accepted best restaurants, bars and cafes across the country. It's available (1996 price, R8) from *Living*'s publisher, Penta Publications; PO Box 597, Green Point 8051, telephone (021) 439 8167, or fax (021) 439 8196.

Recommended

Given these complexities, what follows can be no more than a personal list of favourites. The selection criteria are simple; high-quality food, good service, sensible prices. Expensive = R80+ per head; Moderate = R50-R80 per head; Cheaper = R30-R50 per head (excluding drinks, in all cases). In the expensive bracket most places aim at a kind of South Africanised French cuisine, ie decorative presentation of a variety of meats and fish served with exotic sauces. Many good restaurants don't have an alcohol licence—they operate a 'bring your own' policy; if in doubt, ask beforehand. Many of the recommended hotels, particularly the country lodges, (see **Appendix: Hotels**, page xxx) also have excellent restaurants. Finally, restaurants come and go; always telephone before going, just to make sure last year's hit is still around. Smoking has not become a social taboo; few restaurants have no-smoking areas.

TAKE-AWAYS

The *Chess-Scacchi* chain which produces (and delivers, if you want) excellent pizzas and pastas; at the last count, it had four outlets in Johannesburg's northern suburbs, one in Cape Town and another in Durban; in Johannesburg, telephone (011) 442 6276/7, for the Hyde Park branch. Cheap.

For both take-away and sit-down good food there are several nationwide chains of burger, grills, ribs (etc) joints; *Mike's Kitchen*, *Spur*, and *Steer* are all good family restaurants at competitive prices; for example take-away prices at *Spur* for huge burgers with french fries and salads are R15, and for 500 gramme steaks R45.

On Belgravia road in Athlone, a suburb of Cape Town, there is the *Wembley Roadhouse*, an unprepossessing name for what is certainly South Africa's finest take-away diner, serving everything from burgers, pizzas, curries to grills and salads; superb food, remarkably low prices, great fast service; telephone (021) 697 1435.

The Bakery, 90 St George's Street, Simonstown, serves great sandwiches, pies, health food, home-baked breads, cheeses and suchlike; telephone (021) 786 2412.

Look out for the ubiquitous 'cafe,' which is not a cafe in the commonly-understood sense, but a general store selling tobacco, newspapers, magazines, tinned produce, cold drinks and other bits and pieces. The take-aways available from such cafes are much patronised by black South Africans, essentially because of the very low prices. Try them; there's no pretence at gourmet fancifulness, but the food is usually good, extremely cheap, and nourishing.

Try also the pie-shops, now very common in urban areas and again, much patronised by black South Africans. Delicious pies on sale at what is (for foreign tourists) the ridiculously low price of R2-R3—just about what many black South Africans can afford to pay for a wholesome meal.

BLOEMFONTEIN
❏ Moderate
De Oude Kraal; 40 kilometres south of Bloemfontein on the N1 highway; telephone (05215) 636. Need to book for dinner, Sunday buffets a speciality, booked weeks ahead. Traditional South African country cooking.
Die Plaaskombuis: Jagersfontein Road, telephone (051) 441 8535. Traditional South African hearty cooking.

❏ Cheaper
Stephan Pieterse Restaurant: Hotel School, OFS Technikon, lunches only, Mon-Fri; telephone (051) 407 3231. Unusual; cooking and service by training students, tasty food and great service at excellent prices; need to book in advance.

CAPE TOWN/CAPE PENINSULA
❏ Expensive
Buitenverwachting: Klein Constantia Road, Constantia; telephone (021) 794 3522. Continental European style cuisine, formal.
The Cellars Restaurant: Cellars-Hohenort Hotel, 15 Hohenort Avenue, Constantia; telephone (021) 794 2137. Broad menu, Continental-style cuisine, formal.

❏ Moderate
Alphen: Alphen Drive, Constantia; telephone (021) 794 5011. Good for both lunch and dinner. French-style.
Kaapse Tafel: 90 Queen Victoria Street, Cape Town; telephone and fax (021) 23 1651. Relaxed, informal, serves a variety of Cape specialities.
On The Rocks: 45 Stadler Road, Bloubergstrand; telephone (021) 561 988. Excellent seafood, al fresco in fine weather.
Rozenhof: 18 Kloof Street, Gardens, Cape Town; telephone (021) 241 968. Continental-style.
Shrimpton's: Shrimpton Manor, 19 Alexander Road, Muizenberg; telephone (021) 788 1128. Renowned for seafood.

Tantina's Restaurant: Corner of Belvedere and Keurboom Roads, Claremont; telephone (021) 683 2456. French-style.

❏ Cheaper

Africa Cafe: 213 Lower Main Road, Observatory; telephone (021) 479 553. Note—this is a no-smoking restaurant. Dishes from Cameroon, Malawi, Mozambique, Senegal et al.

Barristers Grill Room and Tavern: Castle Building, corner of Kildare and Main Street, Newlands; telephone (021) 641 792. High quality steakhouse.

Bistro La Boheme: 52 Barnet Street, Gardens, Cape Town; telephone (021) 452 550. A no-nonsense French country cooking place.

Brass Bell: Waterfront, Kalk Bay; telephone (021) 788 5455. Excellent hearty fresh seafood dishes.

Cape Manna: 34 Napier Street, Cape Town; telephone (021) 419 2181. Traditional Cape Malay food such as bobotie, denningvleis, breyanis, waterblommetjie bredie.

Europa: 78 Regent Road, Sea Point; telephone (021) 439 2820. Fresh seafood, no-frills meat dishes, unpretentious.

Wangthai: 31 Heerengracht, Adderley Street, Foreshore, Cape Town; telephone (021) 418 1858. Authentic Thai food.

CAPE WEST COAST/SALDANHA
❏ Moderate

The Breakwater Boma: Near Saldanha. A 90 minute drive from Cape Town up the west coast is this unlicensed (so bring your own) informal beach braai, serving all kinds of seafood; you eat as much as you like for a set price. Arrive at 12.00, stay as long as you like. Bookings absolutely essential, as it's a (deservedly) very popular venue with locals. Telephone (02281) 42547, fax (02281) 43421.

Strandkombuis: At Yerzfontein, 80km up the west coast from Cape Town, another seafood braai establishment similar in all essentials to that listed immediately above. Booking again essential. Telephone (02245) 206, fax (02245) 716.

CAPE WINELANDS
❏ Expensive

Bosman's: Grand Roche Hotel, Plantasie Street, Paarl; telephone (02211) 632 727. Winner of numerous accolades, formal, judged by many the best (European-style) cuisine in the country. It's all a matter of taste.

❏ Moderate

Boschendal: Pniel Road, Groot Drakenstein, near Paarl, off the R310 road; telephone (02211) 41 252. Set on a wine estate, formerly Cecil Rhodes' country home.

Restaurant—hot and cold buffet—and picnic baskets.

De Volkskombuis: Wagenweg, off Dorp Street, Stellenbosch; telephone (021) 887 2121/887 5239. Traditional Cape cooking.

Doornbosch: Old Strand Road, Stellenbosch; telephone (021) 887 5079/886 6163. French and Italian.

Decameron: 50 Plein Street, Stellenbosch; telephone (021) 883 3331. Very popular; simple, first rate Italian cooking.

Le Ballon Rouge: 12 Reservoir Street, Franschhoek; telephone (02212) 2651. Superb fresh locally produced ingredients, exceptionally good value.

Le Quartier Francais: 18 Huguenot Road, Franschhoek; telephone (02212) 876 2151. Attached to excellent country hotel, good local produce, renowned cooking.

❏ Cheaper

Mamma Roma: Stelmark Centre, Merriman Avenue, Stellenbosch; telephone (021) 886 6064. Family-style Italian specialties.

Nautilus: Grotto Beach, Hermanus; telephone (0238) 770 090. Good fresh seafood, excellent location overlooking Walker Bay.

Paddagang Wine House: 23 Church Street, Tulbagh; telephone (0236) 300 242. Lunches only; traditional Cape cooking.

DURBAN
❏ Expensive

Royal Grill: Royal Hotel, 267 Smith Street; telephone (031) 304 0331. Still the classiest dining experience in Durban; international cuisine.

❏ Moderate

Christina's Restaurant: 134 Florida Road; telephone (031) 303 2111. Interesting French-inclined international cuisine, an off-shoot of an established cooking school.

Roma Revolving Restaurant: John Ross House, Victoria Embankment; telephone (031) 376 707. Panoramic city/harbour views in slowly-revolving setting; good Italian food.

St Geran: 31 Aliwal Road; telephone (031) 304 2018. French-Mauritian spicy cooking.

Ulundi: Royal Hotel, 267 Smith Street; telephone (031) 304 0331; the best place in Durban for classic Indian food and game dishes.

❏ Cheaper

Lord Prawn: 47 West Street; telephone (031) 372 978. Lashings of fresh seafood.

O'Cacador: 546 Point Road; telephone (031) 377 214. Popular, lively; Portugese-style seafood.

Swiss Chalet: Tinsley House, 225 Musgrave Road; telephone (031) 21 3508 (and two other outlets). Generous portions of interesting Swiss-style food.

JOHANNESBURG
❏ Expensive
Cullinan: 115 Katherine Street, Sandown; telephone (011) 884 8544. Extensive international menu, well-heeled patrons.
Three Ships: Carlton Hotel, Commissioner Street; telephone (011) 331 8911. International. Very good food, classy setting.
Zoo Lake Restaurant: Zoo Lake, Parkview. International cuisine. (011) 646 2991/646 8807.

❏ Moderate
Coachman's Inn: 29 Peter Place, Lyme Park, Sandton; telephone (011) 706 2976. French. Extensive menu, also carvery.
French Bistro: Shell Court, corner of Baker Street and Cradock Avenue, Rosebank; telephone (011) 442 5965/6. French. Bistro-style ambience.
Leipoldt's: 94 Juta Street, Braamfontein; telephone (011) 339 2765. Excellent traditional South African dishes.
Longhorn: Hyde Park Centre, Hyde Park; telephone (011) 442 7345. Good for families, famous for meat.
Mary-Anne's Whole Food Emporium: Shop 5, The Colony, 345 Jan Smuts Avenue, Craighall; telephone (011) 442 3836/7; excellent vegetarian cuisine.
The Carnivore: Muldersdrift Estates, Plot 69, Muldersdrift; telephone (011) 957 2099, fax (011) 957 3132. African-style dishes, including exotic meats such as ostrich, crocodile, cooked over an open fire in the restaurant, as well as unusual vegetarian food. On arrival you are promised a Dawa—a blend of vodka, honey, lime chunks, sugar and ice.

❏ Cheaper
Cranks: Shop 52, Rosebank Mall, Cradock Avenue, Rosebank; telephone (011) 880 3442. Thai/Indonesian.
Franco's Pizzeria and Trattoria: 54 Tyrone Avenue, Parkview; telephone (011) 646 5449; good quality Italian food.
Guildhall: 88 Market Street, on the corner of Harrison Street; telephone (011) 836 5560. Good for an unpretentious pub lunch, where if the weather is fine you can sit on an outside balcony (rare in Johannesburg).
Iyavaya: 42 Hunter Street, Yeoville; telephone (011) 648 3500. African. Marinated baby crocodile, mopani worms stewed in milk, ostrich in pepper sauce—and much else.

PRETORIA
❏ Moderate
Gerhard Moerdyk: 752 Park Street, Arcadia; telephone (012) 344 4856. Traditional South African food.

La Madeleine: 258 Esselen Street, Sunnyside; telephone (012) 446 076. French-style bistro.

Lombardy: Lynnwood Road East; telephone (012) 87 1284. French-style, small menu but high quality.

Vivaldi: New Muckleneuk Centre, Bronkhorst Street, New Muckleneuk; telephone (012) 46 8828. Good Italian.

❏ Cheaper
Taormina: 654 Jacqueline Drive, Garsfontein Park; telephone (012) 998 9204. Italian.

GENERAL
❏ Cheap
Knysna; Grey Street, telephone (0445) 826 514. Roast House. Astonishing good value for money; simple roasts, carvery, soups, desserts at a very low set price, second helpings included.

Mossel Bay; Santos Road, telephone (0444) 911 995. Santos Express. Family restaurant in a railway carriage on the beach. Excellent straightforward food, exceptionally cheap.

Port Elizabeth; 35 Westbourne Road, telephone (041) 331 707. Sabatinos. Excellent traditional Italian cooking.

East London; King David Hotel, 25 Inverleith Terrace, Quigney, telephone (0431) 23 174. Casbah. Middle eastern and Mediterranean cuisine.

❏ Moderate
Port Elizabeth; 5 George Street, telephone (041) 555 534. Sir Rufane Donkin Rooms. Cape-style influenced small but interesting menu, regularly changed.

Port Elizabeth; corner of Russell and Rose Streets, telephone (041) 559 684. Ranch House of Steaks. Steaks, Turkish and Greek fare.

Grahamstown; 10 Market Street, telephone (0461) 311 287. The Cock House. Also a comfortable small hotel; blend of British and eastern cookery.

Knysna; 57 Main Street, telephone (0445) 21616. La Loerie. French-style nouvelle cuisine.

Knysna; Rheenendal, telephone (0445) 4804. Portland Manor. Good value three course set menu of local produce.

BUSINESS AND ECONOMY

O ne of the quips doing the rounds of South African dinner parties in 1996 was that while the rest of Africa was spiralling into unmanaged decline, South Africa was much better off—at least its decline was being managed. That grim joke doesn't detract from the fact that South Africa possesses all basic necessities for conducting business. Telephones, faxes, the Internet, the making and keeping of appointments, availability of research information, reliable statistics, a network of skilled corporate support services—all exist and function well. Superficially, the South African economy feels vibrant; certainly the entrepreneurial spirit is alive and kicking.

But on deeper levels there are worries. South Africa is by far the continent's most powerful economy, but it's an economy utterly distorted by apartheid. The historian Charles van Onselen sums up the kernel of the problem: 'The resources of this country have so far been harnessed to serve the needs of just four million people. Now they are having to stretch to meet the demands of forty million people.'

South Africa requires an annual, sustained growth rate of as much as six per cent, simply in order to absorb each year's new entrants to the job market and begin emptying the vast reservoir of long-term jobless—in 1996 as much as 40 per cent of the black population was unemployed. That sort of growth rate is a tall order; real gross domestic product grew by little more than three per cent in 1995, and was unlikely to be more in 1996. Inflation is likely to return to double figures in 1997, and will bring with it strong pressure from the powerful unions for rises neither the public nor private sectors can afford. Without strong economic growth and low inflation, the uneasy political stability will not last.

At the heart of the government's policy to redress the socio-economic damage caused by apartheid is a Reconstruction and Development Programme (RDP), aimed at fostering democracy, stimulating urban renewal and rural development, and creating a mass culture of paying for services. Many black South Africans, so long excluded from the formal economy, are unaccustomed to paying taxes, or paying for services such as electricity, water, sewage disposal, and health care. The government sees itself as having a responsibility to bring such basic necessities to all members of the community; but someone has to foot the bill.

A key test for the government—which it is so far failing—is its house-building programme. There is a desperate need for housing, as a cursory glance at almost anywhere in the country reveals. The RDP plans to spend more than R40 billion before the year 2000 on a host of schemes, including building 200,000 new houses a year, schools, hospitals, and providing electricity and water to under-developed areas. In 1993 there was an estimated national housing shortage of almost 1.45 million dwellings, with demand growing at an estimated 200,000 units a year. Even if the RDP succeeded in its housing provision aim, it would still only be standing still; by 1996 it had already fallen far behind its target.

There is also the question of where the R40 billion for the RDP will come from. So far the government has exercised fairly tight fiscal controls, but with just nine per cent of taxpayers paying 94 per cent of direct taxes, and income tax rates already relatively high by international standards, it was (in 1996) difficult to see the additional finance necessary for the RDP coming from internal sources. As far as external lenders are concerned South Africa is a low priority, given the world's many catastrophic basket cases. In the next few years there will be tremendous pressure to loosen fiscal controls, in order to satisfy the RDP's needs and fend off a political backlash against the ANC-dominated government.

There are other pressures, too, not least Cape Town's ambition to stage the 2004 Olympic Games. Organisers of Cape Town's bid for the games are, according to reports in 1996, lobbying for national government to spend as much as R1bn—more than £170m—in capital expenditure for this project. Those pushing for Cape Town to stage the games argue that the investment will create much-needed jobs and houses, but it's a very speculative enterprise and doubt must be cast over its wisdom; are the Olympics really a priority, when so much else needs urgent attention?

One optimistic sign is, oddly enough, the explosion now happening in the informal sector. Arguably the biggest employment programme of the 1990s has nothing to do with government initiatives; to see it, you just need to take a walk around downtown Johannesburg, or the streets of any large urban area; the pavements are packed with street hawkers selling a whole range of goods and services. According to a government report in March 1995, South Africa then had about 800,000 small and medium enterprises (SMEs), with an estimated 3.5

million people working for them, involved in what it termed 'survivalist enterprise'. Some of these SMEs could eventually grow into major businesses, providing much needed jobs and taxes. But such street entrepreneurs might also be content with lesser ambitions; a barber in Johannesburg in 1996 was earning as much as R3,000 a month, three times the wage of an average goldmine worker—and no income tax. Even a street-level banana-seller was making more than the goldminer.

In other ways, too, a massive redistribution of wealth was going on after 1994, almost unnoticed. In 1995 car theft in South Africa was estimated to have had an annual turnover equivalent to $1.15 billion. Stealing cars had become an industry larger than many of the country's biggest companies. In that year alone, car thieves accounted for turning over almost two-thirds of the legitimate car industry, which sold 163,858 new cars. Crime is not completely negative for the economy. Car sales increase (many of the stolen vehicles disappear); insurance premiums go up; and the security business in 1996 employed some 200,000 people, almost half as many as were working in mining.

While South Africa is an economic giant on the African continent, in global terms it is a relatively small player; its GDP in 1995 was some $135 billion, and GDP per capita just over $3,200. Some of its traditional economic strengths are weakening. Mining is still a highly important aspect of the country's economy, accounting for about 50 per cent of foreign exchange earnings, employing some 12 per cent of the workforce directly, and as much as a third, indirectly. South Africa is still the world's number one gold producer, annually extracting some 550 tonnes. But this is a significant drop from the 1,000 tonnes of 1970, and mining overall shed more than 200,000 jobs in the first half of the 1990s. Other sectors of the economy—such as manufacturing, agriculture, financial services and tourism—are well-developed, but in the mid-1990s only tourism looked to be an area where dramatic growth was possible. The Johannesburg Stock Exchange—the 12th largest in the world—suffers from very low liquidity and widespread suspicion that it is a cosy old boy network, not least because five large conglomerates control as much as 80 per cent of the quoted stocks. Reform of corporate laws and practices is long overdue, but is (inevitably) not a dominating priority for the ANC. Leading figures in the ANC want to see the break-up of the large conglomerates that have dominated the private sector for many years; that is easier said than done.

Hotels, Lodges, and B&Bs

South Africa has some of the world's most luxurious hotels. It also has a fine range of excellent bed and breakfasts (B&Bs), country lodges, and wildlife or game reserves, both state-run and private. An appendix gives details of both private game reserves and National Parks accommodation; this section concentrates on hotels, lodges and B&Bs.

The democratic changes have encouraged tourists to flock to the country in vastly increased numbers, which it turn makes it imperative to book accommodation - luxury or otherwise—well in advance during the peak season, which has expanded to stretch from November to March. Prices for accommodation - even for the very best hotels—are still low by international standards.

A note about **children**. It's one of the more infuriating aspects of travelling in South Africa that some hoteliers appear to wish children did not exist. A surprising number of hotels, country lodges and B&Bs do not accept children beneath a certain age; which age, varies enormously. Most of the major chains are, however, quite happy to accept children. Check before making bookings.

Satour

The South African Tourism Board (Satour) grades hotels on a voluntary basis on a scale of one to five stars. It regularly inspects these establishments. **One star** signifies comfort; **Two stars** indicate very good; **Three stars**, excellent; **Four stars**, outstanding; **Five stars** luxury. This system is quite accurate, though some international travellers may feel five-star luxury in South Africa is not quite as good as five star luxury elsewhere.

Confusingly, lack of Satour stars does not necessarily mean poor quality; indeed, some of the most comfortable, attractive places to stay are small, privately-run hotels that have opted to stay outside the Satour system. Satour also gives accreditations to country houses and B&Bs. The first place to look for guest house, B&B, and country lodge accommodation is Satour's annually updated *National Accommodation Guide*, a very comprehensive and clearly laid-out book, available from all Satour offices (*see* SATOUR APPENDIX, *page 313*).

Satour accommodation inspectors are very fussy people and demand the highest standards. The hoteliers who choose to be in Satour's system pay only a very small levy to do so, meaning (potentially) a more objective account than is perhaps the case with more commercially-minded publications.

Privately-Published Accommodation Guides

There are many specialist publications listing hotels, the most ample probably being the annual *Guide to Hotels in Southern Africa*, published by Struik. It's not completely comprehensive; a number of very fine small hotels and lodges are not included. Struik also publishes a guide to B&Bs.

There are other useful publications, but it must be remembered that most of them are partly advertorials—ie, the hoteliers have paid, in some cases considerable sums—for the privilege of appearing. Nevertheless, the standards of accommodation are usually exceptionally high. Here are some:

The Hotelogue, PO Box 160, Green Point, 8051 Cape Town, telephone (021) 434-1954, fax (021) 434 0489. Fifty of the finest individual hotels and game reserves.

The Portfolio of Country Places, *The Retreats Collection*, and *Portfolio's Bed & Breakfast Guide*, all available from PO Box 483, Swellendam, 6740 Cape. Telephone (0291) 43341, fax (0291) 43337. Each of these lists individual, privately-owned accommodation. The Portfolio collection consists of pocket-sized guides, and the standard of accommodation is unquestionably high. But remember that hoteliers pay a large fee to appear in them; some excellent places don't appear, because they choose not to pay the price.

Bed and Breakfast South Africa: PO Box 91309, Auckland Park 2006, South Africa; telephone (011) 482 2206/7, fax (011) 726 6915. A large number of B&B's across the country.

The Jacana Collection: Jacana publish collections of self-catering country cottages, fully inclusive country homes, B&B's on farms, self-catering coastal cottages, hiking, horse and mountain bike trails. Jacana Country Homes and Trails, PO Box 95212, Waterkloof 0145, South Africa; telephone (012) 346 3550/1/2, fax (012) 346 2499.

The Leading Hotels of Southern Africa: A collection of some of the best (and most expensive) hotels. Central Reservations Office, PO Box 78291, Sandton 2146, South Africa; telephone (011) 884 3583 and 884 3613, fax (011) 884 0676.

Secluded Country Lodges: A smaller outfit but with an interesting selection of lesser-known places to stay. PO Box 2473, Parklands 2121, South Africa; telephone (011) 442 5640, fax (011) 442 5675.

In KwaZulu-Natal Midlands for B&B and self-catering accommodation obtain a brochure called *Selected Mini-Stays*. PO Box 1327, Pietermaritzburg 3200; telephone and fax (0332) 303 343.

There are at least two B&B booking agencies worth trying in Johannesburg; the *Bed and Breakfast Association*, 11 Shaw Road, Blairgowrie 2194; telephone (011) 787 3169/803 7170, and *Home Hospitality*, PO Box 73992, Fairlands 2030; telephone (011) 477 7967.

Hotel Chains

There are several excellent hotel chains, providing superb family accommodation, some at quite reasonable rates. The vast increase in tourist numbers has also sent other international groups hunting for suitable locations; the Hyatt, Hilton, Days Inn and Golden Tulip chains are all planning to build new hotels in the near future, so check with Satour for latest developments.

SOUTHERN SUN
Country-wide network of 60 hotels, resorts and game reserves ranges from highly expensive, five star luxury, through Holiday Inns to the superb value for money Formule 1, ultra-budget hotel. Reservations and brochures: PO Box 782553, Sandton 2146, South Africa; telephone (011) 780 0100, fax (011) 780 0106/7.

PROTEA
The Protea chain has 56 good middle-range hotels dotted across the country, ideal for families and travellers looking for comfort at affordable prices. Reservations via 5th Floor Nedbank Foreshore Building, Heerengracht, Cape Town; telephone (021) 419 8800, fax (021) 419 8200.

KAROS
A smaller network of reasonable hotels. Central reservation information can be obtained from PO Box 87534, Houghton 2041; telephone (011) 643 8052, fax (011) 643 4343.

SUN INTERNATIONAL
These hotels are mainly located in the former so-called homelands, and are dedicated as much to gambling and nightlife as providing accommodation; the quality

can be high, though some are depressingly tacky. Central reservations: PO Box 784487, Sandton 2146; telephone (011) 783 8750, fax (011) 883 5561.

Prices

It's difficult to give precise indications of prices in the context of significant inflation and the continual slow slide of the Rand against other currencies, though the two tend to cancel each other out. Prices fluctuate wildly between high and low seasons; most places charge a "single supplement".

Very good B&Bs can be found for the equivalent of less than £25 per person per night, while a night enjoying the supposedly last word in luxury - such as at the Grande Roche in Paarl or The Mount Nelson in Cape Town - will cost five times that. Unless specified, quoted prices include breakfast but not other meals. A general indication of price is given by the following, based on one person/one night occupation:

> A — Expensive — (R450 and above)
> B — Moderate — (R200–R450)
> C — Cheaper — (below R200).

Satour star gradings and accreditations are mentioned where they exist.

Personal Recommendations

The following is a very small selection of the vast amount of hotels, country inns and B&Bs on offer. All are quite different in style and price, and (almost all) are unreservedly recommended; many have swimming pools and gardens. Apart from some B&Bs, all take credit cards.

EASTERN CAPE
GRAAFF-REINET
Drostdy Hotel. B/☆☆☆. Originally designed in 1804, the Drostdy is friendly, comfortable, though some of its fittings feel a little tired. The staff claim to have seen ghosts wandering the front entrance late at night, but that might be an effort to introduce sparkle into Graaff-Reinet's dismal nightlife. PO Box 400, Graaff-Reinet 6280; telephone (0491) 22161, fax (0491) 24582.

GRAHAMSTOWN

Cathcart Arms. C/✫✫. Claims to be the country's oldest hotel, having applied for its first liquor licence in 1825. Small, comfortable. PO Box 6043, Grahamstown 6141. Telephone (0461) 27111. Grahamstown also has a very useful Bed & Breakfast Association; telephone (0461) 28 001/28 835.

HOGSBACK

Hogsback Inn. C/✫✫. Small, comfortable country-style inn. Telephone (045) 962 1006.

PORT ELIZABETH

The Edward Hotel. B/✫✫. Edwardian-style, built 1900, large, comfortable, walking distance to city centre yet with magnificent view of the city and harbour. PO Box 319, Port Elizabeth 6000; telephone and fax (041) 56 2056.

RHODES

The Rhodes Hotel. C/✫. A tucked-away delight. Small 19th century hotel in a peaceful village popular with skiers who use the slopes of Ben MacDhui (3,000 metres) in winter. Good food, also self-catering accommodation in cottages. PO Box 21, Rhodes 5582; telephone (04542) and ask for Rhodes 21.

UMTATA

Try not to stay in Umtata. It's grim and potentially very hostile.

WILD COAST

There are several small resorts along the coast, most of them in the C category, most of them with good restaurants and rondavel/thatched cottage accommodation. Given the collapse of tourism in this part of South Africa, booking should not be difficult; if you are prepared to haggle you can probably get a good discount on rate-card prices. **Trennery's** (telephone 0474 3293); **Mazeppa Bay** (telephone 0474 3287); **Kob Inn** (telephone 0474 4421); **Umngazi River Bungalows** (contact the East London publicity association for details how to book this exceptionally remote and peaceful beach resort).

FREE STATE

BLOEMFONTEIN

De Oude Kraal Country Lodge. Satour accredited guest house. C. Strictly speaking not in Bloemfontein, but some 40km south; farmhouse, comfortable, excellent food.Telephone (05215) 636/733. Bloemfontein has several of the standard hotel chains but it is not an attractive city to stay in.

FOURIESBURG

Fouriesburg Hotel. C/☆☆. Small, good food, good for an overnight en route break, 50km south-west of the Golden Gate Highlands National Park. PO Box 114, Fouriesburg 9725.

ZASTRON

Maluti Hotel. C/☆☆☆. Small, comfortable, traditional local cooking. Telephone (05542) 107.

GAUTENG

JOHANNESBURG

Gold Reef City Hotel. B/☆☆☆. Gold Reef City is a theme park some 6 kilometres from the centre of Johannesburg. Within it is the hotel, which is modelled on a Victorian-style hotel, fixtures and fittings trying to emulate that period. Comfortable, clean and quiet, the only drawback is that it's inside the theme park. PO Box 61, Gold Reef City 2159, telephone and fax (011) 496 1626.

The Carlton. A/☆☆☆☆☆. Still beyond question the best hotel in Johannesburg, with excellent restaurants, it has everything going for it—except its location, the central business district of downtown Joburg. The Carlton will, if you request it and no doubt at extra cost, provide you with a personal security escort when you walk out during the day, but not at night; downtown Joburg is regarded as being too hazardous after dark even for security guards. A large hotel, it closed several floors in 1996, such was the collapse in demand. Consider haggling for cheaper rates and ask about 'special offers'. PO Box 7709, Johannesburg 2000; telephone (011) 331 8911, fax (011) 331 3555.

Two highly recommended B&Bs, within easy driving distance to either Sandton or downtown Joburg and in the C price category are: **Romney Cottage**, 75 8th Avenue, Parktown North, Johannesburg 2193, telephone (011) 442 7548, fax (011) 792 7341; and **The Cottages**, 30 Gill Street, Observatory, Johannesburg 2198, telephone (011) 648 4279, fax (011) 648 4228.

MAGALIESBURG

Mount Grace Country House Hotel. C/☆☆☆. A small, very comfortable hotel about one hour's drive north-west of Johannesburg. Ideal for a short break away from the city. PO Box 4, Magaliesburg 2805; telephone and fax (0142) 771 109.

PRETORIA

La Maison. C. Excellent Satour accredited guest house; 235 Hilda Street, Hatfield,

Pretoria 0083; telephone (012) 434 341. Other good guest houses (also price category C) are the **Battiss** (former home of painter Walter Battis) telephone (012) 467 318; **God's Window B&B**, telephone (012) 807 0902; **Sherwood Forest Guest House**, 131 Hugh Street, Sunnyside, Pretoria 0132; telephone (012) 344 4850.

Various furnished self-catering apartments are good value if you plan a longer stay or are tired of hotels, price category C: the **Clara Berea Lodge**, telephone (012) 320 5665, fax (012) 322 5601; **Executive Cottages**, telephone (012) 348 8698, fax (012) 997 2222; and **Trafalgar Court**, telephone (012) 344 4100, fax (012) 343 2809.

SANDTON

One of Johannesburg's northernmost suburbs, Sandton is also one of the plushest. As a consequence of the high crime rates in Johannesburg's central business district, many businesses are relocating to the northern suburbs; in the past decade Sandton has altered from feeling a little remote from the action to being prime residential and commercial real estate. Beyond any question the classiest—and priciest—hotel in Sandton is the five star jewel of the Southern Sun chain, the **Sandton Sun and Towers**, A/☆☆☆☆☆. The place where international stars and well-heeled business professionals choose to stay in Joburg. PO Box 784902, Sandton 2146; telephone (011) 780 5000, fax (011) 780 5002.

KwaZulu-Natal

BERGVILLE

Sandford Park Lodge. C. Late 19th century buildings, a cosy lodge in the foothills of the Drakensberg. Good food and wines, swimming pool, pretty setting. PO Box 7, Bergville 3350; telephone (036) 448 1001, fax (036) 448 1047.

DURBAN

Karos Edward Hotel. A/☆☆☆☆. A splendid hotel on the beach front, it recently closed for refurbishing but was due to have opened again mid-1996. It used to be excellent, certainly as good as The Royal, and should be worth checking out. Telephone (031) 373 681.

The Royal. A/☆☆☆☆☆. For those who can afford it, the only place to stay in Durban, largely because of its very central location. Large and comfortable, the fixtures and fittings are beginning to feel a little tired. It also charges guests R20 a day for parking, which is a rip-off. PO Box 1041, Durban 4000; telephone (031) 304 0331, fax (031) 307 6884.

Various B&Bs are all excellent value for money and comfortable, within the C price category: **Stonegarth**, (Satour accredited) - telephone (031) 202 8249; Jill's B&B, telephone (031) 202 7577; **The Villa**, telephone (031) 764 3583; and **Annie's Place**, telephone (031) 847 358.

HIMEVILLE
Sani Pass Hotel. B/✫✫✫ (price includes dinner). A child-friendly hotel 1,500 metres above sea level in the beautiful Drakensberg foothills; lots of activities, 255km from Durban. PO Box 44, Himeville 4585, KwaZulu-Natal; telephone and fax (033) 702 1320.

HOWICK
Old Halliwell Country Inn. B/✫✫✫✫. A collection of well-appointed, extremely attractive cottages, some of the most comfortable beds to be found anywhere. Good food, wide selection of wines, cosy friendly atmosphere. PO Box 201, Howick 3290; telephone (0332) 302602 and (mobile) 082 800 5226; fax (0332) 303 430.

MARGATE
Margate Sands: A/✫✫✫✫. An exclusive self-catering lodge on Margate main beach. PO Box 653, Margate 4275. Telephone (03931) 22 543, fax (03931) 73 753.
Mont-aux-Sources: Five of southern Africa's major rivers rise from this peak of 3,282 metres within the Drakensberg's Royal Natal National Park. Two places to stay in this beautiful area are the Karos Mont-aux-Sources (B/✫✫✫), a very child-friendly, well-equipped hotel - Private Bag 1, Mont-aux-Sources 3353, telephone and fax (0364) 381 035; and the Royal Natal National Park Hotel, (C) which offers thatched cottages and rondavels as well as luxury rooms at excellent value for money—Private Bag 4, Mont-aux-Sources 3353, telephone (036) 438 6200, fax (036) 438 6101.

NOTTINGHAM ROAD
About 60 kilometres north of Pietermaritzburg is Nottingham Road, a small town where there is **Rawdon's Hotel** (C/✫✫✫) a small, comfortable place for a stop-over en route between Johannesburg and Durban. PO Box 7, Nottingham Road 3280. Telephone (0333) 36 044.

PIETERMARITZBURG
La'Bri, B&B, C. PO Box 13144, Cascades 3202; telephone (0331) 473070, fax (0331) 471923.
Rehoboth. C. Victorian-style cottages, self-catering, comfortable, in a peaceful suburb. PO Box 100592, Scottsville 3209; telephone (0331) 962 312, fax (0331) 964 008.

RORKE'S DRIFT

Fugitive's Drift Lodge. Satour accredited country house, B/A, full board. An essential stopping point for those interested in the 19th century Anglo-Zulu wars. Because of its relative inaccessibility and in order to get the full benefit of the historical expertise of its owner Dave Rattray, it's advisable to spend at least a couple of nights here. Comfortable without being luxurious, the price is as much a reflection of the historical expertise on offer; Rattray is a registered battlefield tour guide and knows his stuff. PO Box Rorke's Drift 3016, KwaZulu-Natal; telephone (03425) 843, fax (0341) 23 319.

WINTERTON

Cathedral Peak Hotel. B/★★★, dinner included. High up in the Drakensberg mountains, next to Lesotho, a wide choice of accommodation in beautiful surroundings, with lots of outdoor activities. PO Winterton, KwaZulu-Natal 3340; telephone and fax (036) 488 1888.

Champagne Castle Hotel. B. Built in 1928, an established and attractive hotel with superb views. Moderately expensive but very comfortable, a good retreat. Private Bag X8, Winterton 3340; telephone (036) 468 1063, fax (036) 468 1306.

MPUMALANGA

DULLSTROOM

Critchley Hackle Lodge. B/★★★. Cosy lakeside stone built accommodation, small, good food and wines. PO Box 141, Dullstroom 1110; telephone (01325) 40 145, fax (01325) 40 262.

HAZYVIEW, NEAR WHITE RIVER

Casa do Sol. B/A★★★★. More a collection of cottages than a hotel, set in 500 hectares of virgin bush where non-aggressive game can be spotted. PO Box 57, Hazyview 1242; telephone (01317) 68 111, fax (01317) 68 166.

KIEPERSOL

Blue Mountain Lodge. B/A. Satour accredited country house. A relatively new, extremely comfortable establishment; wonderful pool and cuisine. PO Box 101, Kiepersol 1241; telephone and fax (01317) 68 446.

WHITE RIVER

Carrigans Country Estate. Satour accredited country house. B. One of the best small country retreats you can find to stay in the whole of South Africa—maybe anywhere. Wonderful views, splendidly tranquil gardens, superb breakfasts, and luxuriously equipped, spacious, marvellously-appointed accommodation in the form of Victorian-style cottages, with en-suite bathrooms, sitting rooms and kitchens. A perfect hideaway. PO Box 19, Kiepersol 1241; telephone (01311) 31421 (24hrs) or 43451 (day time only); fax (01311) 51390.

Cybele Forest Lodge. A/☆☆☆☆. Small—a maximum of 30 guests, this lodge has gained a deservedly high reputation for quality of service, food and comfort. Some suites even have their own private swimming pools. PO Box 346, White River 1240, telephone (013111) 50 511, fax (01311) 32 839.

Frangipani Lodge. Satour accredited country house. B, including splendid ample dinners. Very small, cosy, comfortable, excellent value, wonderful food. PO Box 1236, White River 1240; telephone (01311) 33224, fax (01311) 33233.

Hotel Winkler. B/☆☆☆☆. As with other White River hotels, very well placed for the Kruger Park. Spacious comfortable rooms and excellent pool. PO Box 12, White River 1240; telephone (01311) 32 317/8/9, fax (01311) 31 393.

NORTHERN PROVINCE
HAENERTSBURG
Glenshiel Country Lodge. B. Established in 1887, John Buchan and Rider Haggard were friends of the original owner, John Swinburne, and stayed here at various times. Comfortable, spacious rooms, good food, intimate. PO Box 1, Haenertsburg 0730; telephone and fax (0152) 276 4335.

TZANEEN
Coach House Hotel. Utterly magnificent accommodation, food, views, staff and service, the only criticism is that (like so many of the class country house hotels) it permits no-one under the age of 14. Medium sized, moderately expensive. PO Box 544 Tzaneen 0850; telephone (01523) 307 3641, fax (01523) 307 1466.

NORTHERN CAPE
KIMBERLEY
The Kimberley Club. C. There are other places in Kimberley, but the only place to stay is this club. Not because the accommodation is luxurious, but because it has a delightful sense of history.

In the centre of the town, the club is one of South Africa's oldest. Non-members can stay on a B&B basis. Founded by some of the most famous names in early diamond mining, the club has many original fixtures and fittings. Don't be alarmed by regulation 17.2.4 of the club, which states (on a discreet little card in your room): 'Denim clothing of any description, T-shirts, golfing shirts, polo or turtlenecked shirts, sweat shirts, windbreakers, sheepskin-type jackets (whether zipped or not), zippered jackets (other than tailored leather or suede leather jackets), hunting jackets, bush jackets, anoraks, tracksuits (or components of tracksuits), short pants, slip-slops, strops, running shoes and canvas or other types of athletic gym shoes may not be worn by ladies or gentlemen.' Accommodation is comfortable if slightly antiquated, with Victorian-length massive enamel baths. A great experience, and very friendly staff. 70-72 du Toitspan Road, Kimberley 8301; telephone (0531) 824 224, fax (0531) 821 385.

In the rest of the Northern Cape you are probably best advised to stay in one of the various chain hotels in the region. They are not luxurious but are generally at least comfortable.

NORTH-WEST PROVINCE
SUN CITY

The Palace of the Lost City, in the Pilansberg region of north-west South Africa. PO Box 308, Sun City 0316; telephone (01465) 73000, fax (01465) 73111. This is recommended only if you have enough money to indulge in experiencing a unique piece of grotesque absurdity. Cheapest room in early 1996 was R940 a night, up to R13,000 a night for the King Suite.

Much patronized by golfers and hapless package tourists who know no better. Ridiculously expensive restaurants, poor quality pretentious food and worse service. The pool is, however, magnificent. Tacky in the extreme, the completely spurious architectural style can only be described as African Gothic; a life-size sculpture of an elephant graces one foyer. Elevators have hand-rails constructed from plastic, shaped to imitate a carved ivory tusk, a theme carried through to the ballpoint pen in your room.

The charmless vulgarity is given extra piquancy by the fact that the Sun City complex is surrounded by some of the worst rural poverty created by apartheid. The trouble is, this province is very ill-served as far as accommodation goes; which is perhaps why Sun City was built there in the first place—there isn't much else.

WESTERN CAPE

This province is a highly popular tourist destination; there is a vast range of accommodation but, equally, a huge demand, so early booking is advisable.

CAMPS BAY

The Bay. A/✰✰✰✰✰. Very comfortable beach-side hotel in Camps Bay, a short drive from the centre of Cape Town, with a fine mountain backdrop. Medium sized, light and airy rooms with good views. PO Box 32021, Camps Bay 8040; telephone (021) 438 4444, fax (021) 438 4455.

CAPE TOWN

Ambleside Guest House: C. Bargain price small B&B, very close to town centre and on the slopes of Table Mountain. 11 Forest Road, Oranjezicht, Cape Town 8001. Telephone (021) 45 2503.

Holiday Inn Garden Court: B/★★★. There are several Holiday Inn hotels in Cape Town; this one, on De Waal, is modern, comfortable, clean and conveniently located for the town centre. Favoured by local business travellers and families. A small but irritating point is that it charges R5 for 0800 (ie, theoretically 'toll-free') telephone numbers—a way of clawing back revenue from those travellers who avoid paying outrageous premium charges on hotel telephone bills by using telephone charge cards. Telephone (021) 451 311.

Table Mount Lodge. C. Small, conveniently located, comfortable, private. 10A Tamboerskloof Road, Cape Town 8001; telephone (021) 23 0042, fax (021) 23 4983.

The Ambassador. B/★★★★. Wonderful views, perched right on the edge of Bantry Bay on the Atlantic coast, some executive suites with self-catering facilities. A good spot, very close to Cape Town but more tranquil. PO Box 83, Sea Point 8060; telephone (021) 439 6170, fax (021) 439 6336.

The Bunkhouse. C. Good budget accommodation for backpackers, five minutes' drive from city centre. Self-catering, dormitory and single rooms, staggeringly cheap—R22 per night in 1996. Telephone (021) 434 5695.

The Mount Nelson. A/★★★★★. Generally acknowledged as one of the world's finest hotels. Luxurious, excellent service, restaurants, pools, tennis and squash courts. Very expensive; prices started in 1996 at about R800 for single occupancy, depending on the season. Much patronized by South Africa's elite and a favourite with well-heeled international travellers. Easy walking distance to city centre. PO Box 2608, Cape Town 8000. Telephone (021) 23 1000; fax (021) 24 7472.

The Peninsula. B/A★★★★. An all-suite hotel, ranging from the basic unit, a studio suite, comprising an open-plan bedroom and lounge, separate kitchenette and private bathroom with shower, sleeping one-four persons, to royal suites with three bedrooms and spacious accommodation. Better value than The Mount Nelson and greater privacy. A short drive to the city centre. PO Box 768, Sea Point 8060. Telephone (021) 439 8888; fax (021) 439 8886/7.

The Sheiling. C. B&B in traditional Cape Dutch home; 4 Glenugie Avenue, Tokai 7945, Cape Town; telephone (021) 725301.

Victoria & Alfred Hotel. A/★★★★. This is a splendid new hotel, with gigantic, comfortable rooms, situated right on the new Waterfront development, ideal for tourists and business travellers who don't mind a short ride into the centre of town. Very private and quiet, despite its location, this hotel also welcomes children. PO Box 50050, Waterfront 8002; telephone (021) 419 6677, fax (021) 419 8955.

CONSTANTIA

Alphen Hotel. B/✫✫✫✫. Constantia is one of Cape Town's plushest outlying districts but the Alphen is very good value, small, and extremely comfortable. PO Box 35, Constantia 7848. Telephone (021) 794 5011, fax (021) 794 5710.

Cellars-Hohenort. A/✫✫✫✫✫. A superbly comfortable, relaxing place to stay. PO Box 270, Constantia 7848; telephone (021) 794 2137, fax (021) 794 2149.

Franschhoek: Le Ballon Rouge Guest House. C. Exceptionally good value, very comfortable small en-suite accommodation, with the bonus of a superb restaurant attached. PO Box 344, Franschhoek 7690; telephone (02212) 2651 (mobile 082 558 8942); fax (02212) 3743.

MATJIESFONTEIN

Lord Milner Hotel. C/✫✫. A quaint hotel, built in 1899 and used as a hospital during the Anglo-Boer war of 1899–1902. Pleasant gardens, good food, quiet. Situated in a tiny village (all of which has been declared a national monument) in the middle of nowhere in the Cape. Suitable for a quiet weekend away. Matjiesfontein 6901; telephone (02372) and ask for 5203; fax (02372) and ask for 5802.

OUDTSHOORN

Riempie Estate Hotel. C/✫✫✫. Accommodation in thatched chalets; comfortable, clean, no-frills hotel ideal for families and groups. PO Box 370, Oudtshoorn 6620; telephone (0443) 22 6161, fax (0443) 22 6772.

PAARL

Grand Roche. A/✫✫✫✫✫. South Africa's hotel of the year in 1995, this luxury estate is exceptionally comfortable and has achieved great accolades; its Bosman's restaurant is highly esteemed. Some find it brash. PO Box 6038, Paarl 7622; telephone (02211) 63 2727, fax (02211) 63 2220.

Roggeland Country House. B, including all meals and wines. Quietly eccentric, the Roggeland has a rotten location for such a beautiful part of the country. The British magazine Tatler a couple of years back asserted that the Roggeland was one of the 50 best hotels in the world, an exaggeration that can only have resulted from over-indulgence in the chardonnay. It is however a comfortable, welcoming and intimate place to stay, priding itself on using only the freshest of ingredients for its somewhat unusual cuisine. PO Box 7210, Northern Paarl 7623; telephone (02211) 68 2501, fax (02211) 68 2113.

RIEBEEK WEST

Carolann's Guest House. Satour accredited guest house, C. 50 minutes drive from Cape Town, a comfortable Victorian house with good cooking. 10 Long Street, Riebeek West 7306; telephone and fax (02246) 245.

SALDANHA

Saldanha Bay Protea Hotel. C/B✩✩✩. On the west coast, an hour's drive from Cape Town, a good example of the Protea chain; convenient for many of the nearby coastal activities. PO Box 70, Saldanha 7395; telephone (02281) 41264/5, fax (02281) 44093.

SIMONSTOWN

The British Hotel. C/B.This is one of the best-kept secrets of the Cape Peninsula. Four self-contained, self-catering serviced apartments, each with three bedrooms. Each is huge, light and airy, capable of swallowing without any trouble a couple of families, with wonderfully comfortable fixtures and fittings and each with sea-facing balconies. Because Simonstown is rather off the well-beaten tourist run, renting an apartment here is exceptionally good value. Yet the train station is just a few minutes walk away (with regular good services into Cape Town) and if you have your own transport, Cape Town is just 20 minutes away. PO Box 78, Simonstown 7995, or 90 St George's Street, Simonstown; telephone (021) 786 2412, fax (021) 786 2214.

STELLENBOSCH

D'Ouwe Werf. C/B✩✩✩. Another claimant to the title of South Africa's oldest hotel, having been established in 1802. Small, very comfortably furnished. 30 Church Street, Stellenbosch 7600; telephone (021) 887 4608/887 1608; fax (021) 887 4626.

Dorpshuis. Satour accredited guest house. C. Conveniently near the centre of town, this is a comfortable, friendly hotel with well-fitted rooms and service. An excellent base from which to explore both town and wine estates. PO Box 999 Stellenbosch 7599; telephone (021) 883 9881/2/3, fax (021) 883 9884.

Lanzerac Hotel. B✩✩✩✩. Situated on a wine estate, a comfortable hotel, with good food and wines. PO Box 4, Stellenbosch 7599; telephone (021) 887 1132, fax (021) 887 2310.

STRAND (FALSE BAY)

The Beaches. C. 14 self-catering apartments, all with a sea view. Private, comfortable, secure, extremely good value for money. PO Box 839, Strand 7140; telephone (024) 854 8673, fax (024) 854 8694.

SWELLENDAM

Pond Cottage. C. Self-catering comfortable cottage, excellent value at R90 a night for single, R150 for two, breakfast included. 21 Buitekant Street, Swellendam 6740; telephone (0291) 42036.

AFRICAN NATIONAL CONGRESS

The welding together of all the disparate black South African peoples into a single protest organization took many years of struggle. In the late 19th century various societies and congresses aimed at promoting Africans' rights flowered and died, with little to show for their efforts.

Indeed, the first resistance organization of lasting consequence was the creation of Mohandas K. Gandhi, (who lived in South Africa between 1893 and 1914, working as a barrister). In 1894 he established the Natal Indian Congress, an organization emphasizing non-violence and obedience to the law in the fight to protect trading and commercial rights of Indian merchants. Gandhi's principle of satyagraha or passive resistance became widely adopted by black, coloured and Indian movements. Not until the 1960s did modern black Africans sporadically take up a military struggle against their repression.

A rare 20th century exception to passive resistance erupted in 1906, when an African chief called Bambatha waged a six-week war against white authorities in Natal, protesting against a new hut tax. Bambatha's small bands of poorly-armed peasants spent all their time simply trying to evade capture. On 10 June 1906 they were finally trapped in a small Natal valley, Mome Gorge, where 500 of them were slaughtered by machine-gun fire, including Bambatha himself—whose head was cut off and put on display by the victorious white troops.

Black African nationalism had its roots in Christian mission schools, particularly Lovedale, established in the eastern Cape in 1841. Such mission schools were generally the only means whereby blacks could obtain an education; they played a vital role in forming the early black political leadership. Tiyo Soga, a Xhosa who at the age of 17 in 1846 first travelled to Scotland to start his training as a Presbyterian missionary (in 1856 he was formally ordained) was a founding figure of African nationalism. He married a Scot, Janet Burnside, and returned to South Africa. He advised his children to 'take your place in the world as coloured, not as white men; as Kafirs, not as Englishmen [...] For your own sakes never appear ashamed that your father was a Kafir, and that you inherited some African blood. It is every whit as good and as pure as that which flows in the veins of my fairer brethren.'

By 1912, African nationalists had lost hope that Britain would give them equal rights. The small black elite of the new Union decided it was necessary to organise more formal resistance. On 8 January 1912, in Bloemfontein, several hundred black leaders and observers gathered together to form the South African Native National Congress (SAANC), which in 1923 changed its name to the African National Congress (ANC).

Some of the founders of the SAANC clearly were ahead of their time. Pixley Ka Isaka Seme, a young Oxford University-educated lawyer, had once been found guilty of using a gun in a threatening manner on a train, when white passengers had objected to his travelling first class. Seme's defence was that 'like all lawyers, I, of course, travel first class.' In the black newspaper Imvo Zabantsundu (Native Opinion) he wrote in October 1911: 'The demon of racialism must be buried and forgotten; it has shed among us sufficient blood. We are one people.'

The first president of the SAANC was the US-educated teacher and editor John Dube. Seme was elected treasurer, and Solomon Plaatje secretary-general. In 1914 Plaatje led a SAANC delegation to London to protest against the 1913 Land Act, which barred black Africans from buying land except from other black Africans or in existing tribal reserves. The London government shunned

Tiyo Soga, the Scots-trained priest and intellectual founder of African nationalism

the SAANC representatives, some of whom (though not Plaatje) were so placatory they actually signed a submission to the British government, accepting the principle of segregation.

In the 1920s and 1930s, the ANC tried various protest actions—such as mass burnings of the hated pass-books all blacks were required to carry—but, battered by a plethora of racist legislation, demoralized by the lack of any visible sign of success, and faced by an implacable and powerful white society (where opposing politicians joined forces to deny black enfranchisement), it lost ground to more radical organisations, such as the Industrial and Commercial Workers Union, or ICU. Under its founder Clements Kadalie the ICU became the most potent African mass-action force between the two world wars. The ICU also eventually collapsed, its leadership bitterly split.

All African attempts to reason with white government fell on deaf ears. Barry Hertzog, founder of the National Party, the Afrikaner movement formed to oppose British interests in the Union, told a delegation of black leaders in Cape Town in 1936 that 'it is not that we hate you, but if we give you the right to vote, within a very short space of time the whole parliament will be controlled by natives. I must tell you point blank, I am not prepared for this.'

During World War II black trade unionism began to develop. By 1941 most black trade unions had affiliated with the Council for Non-European Trade Unions (CNETU). Two prominent black members of the Communist Party of South Africa, Edwin Mofutsanyana and Gaur Radebe, formed the African Mineworkers' Union, which by 1944 claimed a membership of 25,000. In August 1946 more than 75,000 black mineworkers went on strike. It took 16,000 police to crush the strike leaving 12 dead and many more injured; in one sense it was a complete failure. But it radicalized black opinion far more than decades of peaceful lobbying by the ANC.

The ANC also underwent radical change in 1943, with the formation of the Congress Youth League, an internal wing developed by younger, impatient activists such as Peter Mda, Anton Lembede, Nelson Mandela and Walter Sisulu. The Youth Leaguers pressed for direct mass action. In 1948 Mda proposed a programme of action including boycotts, strikes, stay-at-homes, civil disobedience and generalized non-cooperation with white authority. After some fierce internal debates, this programme was accepted in 1949 as official ANC policy.

The tercentenary of Jan van Riebeeck's landing at the Cape in 1652 gave the ANC a perfect opportunity to demonstrate its new-found spirit.

The Afrikaner government planned 1952 as a year of triumphalist celebration; the ANC warned of a 'Defiance Campaign' if all racist legislation had not been abolished by February that year. No such abolition happened, and a week of mass action was staged at the start of April. The government responded by 'banning' known communists. On 26 June 1952, non-violent demonstrations and peaceful violations of apartheid laws took place, nationwide. By the end of the year more than 8,000 protesters had been arrested—and the ANC's membership ballooned from 7,000 to more than 100,000. There were riots in Port Elizabeth, East London, Johannesburg and elsewhere. But the government lopped off the ANC's head, arresting 20 of its leaders under the Suppression of Communism Act, which gave widespread powers to the police and heavily-biased judiciary.

Despite that, the ANC rump managed to stage in June 1955 a 'Congress of the People' in a field at Kliptown, near Soweto, on the outskirts of Johannesburg. More than 2,800 delegates arrived to applaud the adoption of a 'Freedom Charter', comprising 10 clauses calling for, among other things: votes for all, regardless of colour, race or sex; widespread nationalization of major industries; land redistribution; and equal rights before the law. In December 1956 the government arrested 156 leading activists and put them on trial for alleged treason. The Treason Trial dragged on until 1961; it was perhaps the best publicity for the ANC in many years. At one point the chief prosecution witness, professor Andrew Murray of Cape Town University, an expert on communist affairs, was asked by a defence lawyer if he could identify a communist, merely from reading a passage of the person's writing. Murray said he thought so, and listened as the lawyer read a passage. Undoubtedly a communist, opined Murray—only then to be informed by the lawyer that the extract was from one of Murray's own books. The trial collapsed.

In late 1958 a breakaway group split from the ANC to form the PAC, or Pan-Africanist Congress, following serious internal dissent over to what extent there should be cooperation with non-black protest groups. The PAC was formally established on 6 April 1959, under the slogan 'Africa for Africans'. The ANC leadership regarded this philosophy as merely a different form of racism, but the radicalism of PAC leaders such as Robert Sobukwe, who argued for no compromise with either white liberals or racists, was understandably attractive to many young, more radical blacks. In 1960 the PAC announced that 21 March was to be an Anti-Pass Day; the ANC had a similar protest action planned for 31 March. On 21 March in the township of Sharpeville, about 50 miles south of Johannesburg, some 5,000 demonstrators assembled outside the police station. Scuffling broke out and the police began shooting into the crowd. 69 protesters were killed, 180 wounded, mostly shot in the back.

The Sharpeville massacre was international headline news—a deep shock to the world, which had largely ignored the more deep-seated wrongs of apartheid. The PAC still exists today, though a very much weaker electoral party than the ANC.

Following Sharpeville, Hendrik Verwoerd outlawed both the ANC and the PAC; some 18,000 people were detained under drastic new emergency powers. Oliver Tambo, partner in Nelson Mandela's law firm, left the country to start an exiled ANC mission in London. The ANC leadership decided that the time of peaceful protest was over. In 1961 it formed an underground military wing, Umkhonto we Sizwe (Spear of the Nation). The PAC set up its own armed unit, Poqo, a Xhosa word which may be translated as 'standing alone' or 'pure'. Umkhonto committed itself to attacks on strategic targets, such as bombings of power lines, but Poqo immediately began random terror attacks on white civilians. Both groups were riddled with informers, and their captured cadres were regularly tortured. Under these conditions, neither played much more than a symbolic, irritant role, Poqo in particular soon ceasing to exist in any real sense.

Nelson Mandela left the country in January 1962, to undertake a period training in guerilla warfare in Algeria. He returned home on 20 July and was arrested while driving through Natal on 5 August. At his trial—which became known as the Rivonia Trial, after a northern Johannesburg suburb where several senior ANC figures were arrested—Mandela was sentenced to life imprisonment, along with Walter Sisulu, the ANC secretary-general. Ten more defendants were brought to trial in October 1963, charged with attempting to overthrow the state by force. The ANC had ceased to exist as a legal entity, except in exile; Umkhonto was to wage its own unceasing little war, a car bomb here, a litter-bin bomb there. From abroad, it called—with increasing success

Nationalist Party celebrations, De Arr 1994

through the years—on the international community to impose an economic, diplomatic and cultural boycott against South Africa.

In 1995 Nelson Mandela, by now South Africa's president, met Percy Yutar, by then a small, wizened little figure, but who in 1963 had been deputy attorney-general of the Transvaal, and Mandela's main prosecutor. At Mandela's trial Yutar said it was a great pity that ordinary Africans 'have been duped by false promises of free bread, free transport, free medical services, free housing and free holidays to have embarked upon a policy of violence.'

Thirty-two years later, Mandela shook Yutar's hands warmly; and they shared a cup of tea.

DO NOT ASK ME

Do not ask me, mother, if they're gone
I fear to tell you
they left in the middle of the night
turned their backs on the warmth of the hearth
and for the last time
heard the home rooster crowing

Do not ask me, mother, where they went
Tracks on watery dew-bells
as puny feet brushed the morning grass
have evaporated in the heat of the sun's kindness
and the hunting bloody-snouted hounds
have lost the trail

But to you I will whisper:
Look where the willows weep
The willows of the Mohokare River
have seen the forbidden sight
tiny feet in a mad choreographer's dance
from shore to shore
wading on the sandy bed
And the waters washed and levelled up the sands
Nor will the willows point their drooping limbs
to say where they've gone

(above) *Funeral at Munsieville Township, Krugersdorp*

Do not ask me, mother, why they left
Need I tell you
They took the amasi bird out of the forbidden pot
and bade it fill their clay-bowls to the very brim
they'd been so hungry
so long

Then an army with giant boots
came towering over them
Brand new guns
made to silence little children who cry
glinting in the African sun
The gun-toters threw the amasi bird
back into the pot
and wrote on it with the government's ink
For white children only
and henceforth it was guarded night and day
by one hundred bayoneted soldiers

And the children raised their fists
and shouted
Amasi! Amasi! We demand the amasi bird!
Amandla! Amandla! Ngawethu!

Now they've been gathered up
in the wings of the Giant Bird
to the place of circumcision
far, far away

Soweto 1990: Migrant
Zulu workers perform
traditional dances

And the village awaits
for the day of their return
to conquer.

Daniel P Kunene

Appendix I: National Parks

If nature here wishes to make a mountain, she runs a range for five hundred miles; if a plain, she levels eighty; if a rock, she tilts five thousand feet of strata on end; our skies are higher and more intensely blue; our waves are larger than others; our rivers fiercer.

Olive Schreiner

South Africa's many private and state-run game and nature reserves, parks and conservation areas—there are more than 500 in Mpumalanga alone—are only beginning to be explored by travellers from outside the country. You can rush through them; but they are much better appreciated by lingering a few days. Most of them are remote and require lengthy journeys by road, and are inaccessible to travellers without their own means of transport.

At the last count (in 1996) there were 20 parks administered by the National Parks Board—the **Cape Peninsula** and **Table Mountain** being the latest additions. More will undoubtedly follow. Many have excellent, great value, self-catering accommodation, as well as space for caravans and camping. Nearly all are well-supplied with simple but high-standard restaurants, shops where you can buy food and drink, information bureaux and petrol stations. Their accommodation ranges from the expensively luxurious to the very cheap and basic, but all is such exceptionally good value that it's wise to book as early as possible; most of the parks accept bookings up to a year in advance. In low season quite a few offer discounts of up to 30 per cent on high season prices. Most parks and reserves charge a small entrance fee, in addition to any accommodation costs.

A sour note is that some of the smaller parks were created under the worst days of apartheid; communities who had lived in the areas for many years were forcibly removed to make way for animals, plants and rangers.

For further general information, enquiries, and applications to stay in park accommodation, you can contact the individual park or the **National Parks Board** at either

PRETORIA
PO Box 787, Pretoria 0001
telephone: (012) 343 1991
fax: (012) 343 0905
or

CAPE TOWN
PO Box 7400, Rogge Bay 8012
telephone: (021) 22 2810
fax: (021) 24 6211

GENERAL RULES

- In those with larger animals and predators you must not, for your own safety, get out of your vehicle except at designated spots (such as restcamps or viewing points)
- Some recommend anti-malarial precautions
- Check your vehicle is well-serviced before entering the park
- Firearms must be declared and sealed at entry gates
- Take a torch for after-dark use
- No feeding any animals
- No littering
- No removal of any plants or wildlife
- No pets
- Maximum speed limits of 50 kilometres per hour on tarred roads, 40 kilometres on dirt roads
- Some cover vast areas; don't under-estimate the time it takes to get from one point to another, particularly if using dirt roads
- Several specify no driving between dusk and dawn (when entrances are normally closed), to permit the animals some peace and quiet

National Parks

The following have accommodation:

ADDO ELEPHANT:

PO Box 52 Addo 6105. Telephone (0426) 400 556, fax (0426) 400 196. 72 kilometres north of Port Elizabeth. 14,551 hectares set aside in 1931 to preserve at that time the 16 remaining Cape elephant population from extinction; a professional hunter, Jan Pretorius, had been hired by the Cape administrator in 1919 to slaughter the whole herd. He took a year to shoot 120, then a public outcry forced him to desist. Now the herd is above 130 animals, in dense thorny bush. Beside elephant, there are buffalo, kudu, eland, black rhino and a large variety of birds. Accommodation in air-conditioned fully serviced six-bed cottages, chalets with two single beds and two-bed huts, starting at R145 for two persons per night. Total beds: 93.

AUGRABIES FALLS

Private Bag X1, Augrabies 8874. Telephone (054) 451 0050/51/52, fax (054) 451 0053. 120 kilometres west of Upington, 40 kilometres north-west of Kakamas, in Northern Cape. 15,415 hectares. Another 70,000 hectares (not open to the public) have been set aside for breeding of species such as the black rhino. At peak flood 405 million litres of water from the Orange River go over the falls every minute in a direct drop of 85 metres into the largest granite gorge in Africa. In such a flood there are 19 separate waterfalls; the largest is one of the six biggest in the world. Also various bird and animal species; plant species include the quiver tree, camelthorn, wild olive and tree fuschia. The park is centred on Klaas Island, which has accommodation in air-conditioned, fully serviced four-bed cottages, chalets of two or three single-beds, starting at R215 for two persons per night. Also in the park is the Klipspringer Hiking trail—three days of hiking (maximum of 12 people) with two overnight huts. Total beds: 180.

BONTEBOK

PO Box 149, Swellendam 6740. Telephone (0291) 42 735, fax (0291) 42 646. 6 kilometres from Swellendam, 238 kilometres from Cape Town in Western Cape province. 2,786 hectares, established to preserve the bontebok antelope from extinction; just 17 breeding animals survived by the 1930s. The small herd is now well-established. Also you can see Cape mountain zebra, Cape grysbok and other antelope species, as well as more than 200 species of birds. In the temperate climate some 500 different plant species thrive. Accommodation is in the form of six-berth fully-serviced caravans, price R70 for two persons per night, R10 supplement per extra person. Total beds: 24

GOLDEN GATE HIGHLANDS

Private Bag X03, Clarens 9707. Telephone and fax (058) 256 1471. Some 320 kilometres south of Johannesburg, an 11,600 hectare scenic reserve of impressive, naturally-formed red, orange and yellow-brown sandstone ridges, cliffs and caves. Black wildebeest, Burchell's zebra, oribi, blesbok and other grazing mammals, as well as many bird species, such as jackal buzzards, bearded vultures, black eagles and orange-throated longclaws. Two restcamps: Brandwag, full-serviced rooms, chalets and dormitory accommodation; and Glen Reenen, with a single house and several rondavels. Also the two-day 30 kilometres Rhebok Hiking Trail over mountain streams and peaks, including the 2,837m Generaalskop, highest point in the Orange Free State. Overnight stops in basic huts; all cutlery, crockery and bedding must be taken en route by hikers, though kitchens are provided. The most comfortable accommodation is R265 for two persons per night. Total beds: 200.

KALAHARI GEMSBOK

Private Bag X5890, Gemsbokpark 8815. Telephone (054) 561 0021, fax (054) 561 0026. 358 kilometres north of Upington in Northern Cape province. The park is in a vast conservation area—more than 2m hectares of desert; red sand dunes, sparse grassy vegetation. Waterholes attract large quantities of game such as lion, leopard, cheetah, spotted hyena, brown hyena, wild dog, black-backed jackal. 215 species of birds. Three restcamps with fully-serviced chalet, cottage and hut accommodation; Twee Rivieren, Mata Mata and Nossob. Total beds: 169.

KAROO

PO Box 316, Beaufort West 6970; telephone (0201) 52 828/9, fax (0201) 51 671. 471 kilometres from Cape Town, 4 kilometres from Beaufort West, in Western Cape province. 46,119 hectares of mostly arid vegetation in the Great Karoo. 64 species of mammals including bat-eared fox, springbok, Cape mountain zebra, kudu, gemsbok, red hartebeest, black rhino. 196 species of birds, including black eagles. 59 species of reptiles, including five species of tortoise, one-eighth of the world's land tortoises. One restcamp with fully-serviced air-conditioned Cape Dutch style chalets and cottages; one restcamp with basic facilities, only beds and mattresses provided, communal ablutions; and a 4x4 Trail (use your own vehicle or that supplied by the Park, plus a guide; one overnight hut, mattresses only, outside toilet and drinking water). The most comfortable restcamp chalets start at R200 per night for one or two persons. Total beds: 99.

KRUGER

All enquiries and reservations should be made to either of the two main National Parks Board offices, in Cape Town and Pretoria (**see earlier**). Approximately 500 kilometres east of Johannesburg, the Kruger Park is South Africa's oldest (established in 1898 by Paul Kruger) and largest national park. There are eight entrance/exit gates, four of which (Crocodile Bridge, Malelane, Numbi and Paul Kruger) can be reached via Nelspruit; the two middle gates are Orpen and Phalaborwa; the northern area gates are Pafuri and Punda Maria. At the entrance gates you will be given an excellent map of the whole park, showing precise locations of all its restcamps.

The best time to visit is winter, when surface water is scarce—the bush is low, trees are leafless, and the larger animals tend to congregate around waterholes and rivers. From top to bottom the park is 350 kilometres. Apart from the 'big five' the park has a host of other animals, birds and plant-life; the size of the park means there is a wide range of landscapes and eco-systems. The park also has seven, three-night hiking trails, with huts en route, at which simple meals are served.

It has 4,000 beds, in 14 restcamps, five private camps and six bush camps; certain camps are equipped to accommodate paraplegics. Some of the restcamps are the size of small towns; others are very small and private. Prices range from R35 to pitch

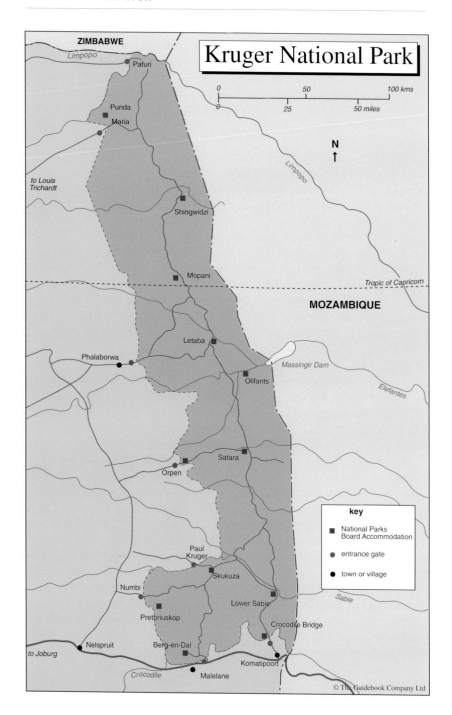

Kruger National Park

ZIMBABWE

Limpopo

Pafuri

Punda
Maria

to Louis
Trichardt

Shingwidzi

Mopani

Limpopo

Tropic of Capricorn

MOZAMBIQUE

Letaba

Phalaborwa

Massingir Dam

Olifants

Elefantes

Satara

Orpen

Paul
Kruger

Skukuza

Numbi

Lower Sabie

Sabie

Pretoriuskop

Crocodile Bridge

Nelspruit

Berg-en-Dal

to Joburg

Komatipoort

Crocodile

Malelane

key

■ National Parks
Board Accommodation

● entrance gate

● town or village

0   50   100 kms

0   25   50 miles

N
↑

© The Guidebook Company Ltd

a tent to R1,880 to rent a splendid cottage accommodating 12 people. Excellent two-bedded rondavels and chalets, with bathroom and kitchen and ample space for four, can be had for about R250 a night. If you wish to stay in one of the five private camps—called Boulders, Jock of the Bushveld, Malelane, Nwanetsi and Roodewal—you must book all of it; each can take 12-19 people; all are self-catering.

MARAKELE
Telephone (014773) 71745, fax (014773) 71866. A small, relatively new park high up in the Waterberg range of mountains, 20 kilometres north-east of Thabazimbi in the Northern Province. In 1996 it was due to have a tented camp large enough to accommodate four people; but a four-wheeled drive vehicle is essential.

MOUNTAIN ZEBRA
Private bag X66, Cradock 5880. Telephone (0481) 2427/2486, fax (0481) 3943. 25 kilometres south-west of Cradock in Eastern Cape province. A 6,536 hectare park designed to conserve the Cape mountain zebra, still threatened with extinction; there are some 200 in the park, the optimum number for the area. Surplus zebra are placed in other reserves. Smallest of the zebras—standing a little more than one metre high—its brilliant striped markings made it much hunted by trophy-seekers. Also home to other herbivores and more than 200 species of birds. Accommodation in excellent fully-serviced guest cottage, at R355 per night for up to four people, or chalet at R180 per night for two people. Also a three-day, 26 kilometres hiking trail, with basic overnight huts. Total beds: 78.

PILANSBERG
PO Box 937, Lonehill 2062. Telephone (011) 465 5423, fax (011) 465 1228. Approximately 250 kilometres north-west of Johannesburg, set in the Pilansberg range of mountains within an extinct volcanic alkaline crater this 50,000 hectare reserve has a variety of big game including the 'big five'. Accommodation is in two rather expensive lodges and one cheaper tented camp. Total beds: 730.

TSITSIKAMMA
PO Storms River 6308. Telephone (042) 541 1607, fax (042) 541 1629. A coastal marine park 68 kilometres east of Plettenberg bay in Western Cape province. Its name derives from the Khoikhoi word for sparkling or clear water. 80 kilometres of rocky coastline, sea and landscapes, fynbos, evergreen forest, deep river gorges. Restricted angling, scuba-diving and snorkelling, nature trails, water sports. A 42 kilometres hiking Otter Trail over five days with four night stops in basic hut accommodation. Other accommodation in fully-serviced log cabins, 'oceanettes'

and very simple forest huts. Prices start at R100 per person per night.Total beds: 233.

WEST COAST
PO Box 25, Langebaan 7357. Telephone (02287) 22 144, fax (02287) 22 607. A wetland reserve of some 27,000 hectares 122 kilometres north of Cape Town in Western Cape province. Important wading bird sanctuary; 50 per cent of the world's swift terns, 25 per cent of its Cape gannets, 15 per cent of its crowned cormorants, and 12 per cent of its African black oyster-catchers. Also flower-viewing in the wetter Spring season. Comfortable accommodation at Langebaan Lodge, starting at R200 for two per night, each additional adult an extra R50. Total beds: 40.

WILDERNESS
PO Box 35, Wilderness 6560. Telephone (0441) 877 1197, fax (0441) 877 0111. A short distance from George in Western Cape province, on the N2 Garden Route highway. 2,612 hectares, incorporating five rivers, four lakes, two estuaries and 28 kilometres of coastline. Surrounded by a National Lake Area of 10,000 hectares. Temperate coastal climate. Large numbers of waterbirds; various nature trails. Several restcamps with a wide variety of fully-serviced accommodation, prices start at R70 a night for a rondavel. Total beds: 146.

The following National Parks do NOT have accommodation but are open to visitors:

KNYSNA NATIONAL LAKE
Telephone (0445) 22 095, fax (0445) 825 801. A protected area around Knysna lagoon, which is almost cut off from the sea by cliffs.

RICHTERSVELD
PO Box 406, Alexander Bay 8290. Telephone/fax (0256) 506. A 600+ kilometres drive north of Cape Town, in the far north-west corner of the country, is this relatively new park.

TANKWA-KAROO
Telephone (0273) 412 322. Close to Calvinia in the Western Cape, a small park still under development, established to restore part of the Karoo to its original state.

VAALBOS
Telephone (053) 561 008. Close to Barkly West in Northern Cape province; rhino and buffalo are being introduced.

ZUURBERG

Telephone (0426) 400 581. Now administered by Addo National Park, which is 12 kilometres south. Of special interest is the Zuurberg cycad, found nowhere else. It's also a sanctuary for the endangered blue duiker antelope. There is a small lodge nearby which must be booked through the Addo National Park.

Natal Parks Board

While all the provinces manage their own parks and reserves, the most interesting are all to be found in KwaZulu-Natal province, under the management of the Natal Parks Board. It's impossible here to give details of any but the most interesting and well-established. For full information, including brochures, further details and accommodation reservations contact the Natal PB at PO Box 1750, Pietermaritzburg 3200, telephone (0331) 471 982, fax (0331) 471 980. For details of other provinces' reserves, contact Satour or the relevant provincial publicity association.

The Natal PB controls and manages 80 protected areas in this province, which has some of the most interesting wildlife and beautiful scenery in the country. In many of them you can take hiking trails under supervision of experienced armed rangers—a superb way of experiencing the bush. There are often pony-trekking trails too. Many of the reserves are in the Drakensberg and make excellent places from which to go walking and hiking.

Once again, it's imperative to make early bookings for accommodation in the board's parks—they are all very popular. In most Natal PB accommodation all you need bring with you is food and drink, everything else is provided. In a number of these reserves there are bilharzia and malaria warnings; you should also be alert for crocodiles and hippos.

The oldest-established game reserves in Africa—**Hluhluwe**, **St Lucia** and **Umfolozi** were 100 years old on 30 April 1995—are in this province. In the large Hluhluwe and Umfolozi reserves you can see the 'big five' and many other large animals; St Lucia is a large wetland area, ideal for fishing, swimming (shark nets protect the beaches) and bird-spotting. The three of them are quite close together, about 250 kilometres north of Durban, easily accessible from the N2 highway which runs parallel to the northern KwaZulu-Natal coastline. They have some of the best game reserve accommodation to be found anywhere. Further up the coast, and entailing lengthy dirt-road drives, are **Sodwana Bay** and **Kosi Bay**, both ideal for anglers or simply to get away from it all; it's a good idea to have four-wheel drive vehicles for both these reserves. Kosi Bay is just south of the Mozambique border;

don't swim there because of bilharzia, crocodiles and hippos.

Other Natal PB reserves you should look out for include: the **Royal Natal**, on the Bergville-Harrismith road (R615), which has a stunning feature, a 5 kilometres-long rock wall about 500 metres high, called the Amphitheatre, which has a series of magnificent waterfalls; the **Albert Falls**, 24 kilometres north of Pietermaritzburg; the **Oribi Gorge**, which has a 400-metre gorge, home to much unusual bird-life—it's 21 kilometres inland from Port Shepstone on the south KwaZulu-Natal coast; the **Kamberg**, about 50 kilometres west of Nottingham Road, off the N3 highway that links Durban with Johannesburg—a good spot for trout fishing.

Private Game Reserves

Private game reserves are now big business in South Africa; most of them are situated in or near the Kruger Park, for a (commercially very sensible) reason—most tourists head for the Kruger because they are obsessed with seeing the 'big five' and as many other animals as possible. But the Kruger can often feel like a very crowded place; there are many other reserves offering much greater sense of freedom, despite lacking the size of the Kruger. If you are not besotted with the 'big five' but simply want to escape into a wilderness, consider going elsewhere. Even if you want to see the 'big five' there are many reserves where they can be found other than the Kruger.

The choice between accommodation in a private or national or provincial reserve is largely but not entirely a question of money. With national or provincial-managed reserves you will get excellent no-frills accommodation at moderate cost—an average of R250 for a self-catering cottage for two people per night. You will also be able to take your children along, whatever their ages. But you might not spot as much game as you would like, because you are restricted to staying in your (hard-topped) vehicle, cannot do any off-road driving, and because you probably don't have the experience to know where the game might be hiding.

With a private reserve/game lodge you get luxury, full-frills accommodation, at extremely high prices—R1,500 per night (about £250, or $375) for one person, meals (but not drinks) included, is not uncommon. Most private reserves also ban children under 11 or so. The high prices are not so much a reflection of superior accommodation—it often isn't that much better than national park accommodation—but largely because you also get a couple of game drives thrown in each day, one at dawn and the other at dusk, when you will travel in a large, open-topped four-wheel drive vehicle, accompanied by a tracker and an armed ranger, both of whom are expert naturalists and whose job is to ensure (as far as possible) that you see the 'big five' and get a full 'bush experience'—in comfort.

It has to be said that many of the National Parks also have ranger services, so you can, if you pay a bit more and spend a little longer time, get a good bush experience that way, too.

There are suspicions that in some of the private reserves some pack leaders of the larger game are electronically tagged, which, if true, would make life much easier for the hapless ranger who has a bunch of impatient tourists in the back, wanting to see something big, to justify the amount of money they've spent. That practice seems unlikely in the Kruger Park, where the internal fences that once separated the park itself from the private reserves are now down, and the animals are free to roam both Kruger's huge, 19,485 sq kilometres area, and the neighbouring private reserves.

However, in some newer reserves, such as the 70,000 hectare **Mandikwe**, about 30 kilometres south of the Botswana border and 300 kilometres north-west of Johannesburg, some animals *are* electronically tagged, in order (it is said) for veterinary surgeons to be able to keep a close watch on how they are faring. Given that Madikwe is very new, that's perhaps understandable. It certainly doesn't seem to make the life of the rangers any easier, since the 10,000 animals released into the reserve are all extremely shy. Madikwe is in fact excellent for animals but very poor for tourists intent on seeing them. That may change in time as the animals become more accustomed to visitors; but if you want to see animals, avoid Madikwe until about 1998, by which time they may have settled down.

On the edge of the Kruger Park are a number of private reserves with excellent accommodation, offering a good 'bush experience' yet at prices which are not outrageous. One excellent small tented camp is **Honeyguide**, inside the 23,000 hectare Manyeleti Game Reserve. Honeyguide takes a maximum of 16 guests, so there's no sense of being crowded. The tents are all en-suite, ranger-led expeditions are arranged, and the food is good. You can contact either the camp direct, telephone/fax (01528) 33581, or via PO Box 786064, Sandton 2146, telephone (011) 483 2734/5, fax (011) 728 3767.

Other highly recommended camps in this reasonably-priced category are **Notten's Bush Camp** (PO Box 622, Hazyview 1242, telephone/ fax 01311 65105), in a 1,700 hectare area where the 'big five' roam. Of much more interest is the special atmosphere created by the camp itself; there's no electricity, you can bring your own drinks—it's very popular and has many repeat visitors. **Leadwood Lodge** is self-catering and excellent value: PO Box 2060, Nelspruit 1200, telephone (01311) 2757/22762: **Khoka Moya Game Lodge**, PO Box 298, Hoedspruit 1380, telephone (01528) 31 729; **Djuma Bush Camp**, PO Box 338, Hluvukani 1363, telephone/fax (01311) 65 118; and **Chitwa Chitwa Game Lodge**, PO Box 784 052, Sandton 2146, telephone/fax (011) 783 1838.

Much more expensive and aiming to capture the wealthy-visitor market are several camps in or near the Sabi Sand area, close to the Paul Kruger Gate entrance to Kruger Park: **Londolozi** (PO Box 1211, Sunninghill Park 2157, telephone 011 803 8421, fax 011 803 1810) has three small camps and room for 48 people; **Inyati** (PO Box 38838, Booysens 2016, telephone 011 493 0755, fax 011 493 0837), catering for a maximum of 20 people; **Mala Mala** (PO Box 2575, Randburg 2125, telephone 011 789 2677); the super-expensive **Singita Lodge** (same contact as Londolozi), with room for just 16 people; and, perhaps best of the expensive reserves, **Sabi Sabi** (PO Box 52665, Saxonwold 2132, telephone 011 483 3939, fax 011 483 3799). All of these offer pretty much the same experience but Sabi Sabi's **Selati Lodge** is exceptionally friendly and intimate, with excellent Shangaan trackers, highly informative, bush-wise rangers who really know their stuff, and an excellent cook called Texan, who rustles up menus like this: peanut soup, stuffed avocado, duck with corn and courgettes, followed by lemon meringue pie.

Appendix II: International and Domestic Offices of Satours

International

AUSTRALIA, NEW ZEALAND
Level 6, 285 Clarence Street
Sydney 2000
NSW
Tel (2) 261 3424
Fax (2) 261 3414

AUSTRIA
Stefan Zweig Platz 11
A–1170
Vienna
Tel (1) 4704 5110
Fax (1) 4704 5114

CANADA
4117 Lawrence Avenue
East, Suite 2
Scarborough
Ontario M1E 2ST
Tel (416) 283 0563
Fax (416) 283 5465
E-mail:
tomelder@idirect.com

FRANCE
61 rue La Boetie
75008 Paris
Tel (1) 45 61 01 97
Fax (1) 45 61 01 96

GERMANY
Alemannia Haus
An der Hauptwache 11
D-60313 Frankfurt/Main 1
Postfach 101940
60019 Frankfurt
Tel (69) 92 91 290
Fax (69) 28 09 50
E-mail: 10075,744@compuserve.com

ISRAEL
14th Floor, Century Towers
124 Ibn Gvirol Street
PO Box 3388
Tel Aviv 61033
Tel (3) 527 2950/2351/2
Fax (3) 527 1958
E-mail: Satour@mail.netvision.net.il

ITALY
Via M. Monti, 8
20123 Milan
Tel (2) 467 121/869 3847
Fax (2) 480 13233/869 3508

JAPAN
Akasaka Lions Building
Second Floor
1–1–2 Moto Akasaka
Minato-ku Tokyo 107
Tel (3) 3478 7601
Fax (3) 3478 7605
E-mail: satourt@bnn-net.or.jp

NETHERLANDS AND BELGIUM,
Josef Isräelskade 48
1072 SB Amsterdam
Postbus 75360
1070 AJ Amsterdam
Tel (20) 662 4623
Fax (20) 662 9761

SWITZERLAND
Seestrasse 42
CH 8802 Kilchberg
Zürich
Tel (1) 715 1815/6/7
Fax (1) 715 1889
E-mail:
satour@dial.eunet.ch

TAIWAN, HONG KONG
Room 1204
12th Floor, Bank Tower
Building
205 Tun Hau North Road
Taipei
Tel (2) 717 4238
Fax (2) 717 1146

UK, EIRE AND SCANDINAVIA
No 5 & 6 Alt Grove
London SW19 4DZ
Tel (181) 944 8080
Fax (181) 944 6705
E-mail:
SATUK@satbuk.demon.co.uk

US EAST

500 Fifth Avenue,
20th Floor, Suite 2040
New York NY 10110
Tel (212) 730 2929
Fax (212) 764 1980
E-mail: satourny@aol.com

US WEST

9841 Airport Boulevard
Suite Number 1524
Los Angeles CA 90045
Tel (310) 641 8444
Fax (310) 641 5812

ZIMBABWE

Mon Repos Building
Newlands Shopping Centre
Harare
PO Box HG, 1000
Highlands
Tel (4) 786 487/8
Fax (4) 786 489

Within South Africa

BLOEMFONTEIN

Sanlam Parkade
Shop No 9
Charles Street
PO Box 3515
Bloemfontein 9300
Tel (051) 47 1362
Fax (051) 47 0862

CAPE TOWN

Shop 16
Piazza Level 3
Golden Acre
Adderley Street
Private Bag X9108

Cape Town 8000
Tel (021) 21 6274
Fax (021) 419 4875

DURBAN

Shop 104
320 West Street
PO Box 2516
Durban 4000
Tel (031) 304 7144
Fax (031) 305 6693

JOHANNESBURG INT'L AIRPORT

Tel (011) 970 1669
Fax (011) 394 1508

JOHANNESBURG

Suite 4305
Carlton Centre
PO Box 1094
Johannesburg
Tel (011) 331 5241
Fax (011) 331 5420

KIMBERLEY

Suite 620
Flaxley House
Du Toitspan Road
Private Bag X5017
Kimberley 8300
Tel (0531) 3 1434
Fax (0531) 81 2937

NELSPRUIT

Tarentaal Trading Post
Corner of Kaapschehoop
Road
and N4 Highway
PO Box 679
Nelspruit 1200
Tel (01311) 4 4405
Fax (01311) 4 4509

PIETERSBURG

Corner of Vorster and
Landdros Mare Streets
PO Box 2814
Pietersburg 0700
Tel (01521) 95 3025
Fax (01521) 91 2654

PORT ELIZABETH

Satour House
21–23 Donkin Street
PO Box 1161
Port Elizabeth 6000
Tel (041) 55 7761
Fax (041) 55 4975

POTCHEFSTROOM

1st Floor
Royal Hotel Building
Lombard Street
PO Box 912
Potchefstroom 2520
Tel (0148) 93 1611
Fax (0148) 22082

Appendix III: International Offices of South African Airways

AMSTERDAM
Transpolis Building
49 Polaris Avenues
2132 jh Hoofddorp
Tel 503 85447 Fax 503 85445

BANGKOK
15th Floor
Maneeya Centre Building
518/5 Ploenchit Road
10330
Tel 254 8206/7 Fax 254 8219

BOMBAY
Interglobe Air Transport
Podar House
Netali Sub Hosh Road
10 Marine Road
Tel 204 7027 Fax 283 3484

BUENOS AIRES
Avenida Santa Fe 794
3rd Floor,
Buenos Aires 1059
Tel 311 8184/5/6 Fax 311 5823

BRUSSELS
4 Finisterstreet
3rd floor
B-1000
Tel 218 0825 Fax 218 1108

CHICAGO
9801 West Higgins Road,
Suite 580 Rosemount
Illinois 60018
Tel 696 440 Fax 696 4768

FRANKFURT
Bleichstrasse 60-62
M-6000 Frankfurt
Tel 299 8030 Fax 293 441

GENEVA
17 Rue Du Cendier
CH 1210
Tel 73 16 740 Fax 73 80 727

HAMBURG
Ballindamm 17
Hamburg 20095
Tel 321 771/2 Fax 324 899

HONG KONG
R702 New World Office Building
18-23 Salisbury Road
Tsim Sha Tsui
Kowloon
Tel 2722 5768 Fax 2311 1174

LONDON
St George's House,
61 Conduit Street
London W1R 0NE
Tel 312 5000 Fax 312 5008

LOS ANGELES
Suite 1530
9841 Airport Boulevard
CA 90045
Tel 641 4111 Fax 641 0860

MADRID
Garn Via 6
1st Floor
Madrid 28013
Tel 41 6429 Fax 41 8378

MIAMI
Suite 100
901 Ponce de Leon Boulevard
Coral Gables
Florida 33123
Tel 461 3484/5 Fax 461 3861

MILAN
Via G. Leopardi 9
20123 Milan
Tel 4801 3682 Fax 4801 5712

NEW YORK
9th Floor
900 3rd Avenue
NY 10022
Tel 418 3700/1 Fax 418 3744

PARIS
350 Rue Sainte Honore
75001 Paris
Tel 42 61 57 87 Fax 42 60 18 15

PERTH
7th Floor Exchange House
68 St George's House
Perth 6000
Tel 322 7388 Fax 324 1724

RIO DE JANEIRO
4th Floor
Avenida Rio Branco 245
Rio de Janeiro
Tel 262 6002 Fax 262 6120

SAO PAULO
6th Floor, Suite 6A
Avenida Sao Luis 165
Sao Paulo 01046
Tel 259 1522 Fax 258 0070

SINGAPORE
179 Union Building
171 Tras Street
Singapore
Tel 227 7911 Fax 221 8810

SYDNEY
9th Floor
5 Elizabeth Street
Sydney
Tel 223 4448 Fax 223 4682

TAIPEI
12th Floor
Bank Tower
205 Tun Hua North Road
Taipei 10592
Tel 717 5169/713 6363 Fax 713 9478

TEL AVIV
Migdal Or Building
1 Ben Yehuda Street
Tel Aviv
Tel 510 2828 Fax 510 2992

TOKYO
6th Floor
Akasaka Lions Building
1–1–2 Moto-Akasaka
Minato-Ku
Tokyo
Tel 3470 1901 Fax 3470 1904

TORONTO
5255 Yonge Street
Suite 1500
North York
Toronto
Ontario M2N 6P4
Tel 512 8880 Fax 512 8877

VIENNA
Opernring 1/R/8th Floor
A–1010 Vienna
Tel 587 1585 Fax 587 158516

Publicity Assocs & Tourist Info

Eastern Cape

ALIWAL NORTH
Tel (0551) 2951,
Fax (0551) 41307.

EAST LONDON
PO Box 533, East London
5200
Tel (0431) 26015,
Fax (0431) 435 091

EASTERN PROVINCE
Tel (041) 558 922,
Fax (041) 561 531

GEORGE
PO Box 1109, George 6530;
Tel (0441) 74 4000

GRAAFF-REINET
PO Box 153, Graaff-Reinet
6280
Tel (0491) 24248

GRAHAMSTOWN
PO Box 124, Grahamstown
6140
Tel (0461) 23241
Fax (0461) 29488

HOGSBACK
Tel (045) 962 1024
Fax (045) 962 1058

JEFFREYS BAY
Tel (0423) 932 588
Fax (0423) 932 227

KING WILLIAM'S TOWN
Tel (0433) 23391
Fax (0433) 22646

PORT ELIZABETH
Tel (041) 521 315
Fax (041) 552 564

UITENHAGE
Tel (041) 994 1329
Fax (041) 994 1342

UMTATA
Tel (0471) 312 885
Fax (0471) 312 887

WILD COAST RESORTS
ACCOMMODATION
Tel (0471) 25344
Fax (0471) 23548/311 980

Free State

BLOEMFONTEIN
PO Box 639, Bloemfontein
9300; Tel (051) 405 8911

FICKSBURG
Tel (05192) 5547/8
Fax (05192) 5449

FOURIESBURG
Tel and Fax (058222) 14

HARRISMITH
Tel (05861) 23525
Fax (05861) 30923

LADYBRAND
Tel (05191) 40654
Fax (05191) 40305

QWAQWA
Tel (058) 713 0576
Fax (058) 713 0691

SASOLBURG
Tel (016) 760 765
Fax (016) 0769

WELKOM
(057) 352 9244
Fax (057) 353 2482

Gauteng

HARTBEESPOORT
Tel (01211) 31949

JOHANNESBURG
PO Box 4580, Johannesburg
2000
Tel (011) 337 6650
Fax (011) 333 7272 or
Tel (011) 336 4961
Fax (011) 336 4965

MAGALIESBURG
Tel & Fax (0142) 771 432

PRETORIA
PO Box 440, Pretoria 0001
Tel (012) 313
7694/8259/7980
Fax (012) 313 8460

Sandton
Tel (011) 881 6911

KwaZulu-Natal

AMANZIMTOTI
Tel (031) 903 7498
Fax (031) 903 7493

COLENSO
Tel (03622) 2111

DRAKENSBERG
Tel (036) 448 1557
Fax (036) 448 1562

DUNDEE
Tel (0341) 22 2121
Fax (0341) 23 856

DURBAN
PO Box 1044, Durban 4000
Tel (031) 304 4934
Fax (031) 304 6196
There is also a teletourist service,
offering 24-hour recorded informa-
tion on events of interest to visitors:
Tel (031) 305 3877

ESTCOURT
Tel (0363) 23 611

GREYTOWN
Tel (0334) 32 735

HOWICK
Tel (0332) 30 5305

LADYSMITH
Tel (0361) 22 992
Fax (0361) 27 051

MARGATE
Tel (03931) 22322
Fax (03931) 21886

NATAL SOUTH COAST
PO Box 1253, Margate,
Kwa-Zulu Natal, 4275
Tel (03931) 22322

NEWCASTLE
Tel (03431) 55 318

PIETERMARITZBURG
PO Box 25,
Pietermaritzburg 3200; Tel
(0331) 45 1348
Fax (0331) 943 535

PORT ALFRED
PO Box 63, Port Alfred
6170
Tel (0464) 41 235

PORT EDWARD
Tel (03930) 32 026

RICHARDS BAY
Tel (0351) 31 111

ST LUCIA
Tel (035) 590 1339

.ULUNDI
Tel (0358) 21 602

UMHLANGA ROCKS
Tel (031) 561 4257
Fax (031) 561 1417

VRYHEID
Tel (0381) 812 133
Fax (0381) 809 637

Mpumalanga

BARBERTON
PO Box 33, Barberton 1300
Tel (01314) 22121
Fax (01314) 25120

BOTSHABELO MISSION STATION
Tel (0132) 23897

CENTRAL LOWVELD
Tel (01528) 35114
Fax (01528) 35055

GRASKOP
PO Box 171, Graskop 1270
Tel (01315) 71316
Fax (01315) 71798

HAZYVIEW
Tel (01317) 67717
Fax (01317) 67414

LYDENBURG
PO Box 61, Lydenburg 1120
Tel (01323) 2121/2501
Fax (01323) 51108

NELSPRUIT
PO Box 5018, Nelspruit
1200
Tel (01311) 551 988
Fax (01311) 551 350

PILGRIM'S REST
PO Box 39, Pilgrim's Rest
1290
Tel (01315) 81211

SABIE
PO Box 494, Sabie 1260
Tel (01315) 43492

WHITE RIVER
PO Box 2387, White River 1240
Tel and Fax (01311) 51599

Northern Province

DUIWELSKLOOF
Tel (0152) 309 9246

HAENERTSBERG
Tel (0152) 309 9246

HOEDSPRUIT
Tel (01528) 31678
Fax (01528) 31912

LOUIS TRICHARDT
Tel and Fax (015) 516 0040

MESSINA
Tel (01553) 40211
Fax (01553) 2513

NORTHERN PROVINCE GENERAL
Tel (0152) 295 9300
Fax (0152) 295 5819

NYLSTROOM
Tel and Fax
(01470) 2211

PHALABORWA
Tel (01524) 85860
Fax (01524) 85870

PIETERSBURG
Tel (0152) 295 2011
Fax (0152) 291 5101

POTGIETERSRUS
Tel and Fax (0154) 2244

THABAZIMBI
Tel (014773) 22 590
Fax (014773) 71 069

THOHOYANDOU
Tel (0159) 21885
Fax (0159) 21298

TZANEEN
Tel (0152) 307 1411
Fax (0152) 307 1507

VENDA
Tel (0159) 21 885
Fax (0159) 21 296

WATERBERG
Tel and Fax (014755) 3862

Northern Cape

COLESBERG
Tel (051) 753 0678
Fax (051) 753 0574

GRIQUATOWN
Tel (05962) 19
KAKAMAS
Tel (054) 431 0838
Fax (054) 431 0836

KALAHARI
Tel (05373) 21001
Fax (05373) 22502

KIMBERLEY
PO Box 87
Kimberley 8300
Tel (0531) 27298

KURUMAN
(05373) 21095
Fax (05373) 23581

NAMAQUALAND
Tel (0251) 22011
Fax (0251) 21421

UPINGTON
Tel and Fax (054) 27064

North-West Province

BRITS
Tel (01211) 589 111

CHRISTIANA
Tel (0534) 3261

KLERKSDORP
Tel (018) 462 3919

LICHTENBURG
Tel (01441) 25051

MAFIKENG
Tel and Fax (0140) 810 023

MMABATHO
Tel (0140) 843 040/1
Fax (0140) 842 524

POTCHEFSTROOM
Tel (0148) 299 5130/1/2
Fax (0148) 294 8203

VRYBURG
Tel (05391) 782 200
Fax (05391) 3482

.
ZEERUST
Tel (01428) 21081

Western Cape

ARNISTON
Tel (02841) 42584

BREDASDORP
Tel (02481) 42584

CAPTOUR (CAPE TOWN)
PO Box 1403
Cape Town 8000
Tel (021) 418 5202
Fax (021) 418 5227

CERES
Tel (0233) 61287

CITRUSDAL
Tel (022) 921 3210

CLANWILLIAM
Tel (027) 482 2029
Fax (027) 482 1933

FISH HOEK
Tel (021) 782 1112

FRANSCHHOEK
Tel (02212) 2086
Fax (02212) 3440

GARDEN ROUTE
Tel (0441) 736 355
Fax (0441) 736 314

HERMANUS
PO Box 117
Hermanus 7200
Tel (0283) 22629

KNYSNA
PO Box 87
Knysna 6570
Tel (0445) 21610
LAMBERT'S BAY
Tel (027) 432 2335

MALMESBURY
Tel (0224) 22996
Fax (0224) 22935

MATJIESFONTEIN
Tel (02372) 5203

MOSSEL BAY
PO Box 25
Mossel Bay 6500
Tel (0444) 91 2202

MUIZENBERG
Tel (021) 788 1898
Fax (021) 788 2259

OUDTSHOORN
PO Box 255
Oudtshoorn 6620
Tel (0443) 22 2221

PAARL
PO Box 47
Paarl 7620
Tel (02211) 23829

PLETTENBERG BAY
Tel (04457) 34065
Fax (04457) 34066

SALDANHA
PO Box 139 Saldanha 7395
Tel (02281) 42 088
Fax (02281) 44 240

SIMONSTOWN
Tel (021) 786 3046

STELLENBOSCH
PO Box 368
Stellenbosch 7600
Tel (021) 883 3584

SWELLENDAM
Tel (0291) 42770

TULBAGH
Tel (0236) 301 348

WESTERN CAPE TOURISM
BOARD
Tel (021) 418 3716
Fax (021) 214875

WILDERNESS
Tel and Fax (0441) 770 045

WORCESTER
23 Baring Street
Worcester 6850
Tel (0231) 71408

Selected Further Reading

History

BEINART, William: *Twentieth-Century South Africa*, Oxford University Press, 1994.
A succinct and authoritative account by a recognised scholar.

DE WET, Christiaan Rudolf: *Three Years War*, Constable, 1902.
A lively account of the South African War 1899–1902 by one of the leading Afrikaner generals.

HEPPLE, Alexander: *Verwoerd*, Penguin, 1967.
An excellent biography of the architect of apartheid.

INNES, Duncan: *Anglo American and the Rise of Modern South Africa*, Heinemann, 1984.
A densely-argued, scholarly analysis of the place and influence of this major industrial conglomerate.

KRUGER, Rayne: *Good-bye Dolly Gray*, Pan Books 1974.
A lively and clear account of the Anglo-Boer war, also known as the Second South African War, of 1899–1902.

LODGE, Tom: *Black politics in South Africa since 1945*, Longman, 1983.
A comprehensive history up to the early years following the Soweto school insurrection of June 1976.

MOSTERT, Noel: *Frontiers*, Pimlico, 1991.
The most authoritative and best-written history of the Xhosa and the 19th century frontier wars.

NASSON, Bill: *Abraham Esau's War—A Black South African War in the Cape, 1899–1902*, Cambridge University Press, 1991.
A scholarly account of the part played by black South Africans in the war.

O'MEARA, Dan: *Volkskapitalisme—Class, capital and ideology in the development of Afrikaner Nationalism 1934–48*, Ravan Press, 1983.
Utilizing sophisticated marxist concepts, this is an extremely dense but seminal analysis of the growth of economic strength within the Afrikaner community.

PAKENHAM, Thomas, *The Boer War*, Weidenfeld and Nicholson, 1979.
One of the best popular accounts of the 1899-1902 war.

PLAATJE, Solomon: *Native Life in South Africa*, P S King, London 1916.
Plaatje, a journalist and political agitator, tours his country and details the devastating effects wrought by legislation aimed at forcing black South Africans off the land.

Reader's Digest Illustrated History of South Africa, 1994, Reader's Digest Association.

REITZ, Denys: *Commando: A Boer Journal of the Boer War*, Faber and Faber, 1929.
Classic Boer account of the South African War 1899–1902.

SIMONS, H J and R E: *Class and Colour in South Africa, 1850–1950*, Penguin, 1969.
Thorough analysis of the rise of South Africa as an economic power.

THOMPSON, Leonard: *The Political Mythology of Apartheid*, Yale University Press, 1985. The ideologies underlying Afrikaner nationalism.

van Onselen, Charles: *New Babylon and New Nineveh*, Ravan Press, 1982.
Two witty prize-winning volumes on the socio-economic history of the Witwatersrand 1886-1914.

VAN ONSELEN, Charles: *The Seed Is Mine—The Life of Kas Maine, a South African Sharecropper*, Hill and Wang, 1996.
Much more than a biography of an unknown black South African, this magisterial work is essentially a history of the way racialism distorted a whole society.

WARWICK, Peter: *Black People and the South African War 1899–1902*, Ravan Press, 1983.
Until quite recently most historians have ignored the role and experiences of black South Africans in the war; Warwick adjusts the balance.

WHEATCROFT, Geoffrey: *The Randlords*, Weidenfeld, 1985.
A lively and entertaining history of the early white mining entrepreneurs.

WILLAN, Brian: *Sol Plaatje, South African Nationalist, 1876–1932*, Heinemann 1984.
An excellent biography of Plaatje and thorough account of the early days of black African nationalist development.

An Illustrated Dictionary of South African History, Ibis, 1994.

WORDEN, Nigel: *The Making of Modern South Africa*, Blackwell, 1994.

Personal Accounts

BIKO, Steve: *I Write What I Like*, Heinemann, London, 1978.
A selection of his writings edited by Aelred Stubbs,

BREYTENBACH, Breyten: *The True Confessions of an Albino Terrorist*; Faber, 1984.
A leading Afrikaner author's shift to radical opposition against apartheid.

CUMMING, R.G: *Five Years of a Hunter's Life in the far interior of South Africa*, John Murray, two volumes, 1851.
An entertaining account of a soldier-turned-game-hunter.

FIRST, Ruth: *One Hundred and Seventeen Days*, Penguin, 1965.
An autobiographical account of the prison detention of a journalist and political activist. A deceptively cool analysis, this ranks among the very finest of such accounts.

HOOPER, Charles: *Brief Authority*, Collins, 1960.
Charles Hooper was a South African born Anglican missionary who went to work with the Bafurutse tribe in the Zeerust district in the far north of South Africa in the late 1950s. It is his moving, detailed story of how apartheid destroyed a peaceful rural community.

HUDDLESTON, Trevor: *Naught for your Comfort*, Hardingham & Donaldson, 1956.
The passionate memoir of Father Huddleston, who was an Anglican priest in Sophiatown in the 1950s.

JACOBSON, Dan: *Time and Time Again*, Andre Deutsch, 1985.
A South African-born novelist's account of his early life.

LELYVELD, Joseph: *Move Your Shadow*, Michael Joseph, 1986.
The author was the South African correspondent of *The New York Times* newspaper in the early 1980s.

MANDELA, Nelson: *Long Walk To Freedom*; Little, Brown and Company, 1994.
Mandela's autobiography.

MATTERA, Don: *Gone With The Twilight*, a story of Sophiatown, Zed Books, 1987.
Life in the 1950s in one of the most vibrant townships.

MODISANE, Bloke: *Blame Me On History*; Thames & Hudson 1963.
A tough and compelling personal account of growing up under apartheid.

PATEL, Essop (editor): *The World of Nat Nakasa*, Ravan Press, 1975.
A collection of writings by one of the great 20th century black South African journalists.

TROLLOPE, Anthony: *South Africa*, London, 1877.
Trollope travelled across much of South Africa during the period when diamonds were first discovered. Critical of the Boer farmers he encountered, he found little to impress him in his journey.

WALLIS, J P R: *Fitz—The Story of Sir Percy Fitzpatrick*, Macmillan, 1995.
Entertaining biography of the author of Jock of the Bushveld, who was also a significant political figure in the early days of the Union of South Africa.

WOODS, Donald: *Asking For Trouble*, Gollancz, 1980.
Woods was editor of the *Daily Dispatch* in East London when in 1977 he became subject to a banning order. A friend of Steve Biko, Woods eventually fled the country.

Literature and Culture

BOSMAN, Herman Charles: *Bosman At His Best; a choice of stories and sketches, culled by Lionel Abrahams*. Human & Rousseau, Cape Town, 1965.
One of the authentic voices of (white) South African literature. His short stories are wry, poignant and self-deprecatory, redolent of the early days of Afrikaners.

BRINK, Andre, and COETZEE, J M (eds): *A Land Apart, A South African Reader* , Faber, 1986.
Stories and poetry.

COUZENS, Tim and PATEL, Essop: *The Return Of The Amasi Bird, Black South African Poetry 1891–1981*, Ravan Press, Johannesburg 1982.
A key anthology of black South African poetry.

CRWYS-WILLIAMS, Jennifer: *Penguin Dictionary of South African Quotations*, Penguin Books 1994. A wonderful book to dip into, full of gems like this, taken from the *Weekly Mail*

& Guardian newspaper on Mangosuthu Buthelezi: 'He holds the Guinness Book of Records entry for the longest-ever speech, a 400-page effort delivered over five days in the kwaZulu legislative assembly.'

FITZPATRICK, Sir Percy: *Jock of the Bushveld*, Longmans, Green and Co, 1907.

This loosely-formed, semi-autobiographical novel has many 'boy's own' adventure yarn qualities, but nonetheless is still a gripping account of early life in the lowveld.

GORDIMER, Nadine: *The Essential Gesture*, Jonathan Cape, 1988.

Gordimer has won a Nobel Literature prize for her novels but this moving collection of essays contains some of her lesser-known political writing.

MACLENNAN, Ben: Apartheid, *The Lighter Side*, Chameleon Press, 1990.

There was little enough to laugh about under apartheid, but the absurdities of its tangle of racist legislation gave rise to vast quantities of inadvertent humour. Maclennan's small book gathers the best examples.

MALAN, Rian: *My Traitor's Heart*, Bodley Head 1990.

The passionate, occasionally purple account of a white liberal who puts his country under the microscope.

MZAMANE, Mbulelo (editor): *Hungry Flames and other Black South African short stories*, Longman, 1986.

Stories by leading black South African writers.

NYEMBEZI, C L S: *Zulu Proverbs*, Witwatersrand University Press, 1954.

A particularly entertaining bedside book, full of folk wisdom such as this: 'Wopheka kuze kuqhakaz uNongidi'—'You will cook until Nongidi shines'. Nongidi is the name of a star which does not exist. Therefore, when the saying is used, it means that one is working to no purpose.'

PATON, Alan: *Cry, The Beloved Country*; Jonathan Cape, 1948.

Not a great novel, but a crucial moral indictment of apartheid.

SCHADEBERG, Jurgen: *The Fifties People of South Africa*, Bailey's Archives, 1987.

An excellent portfolio of black and white photographs of many of the leading characters and personalities in black township life.

SCHREINER, Olive: *The Story of an African Farm*, originally published in 1883, many editions available. This somewhat overwrought novel set in the semi-desert landscape of the Great Karoo has acquired classic status.

SHARPE, Tom: *Riotous Assembly*; Secker & Warburg, 1971.

Sharpe worked in South Africa in the 1950s; this black comedy was hated by the apartheid regime.

UYS, Pieter-Dirk: *P W Botha In His Own Words*, Penguin, 1987.

Pieter-Dirk Uys is South Africa's leading satirist. This little gem collects the wit and wisdom of P W Botha, prime minister and then president prior to F W de Klerk. EG: 'South Africa is not a jellyfish and is in many respects a swordfish.'

WATSON, Stephen: *Presence of the Earth*, David Philip, 1995.

Watson is, for me, South Africa's best contemporary poet writing in English.

Out and About

BRISTOW, David: *20 Best Hikes in South Africa*; LEVY, Jaynee: *Complete Guide to Walks and Trails in South Africa*; PATERSON-JONES, Colin: *Garden Route Walks*—all published by Struik.

CROUS, Hennie: *Saltwater Fishing in Southern Africa*, Struik, 1996.
For all anglers with sections on weather, tackle, bait, inshore, deep-sea and other related matters. Plus 13 detailed area guides with approach maps on where to find particular species of fish.

DE BOSDARI, C: *Cape Dutch Houses and Farms*, A A Balkema, originally published in 1953, third edition published in 1971. An authoritative account of Cape Dutch architecture; packed with useful etymological information.

DOWSON, Thomas: *Rock Engravings of Southern Africa*, Witwatersrand University Press, 1992. Comprehensive, illustrated and intepretative text which also identifies where to find sites.

FOURIE, P F (updated by G de Graaf): *The Kruger National Park, Questions and Answers*, Struik, 1992. A handy factual explanatory book.

Getaway: This is a very useful monthly magazine published in South Africa. Packed with reports on all types of holiday destinations, from hiking trails to hotels and resorts.

HUGHES, HANDS, KENCH et al: *South African Wine*, Struik, 1992.
Excellently illustrated, factual, explanatory guide, covering historical and contemporary developments.

KOORNHOF, Anton: *The Dive Sites of South Africa*, new edition published by New Holland, 1995. Crucial for anyone interested in the subject.

LEARY, PM: *Don't Die in the Bush—a guide to outdoor emergencies and survival techniques in Southern Africa*, Struik, 1996. Handy pocket-sized alphabetically-arranged manual. Invaluable for anyone hiking, backpacking and independently exploring the countryside.

NEWMAN, Kenneth: *Newman's Birds of Southern Africa*, Southern Book Publishers (5th edition, 1996). The field guide recommended by most game wardens.

PLATTER, John: *South African Wine Guide 95*, Mitchell Beazley 1994.
The definitive (and annually updated) exposition of the country's wine. Perhaps a trifle too forgiving. But there's nothing to beat it.

Secret Southern Africa, published by the Automobile Association of South Africa, 1994.
Essential for anyone wanting to explore off the beaten track.

SMITHERS, Reay: *Land Mammals of Southern Africa*, Southern Book Publishers (revised edition, 1994). The field guide recommended by most game wardens.

INDEX